OUGHTOBIOGRAPHY

LEAVES FROM THE DIARY
OF A HYPHENATED JEW

'Surefooted, droll and honest, *Oughtobiography* is a vivid insight into the life and times of one of the most dynamic driving forces behind Irish writing over the past half century.'

Dermot Bolger

'High on his literary flying trapeze, David Marcus juggles with the two realities of being Jewish and Irish and the conundrums of culture, language, table tennis, Cork, the meaning of existence. All done with that grace, humour and intelligence known to a carnival of writers helped by him during his long and distinguished career. His description of encounters with James Stephens and the Somerville clan is worth the price of admission alone. He has done the State some service and all who read this book will marvel at how much.'

Shane Connaughton

'This is a tale of three cities, Cork, Dublin and London, with fascinating glimpses of Sean O'Faolain, Edith Somerville, Frank O'Connor, James Stephens and other legendary figures. Anyone interested in Irish literature of the twentieth century should read this book.'

Michael Holroyd

'This delightful memoir, in its gently haunting way, admits one to the company of a truly good human being, to whom so many Irish writers owe so much.'

Frank Delaney

'David Marcus is truly unique and his brilliant *Oughtobiography* captures that wise, witty uniqueness.'

Brendan Kennelly

'These crowded pages speak of the intimate landscape of literature, yet every sentence here expands into the territory of creativity, and not just of writing. David Marcus's role in modern Irish writing can never be either over-estimated or eclipsed.'

Mary Leland

OUGHTOBIOGRAPHY

Leaves from the Diary of a Hyphenated Jew

David Marcus

Gill & Macmillan

Gill & Macmillan Ltd
Hume Avenue
Park West
Dublin 12
with associated companies throughout the world
www.gillmacmillan.ie

© 2001 David Marcus
0 7171 3250 1
Index compiled by Helen Litton
Print origination by Carole Lynch
Printed by MPG Books Ltd, Bodmin, Cornwall

*The paper used in this book is made from the wood
pulp of managed forests. For every tree felled, at least
one tree is planted, thereby renewing natural resources.*

A catalogue record is available for this book
from the British Library.

1 3 5 4 2

To

Ita, my wife
Sarah, my daughter
and to Vincent Banville

'To live without a past is worse than
to live without a future.'

Elie Wiesel

With grateful acknowledgement to Augustus Young for permission to use extracts from his verse-translation of William Makepeace Thackeray's *Irish Sketch Book*.

CONTENTS

Prologue   xi

Chapter One Memory Bank: First Deposits   1

Chapter Two My First Gentile   11

Chapter Three The Sound of Music   18

Chapter Four The Bird in the Hand   25

Chapter Five Trial by Trauma   33

Chapter Six Irish Writing: First Steps   36

Chapter Seven Irish Writing: First Staggers   42

Chapter Eight A Visit to Drishane House   50

Chapter Nine 'Twixt Cup and Lip   62

Chapter Ten Voice Over   68

Chapter Eleven Carriage Paid   74

Chapter Twelve Cheques and Balances   80

Chapter Thirteen The Exhilaration Elixir   86

Chapter Fourteen Endgames   97

Chapter Fifteen Coming Back for More   106

Chapter Sixteen Where and Wen   118

Chapter Seventeen Work and Play   130

Chapter Eighteen Ups, Downs, and a Family See-Saw   140

Chapter Nineteen Not so Eine Kleine Nachtmusik   151

Chapter Twenty The Midnight Courtship   160

Chapter Twenty-One Annus Mirabilis   167

Chapter Twenty-Two Getting to Know Me   178

Chapter Twenty-Three God Above?   184

Chapter Twenty-Four Getting into the Swing   197

Chapter Twenty-Five Land Ahoy!   217

Chapter Twenty-Six Hyphenated Americans   236

Chapter Twenty-Seven The Joyce of Yiddish,
   the *Oy Vay* of Irish   246

Chapter Twenty-Eight I Remember! I Remember!   251

Chapter Twenty-Nine Going out on a Spin   263

Index   271

PROLOGUE

How oft do my thoughts in their fancy take flight
To the home of my childhood away.
To the days when each Patriot's vision seemed bright,
'Ere I dreamed that those joys would decay.
When my heart was as light as the wild winds that blow
Down the Mardyke through each elm tree,
Where I sported and played 'neath each green leafy shade
On the banks of my own lovely Lee.

Jonathan C. Hanrahan

The leaves of the trees along the Mardyke were astir
and whispered in the sunlight. A team of cricketers
passed, agile young men in flannels and blazers, one of
them carrying the long green wicketbag.

James Joyce

It isn't given to many to be born in a road already celebrated
in song and story – not that I imagine this coincidence had
anything to do with the love for literature that suddenly
seemed to break over me like a tidal wave in my early teens.

Song and story dwelt with me in my home in Cork. And
cricket too, for that matter. Across the elm-canopied

Mardyke Walk was the city's only cricket ground, and a free view of play from my parents' bedroom provided me with a vicarious thrill of involvement, for just as the fielders had to take up new positions each time the bowling changed ends, a tree blocking my sightline made me cross over from one window to the other as if I was one of their team.

The songs of my childhood were mostly my father's beloved operatic arias – he used frequently sing me to sleep with the incongruous information that my tiny hand was frozen; the stories came from the special sets of Collected Works for which my mother used send postal orders to the British newspapers – the brazenly red-jacketed H.G. Wells, the gilt-braided coats of Dickens and the pimpled brown robes of Shakespeare, books which I later augmented from similar outfitters with the *Plays* and *Prefaces* of Shaw in two outsize volumes. And alongside these representatives of Gentile genius stood the twelve huge, black-suited tomes of *The Jewish Encyclopaedia*.

More than anything it was Jewish lore that coloured my pre-teen years. School was Presentation Brothers College, but the texts that have lodged in my memory are not those of my English course there, but the Pentateuch, the Five Books of Moses which, with learning Hebrew and Hebrew prayers, occupied *Cheder* class every day except Friday and Saturday. I pined for the lost Garden of Eden, was aghast at Abraham's preparedness to sacrifice his beloved son at God's behest, fumed at the deception that made Jacob work seven years overtime to win Rachel, and ached for Moses' ability to strike water from a rock.

Cheder took place in a room adjoining the synagogue in South Terrace, on no direct tram route and about a half hour's walk from the Mardyke. A few minutes in one direction from the synagogue was Warren's Place and the rambling, four-storeyed but unresplendent house of my mother's parents; a few minutes in another direction was Hibernian Buildings, Cork's Jewtown and the home of a forbidding-looking great-grandmother.

Like the Israelites who sojourned in the land of Egypt, I seemed at this time only to sojourn in Cork while my real life was lived in a world exclusively Jewish. Family, relations, friends, devotions, celebrations, rituals were all in the ghetto tradition. I ventured not at all into areas of Cork outside my accustomed routes. The north side, the locale of so many of the O'Connor, O'Faoláin and Corkery stories in which I was soon to become immersed, was Indian territory to me; Cork characters such as Klondyke and Andy Gaw could not fascinate me as could my grand-uncle Sopsa, whose *folie de grandeur* hallucinations spun stories of afternoons at Ascot in Lord Rosebery's box followed by tea with the King at Buckingham Palace, or 'Buldings', a shambling, bewildered refugee from ever-darkening Europe who used accost me in the Carnegie Library with his unchanging query, 'From vot izz a philotchofer?'

I have never succeeded in answering that question. Indeed if I had, I would hardly have succumbed to the idea of writing this account. It was only when some literary friends kept insisting that my editorial association since the early 1940s with every Irish writer of note – and with some eminent non-Irish writers too – should be recorded, that I began to wilt. 'You ought to write your autobiography, you really ought to,' was their repeated injunction. So I eventually set to, adapting the book's title in gratitude to their persistence.

But these good friends didn't then know what I knew. They didn't know that of the mountains of unique, historically important letters and analectica that my literary life had produced, not a single page had survived. One postcard alone – but of letters from such as Shaw, Gogarty, Paul Vincent Carroll, O'Casey, Kavanagh, O'Connor, O'Faoláin, Stephens, Edith Somerville, Kate O'Brien and many others – nothing. What became of all this correspondence is for later telling, but for me its loss seemed to present an insurmountable obstacle to the production of a responsible, all-inclusive record. I would have to depend totally on recall.

Fortunately, my recall of my literary life is still extensive and vivid, and though that life occupied more of my waking hours than any other activity, it never reflected the real me. That inner me was formed by two things – music, and the ongoing trauma of having to juggle a hyphenated heritage of being both Irish and Jewish.

Where, in fact, did it all start?

CHAPTER ONE

Memory Bank: First Deposits

It started with the stuff of memory, which for me meant the four most enduring memories of my teen years.

The first one goes back to my time in Pres – Presentation Brothers College – when in history class I learned the significance of the Northern Ireland border and that six counties of the island of Ireland were held and ruled by Britain. As I sat in my desk I had a dream, too intense to be called a daydream, that I would live to see both that Border removed and the Jewish people with a home of their own in Palestine.

I can exactly date the second memory. It was 10 November, 1938, the day after *Kristallnacht,* when the newspapers carried extensive, terrifying accounts of the first widescale Nazi attacks on Jews, and on their synagogues, homes and business premises. I was fourteen at the time, hardly more than a year after celebrating my Barmitzvah, the ritual marking a male Jew's graduation from boyhood to manhood and investing him with the duties and responsibilities of his religion. It was, however, *Kristallnacht* that really brought home to me the fact that I was different, that to be different was to be vulnerable, and that to be vulnerable was to be expendable.

The third memory was the worst one of all. Spring, 1940, when a Nazi invasion of Britain was thought imminent and many experts believed that Ireland, Britain's 'back door', would be its springboard. As speculation grew, one particular dawn was pinpointed by military analysts as likely to offer the invading armies the most suitable climatic and marine conditions for a successful sea journey and any one of the many coves in the vicinity of Cork harbour a perfect landing place. I spent all the previous night sitting up in bed, staring at the clear, starry sky and waiting in terror to hear the streets resound with the rumble of tanks and the stamping of storm troopers' boots.

The fourth memory is associated with the following brief missive:

> Your name or pen-name suggests you are a Jew. If so, I'll pay you three guineas for a good article on the Cork Hebrew Community.
>
> S O'F

S O'F was, of course, Seán O'Faoláin, editor of *The Bell*, the legendary periodical he founded in 1940. I was sixteen when I received that rejection message along with the return of the first short story I had submitted to him. Though one of the most enduring memories of my early life, it caused me far less anguish than the others, probably because having already gathered quite a collection of rejections from various periodicals throughout the world, one more was no shattering surprise. I didn't accept the accompanying offer, but the fact that he made it at all acted as some sort of encouragement.

From the age of fourteen I saw myself as a writer. Before that I had only an unfocused desire, tapping out execrable juvenilia on an ancient Olivetti almost elephantine in its gargantuan architecture. But the ambition and self-belief – the latter a damnable conviction that fooled me for very many years – were engendered one day in class at Pres by my then English teacher, Cornelius ('Pug') Buckley. I almost invariably got an 'excellent' from him for my weekly essay, and from my Irish teacher usually the same for the weekly Irish language essay. Once when the theme for the latter was 'A day in the life of any person or thing of your own choice', finding myself on the Sunday night with not a word written, I cheated by translating into Irish 'The Extraordinarily Horrible Dummy', Gerald Kersh's riveting story about a ventriloquist's dummy, which I had just read in some Penguin collection. But for 'Pug' the English essay theme that gave my ambition its kick-start was 'Patriotism'. As one might expect from a cocky smart aleck whose lack of originality was camouflaged by a glib pen, my effort was a melange of naïve hand-me-downs and empurpled schoolboy rhetoric. 'Pug', however, very much belying his pugilistic nickname, was bowled over, and rewarded me by sending the essay to the editor of the *Irish Independent*, the most widely read daily newspaper in the country. Of course it came back, and of course I was disappointed, but what shocked me was not just the terse, printed rejection slip pinned to my script like a mass card, but the fact that it offered not a single word of comment, much less encouragement. I later realised how naïve I had been to expect anything else, but when in time I undertook editorial responsibilities myself, I remembered that shock and learned from it.

There are, of course, some other teenage events that still stoke my memory with the ineffable warmth and glow of nostalgia. Like the change of the clock that marks the arrival of summer time, I can rely on every June to bring back the

3

most nostalgic one of all. It is the trip my father made to London in that month every year, except during the war. His trips were no business visits, but pleasure-bent pilgrimages: Ascot, Royal Ascot. Not that he was a dedicated gambler. Anything but. For him following the horses was an inexpensive hobby, in no way even a minor extravagance. The smallest of small punters, a bob each way was his standard bet – and that not every day – inflated for Ascot to a pound to win or each way. Very often his expenses were covered by his winnings, but as present-giving was unknown in our home, he never brought any gift back. Except, that is, for the year he returned with, bundled up in his pyjamas (presumably to evade Customs), a brown paper bag which he immediately tucked away in his bedroom wardrobe. If he hadn't been so trusting, he would have known better. The wardrobe was never locked, so, predictably, what was in the bag didn't for long remain a secret. It turned out to be a copy of *Lady Chatterley's Lover*. Now that, if you like, *was* an extravagance.

However, what he always did bring back was something which as I grew up I looked forward to – the list of horses he had noted to back next time out. When I started punting myself in my teens I regularly followed those tips and they frequently paid off. What also paid off were his two pieces of punting advice. One was a solemnly-delivered puzzler: 'It's not what you lose that counts, it's what you save.' Unravelled, I took it to mean that the less one staked, the less one lost. His other piece of wisdom was another riddle, repeated whenever his car-owning friends persuaded him to accompany them to the races at the nearest courses, Limerick Junction or Mallow. It became a ritual, with me happily co-operating as his straight man. When he'd return from the meeting I would greet him with 'Well, Boss,' (I

always called him 'Boss') 'how did you do?' And as if struggling to suppress elation, he would always answer, 'I backed
the first five winners.' Then a pause, a change of tone to
mock-heavy lugubriousness. 'And if I had any money left, I'd
have backed the sixth winner too.' He knew that wisdom
delivered with a light touch was infinitely better than a
lecture. Not surprising: his name was Solomon.

Where did he get his interest in horses in the first place?
Almost certainly from his own father; not that he, too, was a
punter. A refugee from Czarist pogroms in Lithuania, my
grandfather founded a successful picture-framing factory in
Dublin, and in due course my father set up his own branch of
the business in Cork. *Zeida* was a mystery who somehow
managed to go through more than one small fortune, but he
always held on to his first major purchase, a carriage and
pair, stabling the horses behind his home in South Circular
Road and caring for them himself. Like father, like son no
doubt, and the gene was further replicated, for when I was a
child my father frequently amused me with stylish pencil
sketches of a horse, as well as teaching me how to emulate
him. However, what I never attempted to reproduce was the
impressive oil painting of a horse in its stable which he did as
a youngster and which, as long as we lived in Cork, hung on
the wall of our living-room.

But Ascot was not his only Mecca. On at least one evening
in London he would go to the Yiddish Theatre where the celebrated Yiddish actor Maurice Schwartz performed. Both my
parents were fluent speakers of Yiddish, though usually they
spoke it in the home only when they didn't want their children to know what they were saying. One of my father's most
treasured possessions was Maurice Schwartz's recording of
A Shikkerah Chazan, 'The Drunken Cantor', the tale of the

synagogue cantor whose young daughter is critically ill but who hasn't the money to pay for the operation to save her life. His appeal to the community's President for a loan is refused, and his daughter dies. Heartbroken, he turns to drink.

That recording gave my father the opportunity to come up with an idea dear to his heart when, one year, the member of the Cork Jewish community who always took it on himself to produce its Social Club's annual concert, asked him if any of his young sons might be up to doing some turn. Including babies and young children, the Jewish population of Cork at that time was about four hundred, so for the annual concert it was always a struggle to find many willing to make fools of themselves before their family and friends. My father transcribed in phonetic spelling every word of the harrowing story, rehearsed me until I was perfect in word and accent, and sat with my mother in the front row at the concert, restraining himself at the end from joining in the audience's tumultuous applause while my mother dissolved into copious tears.

Being possessed, at that time, of a youngster's typical desire to show off, I revelled in my own performance, and when shortly afterwards in Pres I got a further opportunity to display my acting talent, I was in my element. Shakespeare, as usual, was on the Intermediate Certificate course and the teacher, one of the Presentation Brothers, said that the best way to study Shakespeare was to read the words aloud. He announced that he would outline the story of one of the plays, start with the most exciting scene, and give as many of the pupils as possible a part.

The play he chose was 'The Merchant of Venice'. The role of Shylock he allotted to me, and the scene for my debut performance was that which included Shylock's celebrated, oft-quoted speech:

I am a Jew: hath not a Jew eyes? hath not a Jew hands, organs, dimensions, senses, affections, passions, fed with the same food, hurt with the same weapons, subject to the same diseases, healed by the same means, warmed and cooled by the same winter and summer as a Christian is: if you prick us do we not bleed? if you tickle us do we not laugh? if you poison us do we not die? and if you wrong us shall we not revenge? if we are like you in the rest, we will resemble you in that. If a Jew wrong a Christian, what is his humility? Revenge! If a Christian wrong a Jew, what should his sufferance be by Christian example? Why, revenge! The villainy you teach me I will execute, and it shall go hard but I will better the instruction.

The lead-up to the speech was the beginning of the seismic shock I experienced that morning. It immediately wiped out my awareness of the classroom, my fellow-pupils, the Brother standing at his desk. It wiped out also the me I had been, as completely as an equation on a blackboard is erased with one swipe of a duster. It gave me much more than a feel for the part. It gave me a feel for myself, for who I wasn't and who I was. I was no longer the Jew who had always hidden himself on the fringe in non-Jewish company. I was now, at least for those few minutes, a Jew with a voice – and with an audience. And when I reached '. . . hath not a Jew eyes . . .' the bomb planted inside me detonated. Eyes, hands, organs, dimensions, senses, affections, passions – they all fell into place. Many a time and oft, not on the Rialto of Venice, but much nearer home, in the streets of Cork, I had had to ignore young ragamuffins who, crunching a corner of their coat or gansey in their fist, would wave it in front of me, calling

'Pig's ear, wah, wah.' But they had been children and I merely a target for their sport, so their shouts meant no more to me than to themselves. Once they disappeared around a corner, they disappeared from my mind. Or so I thought.

When I finished the speech, I was momentarily drained yet unable to sit down. For seconds the room was silent and cold. And then the pupil in the seat beside me – years later he entered a religious Order – started to applaud. One or two others followed suit, and then the rest of the class, seizing the opportunity for some high jinks, joined in with whistles and hoots. The teacher immediately brought them to order with angry raps on his desk, and the school Superior, Brother Evangelist, who unnoticed had slipped in quietly on one of his daily supervisory visits, took the opportunity to slip out just as quietly. I resumed my seat, too bewildered to think straight, too elated to think at all.

Next day I found myself no longer playing Shylock. I was recast as Portia.

The English class had been the last of that morning and on my way home I was smarting at my demotion. My self-esteem was badly bruised and my new self-confidence derailed. Why had I been replaced? Because I hadn't been good enough in the role? No, that surely couldn't be the reason. And if the change had been made because the teacher wanted to give as many pupils as possible a chance, then why keep me in the cast at all?

The answer suddenly hit me with the certainty that accompanies the flash of recognition of something that all the time has been staring one in the face. The Superior. It had been his decision. That would be typical of Brother Evangelist. He could see around corners. 'Think ahead,' he told every pupil when welcoming him to Pres. 'Learn to avoid trouble before it can come. Nip it in the bud.' The possible trouble he could see around this particular corner was the danger that giving me, a Jew, the role of Shylock could be interpreted as an anti-Semitic act. And what might follow if I should tell my parents? But I had already told them; it was the big news of the previous day. Had they been upset? On the contrary, they had been delighted and proud. In their minds there wasn't the slightest thought of anti-Semitism. Nor in my mind either. After all, given the idea of having pupils act out scenes from the play, with a Jewish boy in the class what more obvious and natural than to cast him as Shylock? It was one of the very few such opportunities any teacher in Ireland would have had. No, it couldn't have anything to do with anti-Semitism. But then my train of thought hit the buffers. If I was to remain in the cast, why demote me to the role of Portia? Any male teenager would feel greatly compromised by such a prospect. He would certainly expect to be guyed by his classmates, perhaps even be saddled with the awful nick-name for the rest of his schooldays. How much better off was I to be released from the stigma of being the cruel, usurious Jew only to be made instead the butt of my fellow-pupils' jokes? That wouldn't have been Evangelist's idea. Shylock's own words suggested an explanation. 'If a Jew wrong a Christian, what is his humility? Revenge?' I had not wronged my teacher, but if he really was an anti-Semite deprived of his full satisfaction and perhaps even reprimanded for his tact-lessness, then, just as in the play, Portia could have been the instrument of his revenge.

Off and on for some time afterwards I brooded on the whole experience, trying to come to a decision on the teacher's motives. It was a decision I could never reach because it entailed a judgement I could never make. Knowing, as I did, what the word anti-Semitism meant was one thing, but to have it used against me by an adult in a position of authority was something else again. I thought about the persecution of the Israelites by the Egyptians. But that had been only a story in the *Haggadah*, and so long ago that it was too remote from me and I too detached from it to feel the deep hurt of anti-Semitism. Then came *Kristallnacht*, and the word was made flesh for me. Shylock may have been only a character in a play, and his words only those Shakespeare had written for him. But I had declaimed them, and in doing so had made them mine. I still, however, had another word to learn. That word was Holocaust.

CHAPTER TWO

My First Gentile

In summer 1941 my time at Pres ended. I had sat two national examinations that year, the Matriculation, which then was mandatory for entrance to University, and the Intermediate Certificate, because Brother Evangelist entered me, believing I could win one of the national scholarships awarded to the top eighty students, which would mean honour for the school and money for me. I passed the Matriculation and also won an Intermediate Certificate scholarship, but my farewell to Pres was anything but celebratory.

One morning shortly after the Inter results had been announced there was a knock on the front door of my home. I happened to be on hand to open it. The caller was Brother Vincent, the Brother whose duty it was to arrange with Guy's, the city's leading photographers, for the group photograph of all the school's winners of scholarships and other distinctions, which would take its place alongside the scores of others already hanging on the stairways and walls of the building. He told me that the photograph had been taken the previous day but that he had completely forgotten to notify me. However, he could arrange for Guy's to photograph me and have my face inset in a circle in the picture. I thanked him but declined his offer. With a list he would have had of all the students to notify, there was no way he could have 'forgotten' me. I have often asked myself whether my omission was a deliberate act of anti-Semitism or just a bizarre coincidence, and in truth I have to admit that the former always seemed to me the more likely.

Unfortunately, that wasn't the only examination misfortune to befall me. A week later I received a note from the school secretary informing me that my mark for the Inter English paper of 369 out of 400 was beaten by one mark for first place in Ireland. He felt it was something I'd like to know. It wasn't. The thought of whether I might be first or one hundred and first had never been in my mind. But knowing I had missed first place by one mark rankled far more than not having my place on the walls. To top it all, it transpired that to collect the scholarship money I had won, I would have to remain in Pres for a further year.

My future, however, was of much greater concern to me than anything relating to my scholastic past. I had no intention of spending more time in Pres. Nor did I want to go to University. Medicine, which my two older brothers were studying, held no interest for me, nor did any other University course. What I had long set my heart on was to go to London and take my chance there as a writer. At that age I had no lack of courage, but courage, like faith, is often blind. Exactly what 'take my chance' meant I hadn't bothered to work out, but in any event, with a war on I knew my madcap idea was a non-starter. My eldest brother suggested that I should do an Arts degree at UCC. I could read English Literature there, get my degree, go on for an MA, become a DLitt, a Professor, a writer – anything at all I liked in that field.

That was when my uncle, Gerald Goldberg, a solicitor with a growing practice, entered the debate. He urged me to study Law and become a barrister. With him to groom me and give me briefs, my future couldn't be brighter. I already had a good relationship with him, for in frequent visits to his home he had given me the run of his extensive library where I first read Eliot, Auden, MacNeice, Day Lewis, Dylan Thomas and the other leading contemporary poets, an experience that triggered off my own prentice efforts. Among the carrots held out in favour of going for the Bar was the fact that the college terms for the two final years had to be spent in Dublin to attend lectures and examinations at King's Inns. This, I thought, was the next best place to London.

In the end I compromised, exhibiting a tendency which I was to display in a pronounced manner in later years, due probably to my inherited ghetto genes. Concealing my complete lack of any interest in Law, my compromise was that, if the lecture courses did not clash, I would do both Law and Arts.

When I went to sign on in UCC, the sun was shining as I crossed the bridge just inside the entrance gates and started to walk up the broad, tree-bordered roadway leading to the College buildings and quadrangle. Halfway up, a man drew abreast of me on a bicycle, stopped, dismounted, and said, 'You're David Marcus?' 'Yes,' I answered. 'I'm Jack Lynch,' he said. 'I'm doing the Bar with you.'

I should have known him, for two reasons. Firstly, he was the judge's clerk, in the District Court, and we would have seen each other when on my uncle's suggestion I often sat behind the solicitors to listen to cases and gain experience.

And secondly, even if I didn't recognise him by sight, I should have known him from his picture in the newspapers — for he was already an established national hero, famous for his prowess both in hurling and Gaelic football. Unfortunately, these games had never held the slightest interest for me. At Pres rugby, which I didn't play, was *the* game, with cricket, which I did play, an unimportant, semi-scratch arrangement, and out of school there was table tennis, which for some thirty years I played constantly, winter and summer, once for Ireland. So the name and appearance of Jack Lynch meant absolutely nothing to me. How all that soon changed!

Together we signed on in the College, Jack for Law and I for Law and Arts. Next day I received a message to see the Registrar, Dr Alfred O'Rahilly, destined to become College President. Known far and wide as 'Alfie', he was a celebrated philosopher, mathematician, government adviser, industrial arbitrator and, amid his many other roles, lecturer in Sociology, one of my first year Law subjects. When I called on him I was faced with a low-sized, almost grey-haired, chunkily-built personage, fully capped and gowned, and faintly forbidding-looking.

'Marcus,' he greeted me, 'I see here you've signed on for both Law and Arts.'

'Yes, sir.'

'Well, of course there's nothing in the Rules against that, but I'll tell you something, boy. You won't get the exams.'

That was the end of the interview, and the end of my hopes of an Arts degree.

At the end of my first Law year, when the results were pinned on the notice-board, I was relieved to find that I had passed all subjects. But within minutes I was told that 'Alfie' wished to see me in his office.

'Ah, Marcus,' he said, somewhat sternly I thought. 'You know, boy, you didn't pass your exam.'

I stared at him, speechless, my mouth opened wide. What could he mean?

'No, boy, you didn't pass Sociology. But you did a good essay on Nazism, so I gave it to you. That's all.'

An act of pro-Semitism? As a future Knight of St Gregory and a monsignor, it made sense. And who knows, perhaps he was also, in his own way, making amends for warning me off my Arts degree hopes.

The Law lectures were themselves somewhat farcical. Only two per week, each of one hour, given by an elderly city solicitor, and it was not uncommon for us to arrive at the lecture room only to find a note pinned on the door to say that the lecturer was in court and couldn't leave. Even on the occasions he did attend, a different farce was always introduced by the only other student apart from Jack Lynch and myself. He was Dr Sperrin-Johnson, the long-time Professor of Botany in UCC, whose hobby was collecting Degrees, among which were BA, MA, MSc, MB, BCh, BAO and DLitt, but who was now aged enough to fall asleep at every lecture. I always helped him out by giving him a copy of my notes, but my hopes that he might reward me by inviting me to Blackrock Castle, his home, and let me listen to him playing Bach fugues on his organ – which he was reputed to do late into the night – never got anywhere, perhaps because he was never awake long enough for me to pop the question.

From the beginning Jack and I got on excellently. Being in effect the whole of the Law class, we very soon began to work together at my home. What struck me immediately about Jack was his athletic build – not until I later learned of his sporting fame did I see the reason for it. In addition, his firm facial bone-structure gave him a handsomeness that was often enriched by a warm smile. And he was an easy talker, whereas I, somewhat unused to engaging in any but the most inconsequential conversation with non-Jews, gave tongue only with a cautious timidity. But gradually, after we began to study together, I found a sense of comfort in his company, a sort of natural-seeming fraternity that shaped the first step I had taken out of my internal ghetto. Jack would arrive on his bicycle on one or two evenings most weeks, and we would spend a few hours together on our books before adjourning to the kitchen for cocoa and sandwiches, where Jack and my father would chat like old friends on the ways of the world.

The last two years at King's Inns in Dublin were an unwelcome contrast. I was lodging in Terenure with my Aunt Molly, one of my mother's sisters, who was married to Bernard Shillman, a barrister and the acknowledged expert on Irish Workmen's Compensation law. On the face of it that seemed a very fortunate placing for me, but it didn't work out that way. That was certainly more my fault than my uncle's. Although he was of a remote, rather preoccupied disposition and constantly immersed in his work, I didn't take advantage of his presence simply because by now my strong distaste for Law had crystallised into near loathing. Nor did I fit in at King's Inns. There were two lecturers whose lectures were extremely exacting, the building had the eeriness of a mausoleum, and I found my co-students cold and unfriendly. They were all male, and all sons of Government Ministers, barristers, prominent business tycoons and other high-profile VIPs, including the brother of a world-famous Hollywood star. In the two years I was there, no more than two or three ever exchanged even the time of day with me. And although

Jack Lynch and I maintained our close friendship, it proved unfeasible for us to continue our joint study sessions, a deprivation that I found extremely unsettling.

As far as my own personal interests were concerned, the enhanced possibilities of indulging them in Dublin showed discernible promise, and so after much agonising I decided I would ask my parents to allow me give up Law but stay in Dublin. I wrote them explaining my unhappiness and putting my request as strongly as I could. They did not reply. They did not reply because they never received my letter. It appeared that my weekly letter home, the envelope of course being in my familiar hand, was regarded as a communal family message to be opened by whomsoever first got to the post. On this occasion it was my eldest brother who opened the letter before anyone else knew it had arrived and it was he who replied. He told me that he would not give the letter to my parents because it would cause them great unhappiness and that I was being ridiculously hasty and must give myself more time to get used to my new way of life and to being away from home. Sensibly, and sensitively, he didn't add that I was being ungrateful. He didn't need to, for at least I had the grace to recognise that he was right. I felt as if I had imprisoned myself in clichés, had driven myself into a corner, would have to take the rough with the smooth, soldier on, etc. I did, and never regretted it.

───── ⌾⌾⌾ ─────

CHAPTER THREE

The Sound of Music

For as long as I can remember, music has always been a sound in my head, constantly buzzing at my inner ear like a bee in my bonnet, if not already reaching my outer one by some mechanical or technological means. It was from my parents that the obsession took hold. My mother was trained locally as a singer, and one year, when Joseph O'Mara brought his opera company on one of their visits to Cork, she went to the final matinee performance with a letter from her teacher suggesting she be auditioned. O'Mara told her that he wouldn't be making new contracts until his visit later in the year, but he sat down at the piano and put her through the usual scales and arpeggios. Then he instructed her to come and see him in September, when he would give her a contract for the chorus at thirty shillings a week and travelling fares. He also told her to learn the chorus parts of six particular operas.

During the summer, by which time she was already going out with my father, she worked hard at the chorus parts. When September came, she was fully prepared for her afternoon appointment with O'Mara before the final matinee performance of *Tosca*. My father suggested that he take her to the performance, and that as O'Mara was not on this occasion appearing himself, she would be able to see him after the curtain came down. She agreed, but when she went to his backstage office he had already departed for his next venue.

Of course she was heartbroken with disappointment, but a few days afterwards my father proposed to her, and later in life she was able to treat the O'Mara debacle as just fate taking a hand. She was also fond of saying that my father had deliberately misled her so as to make sure she wouldn't be hired and have to leave Cork. I doubt that she was serious. My father, however, just smiled and maintained a diplomatic silence, on the basis that if he denied her allegation it might imply that he wasn't that put out by the prospect of her possibly leaving Cork, while if he admitted it, it would mean that he didn't love her enough to help her gain a career in music. Either way he couldn't win, but his smile was of someone who already had.

One day, when I hadn't reached even double figures, two very large boxes, addressed to my father, were delivered while he was at work. My mother and my two older brothers and I waited excitedly for him to come home and put us all out of our misery. When the boxes were opened, the secret was revealed: a portable gramophone and albums of two operas, *Pagliacci* and *Cavelleria Rusticana*, the tenor role in both being taken by Heddle Nash, probably the leading British tenor of the time.

My parents played the records over and over, and the celebrated arias cut their permanent tracks in my subconscious, but as soon as I started going to the cinema it was the songs of the Hollywood musicals that completely captivated me. This was also the era of the big British bands – Joe Loss, Jack

Hylton, Geraldo, Henry Hall and perhaps a dozen others whose evening broadcasts were my favourite programmes. Perhaps if Ireland had then an equivalent U2 or Boyzone or Bewitched, I'd have listened to them just as avidly, but by the time they dominated the scene I was orbiting in the world of classical music, and the pop groups of their day were to me an unknown species. Indeed, in London's Oxford Street one day in the 1960s, seeing an *Evening Standard* poster declare 'Beatles invade New York', I wondered first whether they could do as much damage as the plague of locusts had in biblical Egypt, and then felt amazed that the *Evening Standard* didn't know how to spell 'Beetles'.

I must have been just about entering my 'teens when classical music took me over completely, though I can still happily listen to such as Glenn Miller, Benny Goodman, Louis Armstrong, George Gershwin, Bing Crosby, Frank Sinatra, Art Tatum and the songs of Cole Porter, Irving Berlin, the Hammersteins and others. Some years earlier when there was a series of celebrity concerts in the Savoy Cinema to which my parents went, I went too, but not to a seat in the auditorium. I stationed myself in a lane behind the back of the cinema which was directly behind the stage, put my ear to the wall, and listened. Then, and in that fashion, I heard though could not see Paul Robeson, one of the most ravishingly perfect voices the world has ever heard, the celebrated soprano Toti del Monte, and the renowned violinist Kreisler. It was at the Savoy too, though fortunately on this occasion inside, that I first heard the strangest, most riveting sound in my life – the sound of silence.

It is said that silence is golden. Not for me, however. For me it has always been silver. Just think of the first three letters: S, I, L, sil. Both 'silence' and 'silver' commence with the same three letters, the same syllable. There it is again, sil, the sibilant shush sound, whereas 'golden' is a hard G sound, an explosive, noisy, reverberating gong word.

To say that I actually heard silence may seem a silly, even ridiculous claim. How can one hear what by definition is the absence of all sound? But the kind of silence that for me was an audible entity had a transcendental, levitational quality produced by the combination of a hush and its echo harmonising deep inside me.

The occasion was a recital given by one of my favourite pianists, Solomon, the first recital I had ever been to. As Solomon played, the audience listened enraptured. His programme was made up mostly of pieces by Mozart, Beethoven and Schumann, and when he finished and stood up to take his bow, the applause, the calls, the cheers, resounded to the roof. As soon as the clamour died down, Solomon sat again at the piano to give an encore. The encore was Chopin's 'Berceuse', perhaps the most breathtakingly beautiful of all Chopin's compositions. A cradle-song, with a five note rock-a-bye theme in the bass, its quiet assurance repeated over and over and over again, while above it Chopin weaved an embroidery of the most enchanting, caressing variations. Tenderly, delicately, with consummate mastery, one of the greatest Chopin players of all time spread over us the soft, heart-warm tones of that magical lullaby, until its final dying chords sank to a close as if with the quiet stealth of sleep.

When Solomon lifted his hands from the keys, no one stirred. For full five seconds there wasn't even the slightest crackle of applause. And then the spell broke and the cheering erupted. But for those long five seconds I had heard it – heard for the first time in my life that transcendental, levitational sound, the sound of silence.

From that night on, piano music became my obsession, and soon the instrument itself too. I knew that I wouldn't be happy until I learned to play it. We didn't then possess a piano, but my older brother, Elkan, was already so keen on the instrument that he had been learning from a teacher some distance away and going to his house twice a week to practise. Once I had finished with school and was preparing for University, I appealed to my mother to let me learn along with Elkan. As Gerard Shanahan, one of Ireland's most accomplished pianists who was also a teacher, lived on the Western Road, back to back with our home on the Mardyke, she decided the most practical course was for both of us to become his pupils. So she bought a second-hand piano and the necessary arrangements were made.

Arriving for my first lesson at his studio which was the front room of his house, I looked around me in astonishment. Hanging from the picture rails, leaning against the walls, tucked away in corners where errant steps could not damage them, were paintings, varying in size and startling in their colours. I had never seen anything like them before, nor did they seem to owe anything to the reproductions of famous paintings I had seen in art books. It turned out that they were all by Jack B. Yeats, and Gerard Shanahan turned out to be one of the first to build a private collection of the artist's work before he achieved his wide reputation.

The piano lessons were sheer delight. They usually took longer than scheduled and were interspersed with mini-recitals and discussions about the styles of various pianists as well as some diversions to talk of Art. One day Gerard gave me a book on Picasso to take home and read. I was at the time still trying to write poetry, and the illustrations inspired me to write six poems which I called 'Pictures from an

Exhibition', copies of which I included when I returned the book.

In my second year, after I had learned pieces of increasing technical difficulty, by Bach, Debussy, Grieg, Beethoven, Mendelssohn and Chopin, Gerard asked me what work I would most like to play.

'There are so many,' I said.

'Yes, but name one.'

'Any one?'

'Any one at all.'

'Well,' I ventured. Hesitated. Then plunged, almost losing my voice. 'Mozart's D minor Piano Concerto.'

'Bring the music next week and we'll start it.'

That was certainly the happiest day of my life up to then.

When I went to Dublin to enter King's Inns, that ended my lessons with Gerard Shanahan, but he arranged for me to continue at the Reid School, though the change of teachers and styles was so unsettling that I made little progress. However, one exciting surprise compensated for everything. Going to King's Inns to sign on, I came on a small shop with its window displaying second-hand gramophone records. Behind the counter was a sandy-haired, bespectacled man whose name I later learned was Mr Sage. I asked him if he had any classical records. He said nothing, but smiled proudly and spread his hands wide in invitation. Every spare inch of every wall, and of the low ceiling too, had a record affixed to it with a strong drawing pin through the needle-hole. They were all classical, as were the many boxes of records on the surrounding tables. I became a regular customer there on the days I had a lecture at the Inns, and when I went home at Christmas after my first Law term, I brought back as my luggage two crammed hat boxes of mostly piano recordings.

For two days I played them almost non-stop, one after the other, before I went to the piano. That day I played better than I ever played before or since. For the only time in my life, I felt, and was, inspired.

CHAPTER FOUR

The Bird in the Hand

1945 was for me a watershed year. I turned twenty-one, was called to the Bar, and was published for the first time. Given that I had never regarded birthdays as anything to celebrate and that the prospect of a very much less than desired legal career now seemed inevitable, the third of these events was the only one that made the year special. And even that, something not remotely on the horizon, came about only with the help of a major stroke of luck.

The distraction of living away from home and the drudgery of having to study had stultified my attempts to write. I had been concentrating on poetry, but the lines I produced were stillborn. Casting about for some motivation, some elixir, I suddenly remembered an Irish poem I had learned at school which had so enchanted me with its music and imagery that I had translated it. It was a poem of twenty-two lines by an eighteenth-century poet, Brian Merriman. What, understandably, the school anthology did not disclose was that the twenty-two lines were merely the poem's opening and that there were over a thousand further lines of rollicking bawdiness about the difficulties Irish women were having in enticing Irish males into the marriage bed. The poem, 'The Midnight Court', has by now gone through some seven or eight different translators as well as a number of stage adaptations.

The recollection of my excitement at trying to match as closely as possible the music, metre, rhyme scheme, mood and current of the original opening while still being faithful to the words and their meaning, gave me a new impetus. If I had managed one translation, why not another? But this time I needed a different kind of poem, one that would shake me and wake me with a good story, a strong voice, and perhaps a touch of humour to lighten the load.

The poem I chose was 'The Yellow Bittern' by Cathal Buí Mac Giolla Ghunna – 'Yellow' Caul MacGilligan – about the poet's discovery one wintry morning of the little bird stretched out dead on a frozen lake, having been unable to break the ice and quench its thirst. MacGilligan was any-thing but a stranger to drink himself, and being constantly nagged by his wife that drink would kill him if he didn't give it up, he distilled from the poem the irony of the poor bittern being killed, not by drink, but by 'the lack of a drop'.

Shortly after I finished the translation I happened to meet a former member of the Cork Jewish community, Larry Elyan, who was working in the Dublin Civil Service. He was much older than me, but speaking to me once in Cork and asking what I was going to do with my life, I had disclosed my literary ambitions.

'What are you writing now?' he enquired when we met again in Dublin.

Proudly I showed him my translation. He read it and asked if he could keep it. Much flattered, I of course agreed. A few weeks later he phoned me to come and meet him in

Davy Byrne's pub. When I arrived he introduced me to Frank O'Connor.

I was immediately overwhelmed, not only by Frank O'Connor's physical bigness – big physique, big face, big head of near-white hair, thick black eyebrows, big black-rimmed spectacles – but even more potently by his charm and big, sonorous voice. Of what he said I remember only that he declaimed lines from my translation, praised it inordinately, and then pushed it into my hand, saying, 'I'll tell you what you'll do. Take it straight up to the literary editor of *The Irish Times*, give it to him and tell him I said he's to publish it.'

Spellbound by this heady turn of events, I couldn't but obey his command. More excited than nervous, I made my way to the Irish Times and asked to see the literary editor, saying that Frank O'Connor had sent me. Without ado I was taken up to the literary editor's room.

He was another tall man, but this time dark-haired and spare. With a small smile he sat me down, asking why Frank O'Connor had sent me. I held out my translation and, almost prefacing my reply with 'Please, sir,' answered, 'Mr O'Connor said to give you this and to tell you to publish it.'

Another smile, this one perhaps slightly wry as his glance at my manuscript showed him it was a poem. He carefully, almost respectfully, put it on his desk.

'I can't read it now,' he said. 'But I'll be in touch with you,' and he showed me out.

Every Saturday I rushed to *The Irish Times* book page to see if the weekly poem was mine. It never was, and after some months my inspection of the book page was made with ever-evaporating expectation.

Then luck intervened once more – I almost bumped into Frank O'Connor outside Trinity College. He stopped me immediately and asked, 'Did *The Irish Times* publish that poem of yours?'

'No.'

He grabbed my arm. 'What in the name of God are you waiting for? Go up to that literary editor and tell him I said he *must* publish it. Go on now.'

So I went.

Again I was taken up to the literary editor. Again he sat me down before rifling through some papers in a deep drawer and coming up with what, even at a distance, I could see was my poem.

He looked at it a moment. 'Well,' he said, 'I like it. But it's a bit too long for me.'

I made no reply. True, it was 'a bit long' – five eight-line verses – but that its length might be an obstacle had never occurred to me.

He thought for another moment. 'I'll tell you what. If you let me drop one verse, I'll use it.'

'Yellow' Caul not being around, I raised no objection. A few weeks later the poem, minus a verse, appeared. At last, I felt, at last my career was launched – even if it had taken some luck to get it off the pad. Or was it luck? The fact was that Larry Elyan was from Cork, Frank O'Connor was from Cork, I was from Cork, and the literary editor, Jack White, was also from Cork. Perhaps in Ireland it's not only who you know, it's also where you come from!

Luck, however, is also often another word for coincidence, for in the same year, 1945, Maurice Fridberg's Hourglass imprint published Frank O'Connor's translation of the complete 'The Midnight Court'. I read it and was not only overwhelmed by the superb rendition, but quite stunned by the poem's subject-matter. Who, knowing only its innocent opening, could possibly have imagined what followed? Indeed, for a moment I felt that I had been taken in by the anthology's non-disclosure of the poem's main concern!

For the next four or five years, as well as being increasingly involved in founding my first publishing/editorial venture, I launched a major assault on papers and periodicals all over the world with poems, some more translations, and short stories, being rewarded with sufficiently frequent acceptances – some unpaid – to make me feel that my literary cause was not without hope, however scanty. By then Frank O'Connor's translation had been banned by the Irish Censorship Board and the culturally criminal nonsense of leaving the Irish original unbanned but banning an English version incensed me. Of course the Board was no doubt well aware of how few Irish men and women at that time were interested in the literature of the language, so they were on safe ground. More or less as a one-man protest I decided to thumb my nose at the crass ukase of the establishment and frustrate it with an act of auto-pollution. I sought out the Irish original and read it.

I hadn't got very far beyond the opening twenty-two lines when I knew what I wanted to do. I translated the whole of Part 1 and sent it to Liam Miller at the Dolmen Press, asking if he might be interested in the other three Parts. With his encouragement I completed my translation, and in 1953 it was published by the Dolmen Press in a *de luxe* edition of two hundred copies for subscribers only – perhaps a Liam Miller tactic to forestall another ban – and was launched in Dublin by Benedict Kiely. I stayed at home in Cork, pleading some trumped-up excuse for my inability to attend. The truth was that I feared conversation would be partly, if not wholly, in Irish, and despite my fluency in reading and writing the language, reading and writing it was all I had been taught in school. Only simple linking sentences were the maximum otherwise required and conversation as an ongoing communal exchange did not exist. Consequently, I decided that to expose myself to the likely challenge of having, for the first time in my life, to enter into extended, confident, practised Irish conversation with fluent speakers, was a risk I hadn't the courage to take.

The stultifying, unimaginative attitude to the teaching of Irish in school seems to have continued for some time since then, for a few years ago Medb Ruane wrote in *The Irish Times*, 'My generation was administered Irish the way we were administered cod liver oil. Although I can remember inspirational teachers in French, Latin and English, I cannot recall the name or face of even one Irish teacher at second level.' Such, too, was my own experience. And I have always regretted my loss and blamed compulsion and empty lip-service for the long-lasting, wholesale flight from the language that was the response of students since the foundation of the State. What a tragedy that, given the opportunity to revive Irish over a century after its suppression, the method chosen was, incredibly, further coercion.

In the days after the launch of my 'Midnight Court' translation I began to examine my motivation for translating Irish poetry and to ask myself whether the practice could be justified. The question had been raised for me not long after founding the periodical *Poetry Ireland*, when, deciding to devote an issue to Irish translations, I wrote to a celebrated Irish writer to ask if he would contribute the lead article on the theme of translating Irish poetry. Now this celebrated writer was too busy to write such an article, but being a kind man his reply ran to a couple of thousand words, and with a P.S., 'Make any use of this you like', it was of course the article I wanted. The writer was Seán O'Faoláin and the question he opened with was: 'Why do we translate from the Irish at all? Have we not done enough and more than enough of it?'

He went on to say, 'When I am given a translation of modern Irish poetry (from, say, about 1600) I am being invited, it seems to me, either to take the translation instead of the original, or to enjoy the skill or virtuosity of the translator rather than the poem as a poem . . . I wonder if this habit of translating is not a habit chiefly; a hang-over of the nineteen-hundreds? Is it not an echo of the years when Mangan, or Ferguson, or Yeats *had* to get to Gaelic Ireland through English?' And Seán O'Faoláin continued, '. . . The fashion of translating from Irish was part of the elementary exploration of a Gaelic world that was, then, still living, and that then, because of politics, had a lively value as an excitation and inspiration. That Gaelic note, that Gaelic thought, that emotion, is today a cliché. It is worse when a modern employs it: it is sentimentality . . . All translations from the Irish can now be no more than either the occasional technical amusement of a poet, or a flower cast gratefully on a grave.'

For my own part, not being a native speaker or a Gaelic scholar, my enjoyment of translating Irish poetry was to a great extent para-physical. It always gave me a sense of elation that was more than just spiritual. The sheer hard work, the trial and error of seeking to reproduce as faithfully as possible the vital statistics of a poem was a thoroughly exhausting struggle. Perhaps my translations could nearly be called, in Seán O'Faoláin's phrase, 'the occasional technical amusement of a poet'. I say 'nearly' because, firstly, although my attempts were occasional, they weren't made in any spirit of mere dalliance; and secondly, if they were fashioned only to amuse myself, then I had a rather masochistic sense of enjoyment; and thirdly, if they were only technical exercises . . . but is there such an animal as a translation that is only a technical exercise? Every translation is a Galatea – a representation, or adaptation, or copy even, of some beauty which the translator has known and wishes to possess, but to possess it he must not merely translate, he must recreate – like Pygmalion he must somehow breathe life into what he has fashioned. V.S. Pritchett commented, 'Poetry can be remade but not translated.' And further, as Hilaire Belloc pointed out, the translator must also be translating from a language in which he is very proficient. If a would-be translator fulfils all these requirements, then what he produces may be good or not so good, but it is more than just a matter of technique. If that's all it is, then we can expect the best translations of the future to come from computers.

CHAPTER FIVE

Trial by Trauma

If 1945 was my watershed year, coming home to Cork made me realise that the memories of pre-Dublin years were not only the memories of a different person, water under the bridge, but that the bridge itself had been swept away. The city hadn't changed, the people I knew there hadn't changed, the small world I had inhabited hadn't changed. And looking into myself I knew that I hadn't changed either – yet. The largely isolated nature of my student days both at UCC and King's Inns had produced an arrested adolescence. My ignorance was akin to that of the Irish public under the joke of national censorship, the Irish government's *cordon sanitaire*. The population had been generally kept in the dark about the war engulfing Europe. But not all of us. Not Ireland's five thousand Jews. Since Hitler's takeover of Germany in the mid-thirties the reports of mounting anti-Semitic outrages had not been very seriously regarded by world governments, and later even the stories of Hitler's Final Solution had similarly been discounted. But again not by Ireland's Jews. Cork's four hundred Jews knew, knew from letters and messages smuggled out, what was happening to their co-religionists in

Germany, knew that the five thousand Jews of Ireland had been marked down for slaughter in due course.

For me *Kristallnacht* had been a single incident and in another country. But the Nazi blitzkrieg that overran Europe had in May, 1940, threatened to invade and overrun Ireland as well. By 1945 the war was over and that threat had been banished. But not for me. I still remembered that May night in 1940 – and even today reports of neo-Nazi demonstrations in Germany recall it – when hour after hour I stayed awake listening for the rattle of machine-guns, for the earth-shaking tanks like some reborn dinosaurs, for the tramp of Nazi boots on Cork's innocent streets and the *panzer* divisions raging through the Mardyke. Though the dawn at last rose on untroubled skies with no drone of bombers disturbing the morning silence, no whistle of plunging missiles screaming through the air, no cacodemons of my wideawake nocturnal dreams running riot in a sky fulgent with blazing arrows and a plague of pluvial blood raining down from a new Pharaoh – though there was nothing of that that I could see, my vigil still had not ended. On my way to school I almost dared search for paratroopers hiding behind the Mardyke's elms, for Nazi insignia on the lamp posts, their Stygian swastikas like algebraic symbols that always added up to the same solution: doom, death, oblivion.

But that had been 1940, I told myself, and now I knew the real watershed was that it all really *was* over and I was alive. My family – parents, brothers, sister – were unharmed, our city intact, its streets and buildings undefiled. They were no longer the mere bricks and mortar of my adolescent venues, they were the scaffolding of my new existence, humming their message of rhyme and reason. Other magic cities had known Gehenna – Dresden obliterated, London razed, St Petersburg levelled – but I could walk an unchanged, undesecrated Cork, treasuring its streets and lanes, tonguing the romantic vowels of its exotic place-names: Tivoli, Shanakiel, Montenotte, the Marina. They sounded no clanging hammerblows, unlike the litany scored into my consciousness as ineradicably as if a number had been tattooed on my forearm.

That new existence of mine, what was it to be? The long nightmare that had passed could never be forgotten, but it had to be put on the back burner of my mind alongside the other burners, the crematoria of Auschwitz, Dachau, Belsen, Buchenwald. I had a way to find, a new bridge to build. I examined where the manacles of war – what the government had termed the Emergency – and of misdirected study had brought me in the previous five years, and I recognised that what I had gone through had been my own emergency from which I now had to emerge.

Before 1946 was over I had left the Bar and set about founding a literary quarterly.

─────⊶⊶⊶─────

CHAPTER SIX

Irish Writing: *First Steps*

When or how the short story replaced the poem as my lodestone I cannot exactly date or explain. It was a subterranean, and therefore gradual takeover, probably set off by the subconscious realisation that I would never make a poet. A poet, it is said, is born, not made, whereas my poetry was made, not born – and while it still sang inside me, the manifold worlds of the short story were becoming my university of life.

What, too, must have been an early influence on my change of direction was the discovery that Irish short story writers were among the world's best – Joyce, O'Flaherty, the Cork duo O'Faoláin and O'Connor – but it was not an Irish writer who detonated the charge that blew my devotion to poetry a fair distance back into my literary hinterland and set me instead worshipping among the mountainous ranges of the short story.

One afternoon in the Cork Public Library I came upon an unusual-looking book, its spine now lighting up in my recollection as aglint with silver, and the even more unusual components of its title scarred on with blood-red letters. The book was called *The Daring Young Man on the Flying Trapeze*; the name of the author was William Saroyan. The book, his first, was a collection of short stories. I took it home and swallowed it whole.

Saroyan was born in Fresno, California, in 1908, of Armenian parents. After the classic American succession of undistinguished jobs, he settled in San Francisco and wrote. His stories were an instant literary sensation, although the over-enthusiasm and sentimentality of the early ones would render them indigestible today. But even in the US they were at that time stunningly individual and fresh, and as like as not it was his particular brand of 'newness' that made such an indelible impression on me at an impressionable age, and locked my course onto the short story and its importance to literature in general and Irish writing in particular.

There were then only two Irish periodicals of note that published short stories, *The Bell*, edited by Seán O'Faoláin and later Peadar O'Donnell, and *The Dublin Magazine*, edited by Seamus O'Sullivan. Seated in the Reference Room of the Library, I would take up *The Bell*, its very title an alarm-call, its tall, rectangular cover, always differently coloured, like a doorway out of which every month would spill a galaxy of busy-tongued, free-ranging guests. For *The Dublin Magazine* I had to cross the corridor to the Lending Department where, reposing on a long counter, was this large, always grey, always square, upper-class-looking quarterly, printed on pukka art paper that commanded respect. To read it, however, no seat was provided, and one had to remain standing as if in the company of one's betters. The editors of these two periodicals each gave out a different vibe, *The Bell's* that of being a no-nonsense sergeant, *The Dublin Magazine's* that of a smooth, deceptively languid superior officer.

Research reveals that in 155 issues over 33 years, *The Dublin Magazine* published some 120 stories, quite a few of which were translations from foreign languages, while in 131 issues over 14 years, *The Bell* published 175 stories. Of course I wasn't reading these periodicals throughout their publishing lives – I was only one year old when *The Dublin Magazine* first appeared – but the figures would seem to indicate that, although Ireland's then foremost short story writers appeared in the pages of both, the form was not favoured with any special attention. Certainly not enough to satisfy my appetite for stories, and nothing to compare with the exciting *Penguin New Writing* which gave lavish space to short stories – often by Irish writers – and for which every month I hurried to O'Sullivan's, the newsagent in Oliver Plunket Street, to see if the latest issue was in. Every time I added yet another to the growing collection on my bookshelf I saw them as an example – no, a reprimand – to whatever or whoever was to blame for not cultivating the Irish short story. Without consistent and dedicated encouragement, how could the form survive, where would the new writers of real talent come from?

These questions troubled my mind in the same resigned, but complaining fashion as a government's blundering riles the man-in-the-street.

'At least,' I grouched to my eldest brother, Abraham, on whom I frequently unloaded my grumbles, 'the-man-in-the-street can do something. He has a vote and eventually he can throw out the government.'

'So why don't *you* do something?' he came back at me. 'Why don't you start a short story magazine yourself?'

'With what?'

'Would you if you could?'

'Of course I would,' I replied, comfortably secure in the knowledge that our exchange was as pointless as an empty water-pistol.

During the war one was told that a poster warning 'Loose Talk Costs Lives' was prominently displayed throughout Britain. In a loose sense one could say that my loose talk cost my life, in that it led to everything that followed. My brother was very friendly with a successful business man in the community, and in one of their time-passing conversations he retailed the chit-chat we had had. The result was an offer to finance a short story magazine, not as a business investment, but as a silent, behind-the-scenes involvement in a cultural venture.

I could not believe it. And when I was assured that the offer was genuine, I didn't want to believe it. How could I possibly edit an Irish literary magazine? My inadequacies were glaring – I had never moved in literary circles, had had next to nothing published, was unknown to writers on whose goodwill and co-operation such a venture would depend, was totally ignorant of publishing, printing and editing processes and conventions, was barely twenty-one – not an age to inspire others with confidence – and I lived in Cork, a provincial base from which one having the temerity to address a national readership might be regarded as an upstart. Furthermore, I was a Jew. How could an unknown, Jewish callow youth expect to be taken seriously? I wasn't Leopold Bloom. And even he was only a paper Jew.

Yet the opportunity was too tempting to reject out of hand, and encouraged by my brother, who volunteered to act as business manager as long as his medical studies allowed – which was not at all long – I fell to weighing up and emphasising the risks and pitfalls. Being terrified of what I had set afoot, I thought I was looking for a way out when in fact, as I realise now, I was looking for a way in. And then my innate racial caution floated the idea that failure might be easier to avoid, or to share, if I were to combine forces with someone who was appreciably senior to me in years and had the requisite literary knowledge and experience; and, above all, that he be of the majority religion, for I was very conscious of my unfamiliarity with the susceptibilities of Irish readers. But where and how could I, with no Catholic friends of any sort, find such a person? Uncannily, the question was trailed by its answer.

Early in my study periods in Dublin I had been taken to meet the playwright Teresa Deevy, where she lived in her Ballsbridge flat with her sister, Nell. Nell was her constant companion, Tessa having completely lost her hearing when she was in university. Her deafness was no barrier to her passion for the stage – much of her work, including her two masterpieces, *The King of Spain's Daughter* and *Katie Roche*, was produced at the Abbey – nor indeed did it inhibit her eagerness to meet people, especially if they were interested in or connected with the arts. She held open house most Sunday afternoons and there was no knowing what famous people might casually drop in on such occasions. Two I particularly recall were Thomas MacGreevy of whose work I was ignorant, and Jack B. Yeats, with whose paintings my piano teacher, Gerard Shanahan, had made me so familiar. Yeats's favourite pose was lying back in an armchair, legs stretched out, elbows planted on the arm-rests with his arms raised like the sides of a triangle, fingers meeting at their tips before his eyes. Talking to Tessa was in no way difficult as she was an excellent lip reader. I soon learned to look straight at her, shaping my words, and also got used to her voice dropping away at the ends of sentences as if she had no breath left. Looking at her so intensely I was struck by the vividness of her large, staring, brown eyes and the sharp intake of breath that animated her open-mouthed smile, while Nell, cigarette permanently between her fingers, was always near at hand, on the *qui vive* to turn to her sister with exaggerated articulation of any stray word Tessa had somehow failed quite to gather.

Before very long Tessa became my closest friend in Dublin, and with her encouragement I frequently called during weekday evenings when, with only Nell's often wickedly humorous comments as accompaniment, Tessa opened me up to myself. She often talked to me about my feeling of isolation both in Cork and Dublin, and during my holiday periods at home she wrote multi-page letters about our mutual interests, no page treated as full unless the sentences were allowed chase up and around the margins. Then in the summer of 1945 she paid a visit to Cork and introduced me to someone with whom she felt I'd find a lot in common. The someone was Terence Smith.

CHAPTER SEVEN

Irish Writing: *First Staggers*

Terence was a sub-editor in the *Cork Examiner*, probably at least fifteen years older than I, living with his mother and brother on the Western Road, about five minutes around the corner from my home on the Mardyke. He had fluent French, was very widely read, an art lover and a playwright who, as far as I knew, had never tried to have his plays produced. After Teresa Deevy had introduced us I doubt that we met more than twice. In fact we were not at all well-matched, both of us being shy, which meant that we exchanged more tension-filled silences than conversation, and so he did not at first enter my mind as a likely congenial co-editor. Besides, I had come up with someone whose participation, if forthcoming, would guarantee the new magazine's authority, status and success. This someone was Seán O'Faoláin.

It was April, 1946, just when O'Faoláin had announced his retirement as editor of *The Bell*. To me the timing seemed to be particularly serendipitous and so I immediately wrote him, outlining my plans for a new literary quarterly and asking if he would consider editing it, with me as his assistant. He replied saying that having just relinquished one editorial chair, he didn't see himself jumping straight into another one, but that if I happened to come to Dublin, I could call on him and he would be happy to give me any advice and help he could. I still foolishly hoped that I might convince him and so I arranged to go to Dublin.

We met in the garden of his home in Killiney on what must have been an unusually clement pre-summer day. I felt completely overawed in his presence but he quickly put me at my ease by asking about myself and comparing the Cork of his youth and of mine. This prelude to the real business of my visit gave me a chance to observe him. Knowing he was born in 1900 and so nearly half a century old, I, being less than half his age, had expected to find someone rather elderly-looking. Far from it. His figure was lithe, his smile eager, his eyes sparkling and his voice enthusiastic – the enthusiasm being on my behalf and on behalf of the projected magazine. He thought it was a good idea and that I should go home and edit it myself; as its originator I had the duty to see it through, to which duty I should now add the responsibility. He was sure the writers would support it, and when I asked if he would lead the list with a short story, he agreed without hesitation. He didn't say what fee he would expect, but as I had to know what the leading writers should be paid, I asked him. Twenty-five guineas was the figure he quoted. After various bits of advice and stray tips about dealing with writers – published and unpublished – and literary agents, he wished me good luck and I left. The sun, I remember, was still shining.

On the four hour plus train journey back to Cork, I became depressed, ready to turn tail and forget all my nonsense. This mood lasted until the train entered the very long tunnel that ends exactly where the Cork station platform begins. It was a tunnel with which I was very familiar and which always induced in me a dream-like state. Speed through it was slow – it took most of five minutes to negotiate – and without the carriage lights all would have been pitch black darkness. So to have it end with such a sudden burst of natural light was like awakening into a new day, into an all-will-be-well feeling, the comfort-cushions of hope and dismissed doubts. Next day I went around to Terence Smith, told him my plans, and asked him to be my co-editor. From that moment the die was cast.

I suggested we should meet twice a week, Monday and Friday afternoons, in alternate houses, starting the following Monday in mine. At the outset of that meeting Terence asked if I had a title for the quarterly. I hadn't, so I suggested the first one that entered my mind, *Irish Writing*. After some hesitation, he said, 'It's a bit obvious, isn't it? And perhaps ambiguous too.' I agreed, but every other name we bandied about didn't appeal, and rather than waste time we decided to stay with *Irish Writing*. We also quickly agreed to aim at having five or six stories in each issue, some poetry, three essays or critical articles, and some book reviews. We then put together a list of the prominent Irish writers whom I, as the founding-editor, was to ask for contributions.

My brother's initial business task was to engage a printer. He found a local jobbing printer who, to our shock, pointed out that as paper was still rationed and not easy to get, he would need money to buy it. We were considerably relieved when our sponsor immediately gave us a cheque for the required amount.

By mid-summer the first issue had begun to take shape. One by one the replies came from the authors I had written and, one by one, manuscripts arrived. Frank O'Connor, whom

I went to Dublin to meet, was warm in his enthusiasm and offered us a new story, 'Babes in the Wood'. Unfortunately, we found we would not be allowed use it before its publication in *The New Yorker* and so we had to forego it. O'Connor's reaction was swift: he sent us another story, 'The Stepmother', which was under no such embargo.

On the same visit to Dublin I read in the newspaper that Liam O'Flaherty had just sailed in from America where he had been throughout the war, and was staying in the Gresham Hotel. Taking a chance I called to the hotel early the next morning and asked to see him. Fully prepared for a rebuff, or at best a cross-examination, I certainly hadn't expected the answer that I should come up to his room. I found a tall, finely-built man, standing in vest and trousers before a mirror, his face covered in lather. He told me to sit on the bed because it was more comfortable and tell him what I wanted. While he shaved, I talked, and my request for a story brought an instant promise of one. When I raised the question of fee, O'Flaherty briskly, almost off-handedly, put in, 'Whatever you're paying the others will do me.' He told me that he was off to Aran next day but that he would send me the story in three weeks. Before the time was up I received a telegram from him. It read: 'Story ready. Send money.' The story was one of his masterpieces, 'The Touch', a Gaelic version of which appeared in his Irish language collection, *Dúil*, published in 1953, and which later led to a controversy as to what version came first.

One morning the postman delivered a very large envelope with the address written in tall, graceful script. Inside, in the same hand, was a warmly encouraging note from James Stephens, modestly suggesting that perhaps the story he was sending wasn't half-bad, but if we didn't like it, no harm done. The story was 'A Rhinoceros, Some Ladies, and a Horse'. It was probably the most popular we ever published, and on its appearance was promptly snapped up by the *American Mercury*.

As publication of No. 1 had been planned for September, our printer had been setting the work as it came in, but when I saw the proofs of what he had completed, I was appalled. Apart from the number of typographical errors and dropped or misplaced lines, the type size and style was not at all what had been agreed and very many letters were broken. A fierce argument ensued, but it was obvious that we had no hope of getting any satisfaction. It was also clear that to stay with that printer was out of the question, so we had to pay for the work already done and engage a printer in whom total reliance could be placed. As we expected, a printer with an established reputation would be appreciably more expensive than the one we had left, and as we had already paid the writers who had sent us work as well as the latter, my brother was worried about the reaction he might get from our sponsor. His worst fears were realised. The sponsor, whose ignorance of what his cultural ego-trip might cost him was as total as ours, withdrew. I was faced with ignominious failure and all it would entail.

That blow was the first really serious one I had suffered in my life, and even though worse was to follow financially, being the first it didn't seem as if there could be any greater disaster. But brooding upon it, the weight of my dejection somehow reawakened the memory of a previous experience, a memory which had never revisited me before and which, compared to it, my present setback was hardly more than a stumble.

One day when I was twelve I suddenly developed an unbearable stomach pain. The doctor was called, acute appendicitis was diagnosed, I was taken off to hospital and operated on that evening. Next day, instead of showing improvement, my condition had deteriorated. The following day I was even worse. Very soon my parents were told that I was sinking rapidly, and as no cause could be found, little hope could be held out. Prayers were said for me in the synagogue. As a last resort the surgeon decided to operate on me again. Even though the appendectomy had been completely routine and without apparent complication, an internal investigation was the only course left to him. He found that I was steadily bleeding from a broken blood vessel and would not have lasted another day. He had no idea why it should have broken, but he stitched it up and put a tube in my stomach to drain the blood that had accumulated. My condition immediately improved, but I spent six weeks in hospital instead of the normal two. The surgeon had saved my life – or so he believed ever after, and I couldn't begrudge him his claim of credit. But in fact the man who really saved my life was Mr Morrissey.

Mr Morrissey was the white-haired gentleman sitting up and reading in the only other bed in the room when I awoke after the first operation. The chair next to my bed was empty, though I had been told that a nurse would be there to attend to me the moment I opened my eyes. My only sensation was one of an unbearable thirst, caused by the method used those days of rendering the patient unconscious by pouring chloroform on a mask placed over the nose. On a chest at the other side of the room I saw a carafe of water. I promptly got out of bed and started to cross towards it.

'What are you doing?' Mr Morrissey shouted.

I pointed at the carafe.

'Get back into bed, boy. Get back immediately,' he ordered.

I climbed back into bed and promptly fell asleep.

When I was eventually released from hospital and my parents told me how and why I nearly died, I told them about the carafe of water and Mr Morrissey. Of course my parents put two and two together but decided not to make a fuss. I had completely recovered, I was home, that was all they wanted. Some weeks later, when I was with my mother as she was shopping in the Grand Parade Market, we passed a butcher's stall. Behind it was Mr Morrissey. We recognised each other immediately. It transpired that he had left hospital the morning after my attempted involuntary suicide and had not been aware of its sequel. But it set up a bond between us, and my mother and I visited his stall regularly afterwards until his death some years later. On these visits I had always wished I could explain to him that as we were Jewish and he wasn't a *kosher* butcher we could never show our gratitude by buying our meat from him.

Why had it taken some fourteen years for me to recall, and recall so vividly, the prologue to that whole episode? I had no recollection of suffering physically or mentally, so what was the connection between it and the dejection into which my present crisis had plunged me? The more the question nagged me, the more I nagged it back. I could have died, I should have died, but I hadn't. Why not? I took no account of the prayers in the synagogue or of divine intervention. I had long abandoned belief in such an agency, going through life more or less as circumstances directed. It was circumstances that had presented me with the opportunity of starting a literary quarterly, something I wanted to do, and my decision to take that opportunity and give up the Bar was my first ever act of self-identification. Was the course I had chosen what my life was meant to be about, was that why it had been saved by Mr Morrissey? Yet now circumstances had turned about once more, offering a new alternative which, were I only to accept it, would release me from my folly with only hurt pride. But that I hadn't rushed at the chance of escape, that I was agonising so much over the offer, tended to prove to me that what I was still looking for was not a way out, but a way back in. I knew I couldn't find it by myself. The only person I could turn to was my father, who believed, as did my mother, that their children's happiness was theirs too. So I told him what had happened and asked him what, if anything, I could do about it. He had up to now taken an indulgent, parental interest in my ambitions. Would he still?

'You ask me what you can do about it, yes?'

'Yes.'

'The answer is: nothing.'

Silence.

'You mean I should get out while the going is good?'

'I didn't say that.'

'No, but you said there's nothing I can do about it.'

'Nothing *you* can do about it. But *I* can, if that is what you want. I can sign in the bank for a loan for you, enough to publish the first issue. After that you're on your own.'

CHAPTER EIGHT

A Visit to Drishane House

High on my list of favourite Irish short stories ever since I had first read them were the Somerville and Ross *Irish R.M.* collections, and there was no doubt in my mind that if I could have a contribution from Edith Somerville in the first issue of *Irish Writing*, it would be the jewel in the crown. But she was then eighty-eight and I had no idea what her state of health might be, so when I wrote to her at her Castletown-shend home, Drishane House, I was fully prepared for a polite refusal. The reply, however, was not from her but from her nephew, Sir Neville Coghill, the Chaucer authority and Oxford don, who was at the time on holiday at Castletown-shend. He wrote that his aunt would be happy to discuss my request with me and he invited me to Drishane House to meet her. He went on to say that if I were travelling by train I would have to stay with him overnight as the only train arrived at Skibbereen, the nearest station, at an hour after Dr Edith would have retired. I didn't have a car, and anyway couldn't drive, so the train and an overnight stay it would have to be.

The prospect appalled me. It had never occurred to me that my letter could lead to having to meet and talk with such a literary icon as Edith Somerville, but as the purpose of the visit was only to get her to contribute to the inaugural issue of *Irish Writing*, after a few days the prospect became more exciting than daunting. Unfortunately, the lapse of time allowed the other prospect – the overnight stay with such an august literary personage as Neville Coghill – to become the real terror. How would I possibly maintain any extended, serious conversation with an Oxford don and authority on Chaucer, of whose work I was totally ignorant? He would not be expecting to have on his hands a mere callow youth presenting himself as the editor of a projectedly important literary periodical. I would be exposed as an impostor, a humbug, a charlatan. And altogether apart from conversation, what about comportment? How did one behave in such surroundings? What was the protocol at table? What should I wear, for God's sake? I, who had never in my life been inside a non-Jewish home, and here I was, galloping headlong into the Big House of Irish literature. It was a situation which Leopold Bloom, with some help from Joyce, might have handled, but Leopold Bloom I was not. However, there was no alternative. I had had to write to Sir Neville accepting his kind invitation.

From my home in Cork the train journey to Skibbereen was only ninety miles but it took almost four hours. World War II might have ended, but the Emergency, Ireland's ironic euphemism for that little altercation somewhere off its shores, was still in force, so fuel was scarce and trains were running on what the wags called a mixture of coal-dust, peat, and splinters of wood borrowed from the more outlying parts of the third-class carriages. It was a long and very cold four hours, which I made longer by spending the whole time worrying. The only consolation I could think of – and to call it consolation was a triumph of self-delusion – was that once I was met at the station by Sir Neville, I would be so busy trying to create an impression that I'd have no more time for angst.

Immediately the train puffed to a stop I was out on the platform looking for my host. But this, surely, couldn't be Sir Neville – a small, jarveyish man, touching his cap and stretching his hand out for my little travelling case?

'Mr Marcus?' he enquired in a soft, country voice.

I nodded uncertainly.

'Follow me, sir,' and he led the way.

Ah, of course, the car, with Sir Neville, would be waiting outside the station.

But there was no car there, only a small, round, horse-and-trap affair, like a tub on wheels – and no Sir Neville in it. My guide opened the little door, put in my bag, handed me up and hopped onto the seat in front. Jogging the horse into motion, he said, 'Sir Neville is waiting for you in the house, sir.'

As we jolted and bounced over the miles I tried to keep calm but panic mounted inside me as we drew nearer our destination. I essayed a few conversational sentences. The weather allowed a speculative comment or two. Then our conveyance – 'I bet the horse is used to this journey. He seems to take it easily,' I said. It was an even more inane remark than I suspected. 'Aye,' was the considered reply, 'she's a good oul' mare, is Nancy.' I said no more.

At last we turned into the drive of Drishane House and eased to a stop at the open door where my host immediately materialised. Though I had, of course, seen many pictures of Edith Somerville, I had never seen one of her nephew. I had imagined a dryish, donnish, smallish man. I found before me a giant, large-boned, long-handed, big-headed – a man so tall that his shoulders seemed slightly rounded from continued bending to communicate with his fellow-men.

Even more striking was his face – I couldn't help immediately bringing to mind that old Frankenstein of the cinema, Boris Karloff; a warm, friendly, smiling, even good-looking Boris Karloff, to be sure, but withal a Boris Karloff. Sir Neville betrayed no surprise at my extreme youth but politely showed me to my room, intimating that as soon as I was ready I could come down for a spot of food.

I was now so worried that I had to sit on the edge of the bed to cool off. How long should I delay? Three minutes? Five? Ten? Even before I could decide, there was a knock on the door. 'Ready?' said my host, as he opened it and stooped in. I sprang up and accompanied him, feeling as if I was taking my last walk. Going downstairs he told me that his mother, Lady Coghill, and the other guests and family were in the village, attending the cinema, and would be back late. I heaved a sigh. At least that was something I did not have to face immediately. We entered the dining room. 'I've eaten already,' he said, 'so I'll just sit and talk with you while you have your dinner.'

Dinner, I could see, was cold meat – and that faced me with my first dilemma. As an orthodox Jew I had never eaten non-kosher meat. What should I do? The ordeal of having to keep up a literary conversation with Sir Neville was giving me enough to think about without affronting him at the outset by rejecting his food. I decided to swallow the meat along with one of the fundamental taboos of my upbringing.

If only that had proved to be my only problem! No sooner was I seated at the table than my host's first words struck terror into my very entrails.

'You'll have a drink?' he murmured, and for the first time I spotted a tumbler flanked by a bottle of Paddy, its regimental stance and golden glitter played on by the vying lights of a palatial chandelier and sparklingly reflected in the array of highly-polished silver, like rows of Royal Horseguards, on either side of the place-mat before me. The bottle was already in Sir Neville's hand. 'You'll have a drink?' had really been more statement than question, a conventional politeness to which – so his manner suggested – an affirmative answer was taken for granted.

But, alas, I was an exception. Not only had my Jewish home been strictly kosher as regards food, it had also been strictly non-alcoholic. When I was eight I had found an empty stout bottle and, smelling it, had recoiled almost in a dead faint. The memory never left me and resulted in my never taking a drink in my life. I had never even seen the inside of a pub!

But this was one challenge I couldn't dare reject. I might look a mere youth but I was now playing the role of a literary bloke, and I knew that by reputation any literary bloke worth his salt was supposed to be able to take his liquor. Here was a chance, perhaps the only chance I might have in this company, to separate the man from the boy in me. The whole success of my venture into the Big House would surely depend on the impression I created on Dr Edith's nephew. I couldn't fail for the want of a bit of stomach lining.

The bottle was still being held over the glass. 'Thank you,' I said, trying to suggest by my tone that Sir Neville's hesitation hadn't really been necessary.

The whiskey began to chug into the tumbler.

'Say when,' I heard.

The instruction froze my already panic-stricken mind. When was 'when'? I didn't know. How much would be seemly as well as making the right effect? A quarter tumbler was surely too little, a half tumbler too much. Something in between? 'When,' I jerked out, by which time I had rather more than half a glass.

I pretended nothing but nonchalantly started my meal. Inwardly, however, I was frenziedly debating the next nerve-wracking problem: At what stage does one drink the whiskey? At the start of the meal? At the end? In the middle?

Sir Neville gave me what I thought might be a clue. 'Some water?' he enquired. If the drinking were to be later, he would have delayed that, I told myself. Then I must drink now. But water? Did one take water with whiskey? Surely only immature novices would dare insult such an ancient and aristocratic beverage. In a moment of inspiration I casually covered the glass with my hand and shook my head.

'Certain?' asked Sir Neville. I should have been warned by the strange note in his voice but I was too distracted by yet another dilemma. How did one drink whiskey – in sips or in one swallow? My memory was full of tough-looking, gun-toting screen cowboys who jerked their heads back and drained their glasses at a gulp. Naturally, that was it. Sir Neville was eyeing me. I steeled myself, raised the glass to my lips and downed the drink in a single swallow – then bent to resume my meal.

Nothing happened for perhaps two and a half seconds and I was beginning to congratulate myself on the discovery of a wonderful, unsuspected talent. Then I seemed both to feel and hear something strike the wall behind me. It was the back of my head.

While it was slowly resuming its normal shape I sat speechless, almost transfixed. I could have been one of those Pompeian inhabitants, overtaken even at his meal by the stream of lava and fixed for ever in that common posture. A fountain of fire was shooting up inside me and my face burned like a radiator. I couldn't move – I dared not move! It was as if the room and everything in it were held steady only by my paralytic stillness, and that the very slightest motion on my part would set the whole place in a mad whirl. I could apprehend my host looking at me with a close, wide-eyed stare, evidently wondering if I was still conscious. I was – but only just. By a supreme effort of will I was hypnotising myself into maintaining sobriety. It was the only thing I could think of doing.

Slowly a modicum of self-control returned. I choked back a desire to cough, manfully prohibited my eyes from watering, and offhandedly resumed my meal. Sir Neville's own responses were not, for a few moments, altogether smooth, and he seemed in some doubt. Then after a pause he lifted the bottle again and said, 'Care for another?' But like every good magician, I knew better than to perform one's *pièce de résistance* twice before the same audience. I politely declined, managing, I think, to imply that I really could do it again but wouldn't be such a hog as to do so on his whiskey. Sir Neville didn't press me. He replaced the bottle with a somewhat regretful expression, as if he was sorry he hadn't observed more closely when he had the chance.

Not surprisingly I have absolutely no recollection of the rest of our conversation. Presumably some conversation of sorts did take place, but whatever remained of my mental processes had other things to worry about. What further terrors would I have to undergo when Lady Coghill and her guests would return from the village? O bedtime, blessèd bedtime! Could I survive until then, or would I collapse in the middle of the house-party festivities and be ignominiously packed off first thing in the morning without even seeing Dr Edith?

The return of Lady Coghill and her guests was akin to an invasion. They seemed to number anything up to thirty people between young and old, but possibly in my still muzzy state I was seeing double. Lady Coghill greeted me with friendliness and even a touch of deference, a mixture no doubt calculated to put me at my ease but in fact having the very opposite effect. The resemblance between her and Sir Neville was striking, the same big build and the same Karloffian appearance, without Sir Neville's stoop but including his charming smile. She didn't burden me with introductions, simply throwing my name out to the general assembly. But Sir Neville included me in older conversation groups that immediately came together, seeming to be made up mostly of family members. He would quietly identify for me whoever held the floor at any one moment. More often than not it was a Somerville from the Royal Navy, giving me in my confused state the impression that the place was awash with Admirals of the Fleet. In keeping me from the younger guests I suspect that, having during the few hours we had spent together gauged my limitations and knowing what diversions were planned, he was saving me embarrassment.

Certainly I could not have made any contribution to the histrionics that followed, a succession of erudite charades based largely on classical allusions, Greek to me, sometimes literally as well as metaphorically. This went on to general hilarity and applause with apparently inexhaustible energy and imagination until Sir Neville bent to whisper in my ear that breakfast would be at nine o'clock, after which he would take me to Dr Edith, adding that the high spirits would probably continue for some time, so if I was tired after my long journey no one would mind if I slipped quietly up to bed. Feeling overcome with relief and gratitude, I thanked him for his consideration and bade him goodnight. Boris Karloff he certainly was not.

I slept heavily through the night, remembering just before I dropped off to repeat to my mind the order, 'Wake at eight, wake at eight,' hoping my newly-found gift of self-hypnosis wouldn't let me down. It didn't, and I was able to present myself in the breakfast room at exactly nine o'clock.

Sir Neville was sitting at the table, evidently not yet having eaten and with no food in front of him, though the handful of the older male family members present were happily munching away. I noted that none of the younger people had yet put in an appearance.

'Good morning,' my host greeted. 'Sleep well?'

'Yes, thank you. Capital!' I replied, hoping I was striking the right note.

'How about a little walk first?' he suggested. 'Give us an appetite.'

On one side of the room large French doors were open onto a very extensive garden with a beautifully manicured lawn. No doubt a pre-breakfast constitutional was *de rigeur*, so I stepped out with him, though to keep pace with his Gulliverian steps required unused-to effort on my part.

'I was re-reading the *Irish R.M.* stories recently,' I said, choosing my ground. I had a good knowledge of the stories, and had quickly decided to lead the conversation and play to my strength with my opening gambit. That should keep me out of deep water and possibly earn me some brownie points into the bargain. We exchanged views and preferences, did one circuit of the lawn and arrived back at the breakfast-room. The array of food laid out in trays, bowls and covered dishes on a long sideboard, though momentarily taking me aback, presented me with no new problems.

'What do you fancy? There's . . .'

'No thank you, Sir Neville,' I cut in confidently, 'I never eat breakfast. Just tea and toast is all I ever have.'

My host raised his eyebrows at this non-breakfast – which in truth was my normal one – but made no comment, probably deciding that such exiguousness in the intake of food was no more freakish than might be expected from someone with the capacity for whiskey that I had demonstrated.

After breakfast Sir Neville accompanied me to meet Edith Somerville, who lived in a house of her own in the grounds. He brought me into her studio, introduced me and departed.

Though in her mid-eighties, Edith Somerville still possessed the brightness and mental agility of a woman in her prime, and her charm – evidently a family gift – was magnetic. She was ensconced in a large armchair at the far end of the studio, a long, wide, many-windowed room of brown panelling, the walls like those of a picture gallery prepared for an exhibition, so many were the pictures that covered them. Seeing me gaze about in some awe, she smiled and said, 'Look around, do, before we have our talk.'

I dutifully examined the pictures nearest me, paintings delicately coloured, drawings and sketches, photographs of streets and outdoor scenes.

'Now sit here.' She motioned with her stick to the chair opposite her.

'One could spend hours admiring all these,' I said quite sincerely, for though I had been aware that as a young woman she had studied art, I had never seen any of her work. Gracefully she inclined her head in acknowledgement of my appreciation. Obviously the subject was dear to her, for she was happy to spend almost the first hour of our conversation talking about art and music – at least she talking and I listening as she regaled me with stories of her days as an art student in Paris.

'Now tell me about this *Irish Writing* of yours,' she eventually invited. I told her about my love of literature, of my plans and ambitions, and named some of the famous Irish writers who had already agreed to support the periodical. She seemed happy with my outline and to my delight promised to send me something.

'Nothing very exciting, you understand. Perhaps a piece about my collaboration with dear Martin Ross. Not that there can be anything in it that I haven't said before. Would that suit you?'

I told her what it would mean to the success of *Irish Writing* to have such a distinguished contribution in the first issue. She waved my comment aside, then picking up a book from a small table beside her, opened it at its title page, took up her pen and said, 'I'll sign this as a present for you. One of my more recent efforts.'

As she finished signing I was about to hand her a blotter that was placed nearby, but she quickly forestalled me, saying, 'No, never blot a signature. Let it dry naturally, just like a sentence ending.' The book was *The Sweet Cry of Hounds*.

Then 'Come with me,' she said, rising and tapping me with her stick. 'It's such a lovely morning.'

She rang a bell, had her pony and trap brought out and took me on a descriptive tour through her beloved countryside. On our return, Sir Neville again materialised to greet us, and Dr Edith bade me goodbye, saying, 'I hope you enjoyed that. At least it should fortify you for your horrible journey back to Cork.' It did, it and my memories of a very kind and wonderful lady. I returned home knowing full well how fortunate I had been to have met and talked with a writer of such nobility and fame. I had the feeling that the future of *Irish Writing* could not be more promising.

CHAPTER NINE

⎯⎯⎯◦✺◦⎯⎯⎯

'Twixt Cup and Lip

What fortified me on the train journey home was not only the success of my visit to Edith Somerville but the glow of achievement felt when I reviewed the progress *Irish Writing* had already made. I kept repeating in my mind the contents list so far – Liam O'Flaherty, Frank O'Connor, Seán O'Faoláin, James Stephens, Louis MacNeice, Lord Dunsany, Patrick Kavanagh, and now Somerville and Ross. Such a quarterly must surely attract both a wide readership and critical attention. Now my co-editor, Terence Smith, and I need have no doubt that what at the outset might have seemed, editorially, an over-reaching blueprint had already put down a strong foundation. We could look forward to building on that foundation with an equally distinguished roll-call of contributors for the second issue.

To that end I decided to invite for inclusion some world-famous non-Irish writer, and to continue doing so every now and again in later issues. The name that first sprang to mind was one whose work had a special appeal for me, Dylan Thomas. I offered him five guineas – a not inconsiderable sum in 1946 – for a new poem, and to my immense delight he immediately replied that he would be happy to oblige. To arouse the greatest possible interest in and anticipation of *No. 2* – and also to attract more subscribers from the US – I planned to announce 'A New Dylan Thomas Poem' on the back cover of *No. 1*.

My success in landing such a scoop emboldened me to go after the one Irish writer whose name and incontestable fame had been long established throughout the world – George Bernard Shaw. His reply, on one of his famous postcards, was, 'I'm an old man. You don't want me, you want the young men. G. Bernard Shaw.' I wouldn't at that stage take no – even a definitive no – for an answer, so I wrote back, 'I have the young men. I want you too.' He answered, again on a postcard, 'As soon as I can, I'll send you an article on my early years in Dublin. G. Bernard Shaw.'

It seemed that my policy of daring all was proving a winner and it made me wonder whether an even more am-bitious and far-reaching plan that had been germinating in my mind might not be so mad or outrageous as it had at first appeared. Why not a semi-annual magazine, 'New World Writing', publishing in translation new short stories by famous and unknown writers from all over the world? I was, of course, in danger of getting too big for my boots. I was even having visions – well, at that stage daydreams would be a more honest description – of becoming Ireland's Penguin Books, and to that end I pondered over the idea of searching for one instantly recognisable umbrella imprint under which all my publishing ventures could go out into the world. It would have to be an imprint, a label, that would create the same subconscious reaction as the title 'Penguin' had. Taking my cue from that illustrious predecessor, I deduced that one needed a word of two syllables – the first one strong-sounding

– and embodying some familiar object or creature. To choose an animal would look like copying Penguin – why had they chosen that, was it because of the correlation between the first syllable and writing? – so I steered clear of animals. Between us, my brother and I – I don't know which of us it was – came up with 'Trumpet Books', and *Irish Writing* appeared under that imprint. It had the necessary initial plosive sound, with its role in introducing announcements, rallies, calls, etc., it evoked an answering sit-up-and-take-notice reaction, and it could be as fecund as Penguin in spawning further musical instrument imprints commencing with T for other categories of books: tuba, tambourine, triangle (good for romance stories), tympani, tabor, and probably others.

Publication of *Irish Writing No. 1* was scheduled for September, 1946, and in early August the printers delivered the first copies. I had already contacted a major British magazine distributor who replied that they would certainly handle the magazine but needed to see an early copy so as to decide how many to order. I complied with their request and back came their order – for ten thousand! I could hardly believe what I was reading but my elation was quickly put on hold by their final sentence: 'Please send us the British Board of Trade licence for us to import that number of copies.' What in the world were they talking about? Who ever heard of a licence being required for the importation of magazines from Ireland into Britain? I made enquiries and learned the ghastly truth.

It was all bound up with some lease-lend treaty between the US and Britain which only recently had been negotiated, by which the US made Britain a huge dollar loan to help towards their recovery from the ravages of the Second World War, while in return US exporters would be helped by Britain agreeing to put an embargo on many classes of goods, for which a Board of Trade licence would be required by the British importers. Periodicals were among the many and varied items affected, new magazines being summarily and totally prohibited. By the time the details and rules of this embargo became public it was too late for *Irish Writing* to circumvent it by rushing out a 'dummy issue', selling it in Britain and so being granted a quota for later issues, a device, I was told, that had been successfully employed by some Irish publishers who had had prior information of what lay ahead.

For *Irish Writing* the situation could not have been worse. Almost all the bank overdraft had been spent and the figures revealed that it would have taken all the British sales of the first two issues to recoup the outlay and get out of the red. I wrote letters to the Board of Trade, pleading, begging, explaining whys and wherefores. But all my entreaties received only the same implacable refusal. I decided to make one final, desperate bid. I asked for a chance to make a personal appeal in London. The relevant departmental Head replied that it would be a waste of time but that, if I insisted, he would grant me an appointment. I set out with a heavy heart and copies of the first issue.

The official who received me was tall, balding, immaculately groomed, and dressed in a regulation Civil Service dark suit as if ready to return after his daily office stint to his normal place behind the ropes of Madame Tussauds. He was courteous, sympathetic, apologetic, soft-spoken – but rigidly correct and quite adamant. It was the old story – he did not make the rules and he had no power to act outside them. I showed him the first issue but he barely glanced at it, indeed averted his gaze from where I had placed it on his desk, to make clear, it seemed, that as far as his instructions were concerned no such magazine existed. A tortuous half-hour passed with not an inch of ground given. Then, to signal that discussion of the purpose of my visit was at an end, he lit a cigarette and handed the magazine back to me, but as if to show that he was not a soulless, uncultured automaton, he glanced at the names of the writers on the cover and expressed polite curiosity about their work. I, feeling in no mood for pointless, literary chit-chat prior to being shown out, but perhaps also to give myself the satisfaction of implying the literary benefits British readers were about to be deprived of, mentioned that I would have an article from George Bernard Shaw in the second issue. His eyebrows did not merely rise, they shot up.

'Shaw!' he exclaimed. And almost as if doubting me, 'Really? How did you manage that?'

'I wrote and asked him. How else? After all, he *is* Irish.'

'What did he say?'

'He promised me an article on his early years in Dublin.'

I wondered why the official was showing such an unexpected interest. It turned out that he was a devoted Shavian himself, and after some discussion about the sage's works, he himself suggested a possible loophole that would allow him to help me in at least some little degree. The fact that not a single issue of *Irish Writing* had yet actually been published did mean that under the strict rules it did not qualify for a quota for importation into Britain, but since the process of producing the magazine had commenced before the embargo was announced, we were, he opined, already in existence, even though normal teething troubles might be said to have delayed publication, and so – ahem, ahaw – he could, perhaps, in recognition of that, stretch a point and grant a licence for the importation into Britain of the first issue only. In vain did I argue that if the first issue was already in existence and would be on sale in Britain, our right to a licence for further issues was thereby established.

'Mr Marcus,' he said, resuming his original Civil Service tone of finality, 'I'm offering you an import licence for just six thousand copies of the first issue only, and if you take my advice, you'll accept that before I change my mind.'

I took his advice. There was no alternative. We shook hands and he showed me out.

I left the building with my mind in a blank fog. Restricted to Irish sales alone after the first issue meant that I would still owe my father well over half the money he had signed for in the bank. And for how long would the embargo continue? Irish sales would hardly make enough even to cover ongoing expenses. However, I could see no other course but to keep going at least until the embargo should be raised. It could not last for ever, could it? Had I known it would last for four more years . . . but no, it was better I did not know that then. It was enough to know that Trumpet Books was never to become the Irish Penguin, enough to have to face the fact that my daydream of founding a regular *New World Writing* collection was just that, a daydream. The only kindness fate dealt me that day was not enabling me to look into the future and see that some years later an annual anthology called *New World Writing* would be brought out by the US publishers The American Library, and that I myself would have a story in it. To have known that would have been worse than consolation. It would have evoked only what my mother, relapsing into the Yiddish she used for fate's most ironic blows, would have called *bittera galechter*, bitter laughter.

CHAPTER TEN

Voice Over

I could have gone back to Cork next day, there was nothing to keep me in London any longer, but something held me back. With *Irish Writing* facing slow extinction, I was in no hurry to report what I regarded as the failure of my mission. I would have to do so sooner rather than later, but first I needed a break to absorb the immediate reality, perhaps even a chance to find a way of softening the blow without raising false hopes. Ironically, what floated into my mind was the poem 'How They Brought the Good News from Ghent to Aix', but I knew there was no magic formula in it that might make it easier for me to bring the bad news from London to Cork.

Company, I felt, was what I needed, thus surprising myself, normally a loner. But I knew no one in London apart from relations, and relations were the last people I wanted to see at such a time. Congenial company, a writer perhaps, definitely not a shoulder to cry on but someone new, whom I had never met before, whose conversation might refresh my spirits with the roundabouts of distraction.

I had brought with me to London a list of Irish writers I might contact for future issues of *Irish Writing* if my visit to the Board of Trade should be successful. Under the circumstances, however, I did not see how I could, with justification, call on any of them and talk as if I had a viable periodical with a long-range future.

Going through my list I came on the name of James Stephens. No, I thought, he has already sent me a story so there is no point in bothering him. Besides, although I had once or twice heard him read on the BBC, I had also heard that he was often ill and never welcomed visitors. A pity, but if there was one Irish writer I would have dearly loved to meet, that one was James Stephens. Well, perhaps now I had my chance. I had nothing to lose by trying, and 'taking a chance' had come off for me many times in the immediate past – even, if only to a very small degree, with the Board of Trade – so I went into a phone box and dialled his number.

A woman answered the phone and in reply to my enquiry she told me that Mr Stephens was not available unless the call was urgent. I admitted that my call was not urgent, but I explained my mission and asked that he be given my name, hoping all the while that he would remember who I was and that he had sent me a story. In a moment I heard the sing-song voice of James Stephens greeting me.

I told him that I was anxious to present him personally with a pre-publication copy of *Irish Writing No. 1* if he had time to see me.

'Well, you know,' said he, liltingly, 'I'm a peculiarly busy person.'

I agreed that no doubt he must be just that, but if he were at all available that day, I'd be most grateful. So we arranged to meet at one o'clock for lunch outside a café in Piccadilly.

Just before hanging up I realised that I hadn't the vaguest idea what he looked like.

'How will we know each other?' I asked.

'That's simple,' he answered, and as if he were a child confiding a delightful, exclusive secret, he whispered, 'I'll be the smallest man you've ever seen.'

So at one o'clock I stood in Piccadilly looking for the smallest man I had ever seen. From Oxford Street he came, appearing before me as if squeezed out of the throng of pedestrians like toothpaste from a tube. A soft hat on top, an overcoat draped almost to the ground, with, in between, a head and face five sizes too big for its manikin body – and the whole structure barely reaching to my top trouser button.

He shook my hand with great formality and then ushered me into the café. As soon as we were seated at a table I drew out a copy of *Irish Writing* and laid it before him. The cover of the first issue depicted a large, soft-green map of Ireland surrounded by a sky-blue sea with two thin white lines, like breaking waves, ringing the whole coastline. Stretching from the north-east to south-west corner of the map were the names of the fifteen contributors, headed by Liam O'Flaherty, with James Stephens next. Stephens looked at it, plonked his hand on the cover, and with great relish said, 'Ah, that's Ireland.' Then he put a finger on O'Flaherty's name, saying, 'I'm glad to see him there. You have the right man on top.'

From then on the whole lunchtime was taken up with questions about every writer in Ireland and about the state of the country's culture. At that time James Stephens had already been about twenty years an exile and greatly regretted that he had grown out of touch not only with the Irish people and Irish affairs, but even with contemporary Irish literature.

'I do very little reading these days,' he said. And then, looking rather wistfully past me, added, 'Some day soon I'm going to get down to really serious reading. I'm going to read all my own works again.'

I smiled, thinking he was joking, but he continued, 'That's quite true. What use is it to me, at my time, to read another man's work, doing nothing but judging every line and criticising every judgement? At least with my own work, I know why I said whatever I said and that when I said it I was satisfied. And to write more myself requires energy I no longer have.'

He turned again to *Irish Writing*, picking out the name of Myles na gCopaleen.

'Who is this beautiful person?'

I told him about Myles's column in *The Irish Times* and about his ability to pun in Irish. Stephens's eyes lit up with enthusiasm. 'What a pity,' he said, 'that I've let my knowledge of Irish dry up completely. I shouldn't have. Perhaps you could help me. Are there any books you could send me to brush up the old tongue?' In no time he had me promising to send him a 'Teach Yourself Irish' or some such aid.

By now it was nearly two-thirty and he suggested that we move to another place for afternoon tea. This suited me as I wanted to get him onto the subject of poetry. So we entered a Lyons café and took a table in the corner. We were served by a waitress – at lunch we had been ministered to by a waiter in whom Stephens took no interest – and within a minute he had learned most of her life history. As part of it included the information that she had been born in Ireland, the two of them were quickly firm friends, and he, in some subtle way, made us feel members of a secret and rather aristocratic brotherhood stranded in a dull, alien community. On the strength of it he obtained a little extra sugar – it was then severely rationed – and had no need, as had been necessary at lunch, to draw out of his pocket the little bag of sugar which, he explained, he always carried with him these days.

To get him onto the subject of poetry I asked what he thought of the Welsh poet Dylan Thomas. Stephens repeated that he read little or no contemporary work, and though he knew something of Thomas, he could not say much about him. He invited my opinion, and when I mentioned my admiration for one of Thomas's latest poems, 'Fern Hill', he made me speak it for him. When I finished he said, 'You know, Milton is supposed to have written the longest poem in the English language. Well, I've written the shortest.'

Thereupon he recited the poem in question. Unfortunately, I cannot recall which one it was, but immediately he finished it, he went on without pause, 'And what's more, I've written the only poem in the English language without a verb,' proceeding to recite 'The Main-Deep'.

A Lyons café was at any time a very busy place. Tables were seldom empty for long and, in common with most cafés, were placed very close to each other. Though we were in a corner there were still many tables, all occupied, within a few feet of us – and Stephens had taken the corner chair, thus having a view of the whole floor. Up to now our conversation had been maintained at a normal tone of voice, but once Stephens started to speak his poems, it was as if time and place had disappeared and he were at that moment before a microphone or perhaps once again on a stage, holding a vast audience spellbound, as he had often done with his poetry recitals. I was completely gripped as I watched the rubbery face before me reflect every intonation and mood. The eyes would open wide and then slumbrously peer through almost closed lashes and then be swallowed entirely by the bosomy lids that enveloped them. The hands would draw the poem all about me in the air and the massive-seeming head would sway and float like a barrage balloon on a breezy day. It was sheer magic.

Only when he paused for a moment did I realise that everyone near us must have heard him, and beginning to feel embarrassed I turned to look about me. I found that the whole room had become his audience. Knives were laid quietly aside and cups carefully, soundlessly deposited in their saucers, while the people sat, like statues, hypnotised by the almost unbelievable beauty and fascination of James Stephens's voice speaking poetry. I relaxed and again allowed the spell to envelop me. He continued – 'The slowest poem in the English language', 'The quickest poem in the English language'. Words and rhythms entranced him as much as they entranced his listeners.

Then he said he would have to leave, for he had an appointment at the BBC to broadcast on their Overseas Service to 'the tribes of interior Africa about Donne and Shakespeare'. As we came out of the café a street photographer snapped us and gave the ticket to Stephens. He gave it to me, but as I was leaving London the next day I was unable to collect the photograph. Then he took my hand and thanked me for getting in touch with him. 'God bless you,' he said, 'and when you get home, give my love to everybody in Ireland.'

'Everybody!' I replied. 'That's a tall order.'

'Maybe 'tis and maybe 'tis'nt,' said James Stephens, 'but that's the way I want it. For you're young and I'm old, and as between us it's likely that you'll have much more time to do it than I will.'

He turned, ambled off, and in a moment was swallowed up in the crowd.

CHAPTER ELEVEN

---∞∞∞---

Carriage Paid

The only way I was ever able to enjoy a train journey was to have a carriage to myself, a lucky privilege that very seldom came my way. On this occasion, the second part of my trip home, the journey from Dublin to Cork, I searched out an empty carriage and took my favourite seat in a corner by the window with my back to the engine, the place my father advised me always to make for so as to avoid smuts blown in if the window had to be opened at a fellow-traveller's request. Sitting there also meant that I could comfortably look out at the countryside we passed instead of having to meet the eyes of any passenger directly facing me, a danger from which one knew not what unwanted conversation might follow. Unfortunately, only a minute before departure time, a woman whom I had seen pass the carriage a few times came in, put her case on the luggage rack and took the seat opposite me, the very place I had hoped would remain empty. It struck me that she might have deliberately chosen me as her travelling companion so as to have someone she could talk to, or at, without interruption. How right I was!

Unsurprisingly, she began with the weather, being thoroughly acerbic about the summer that had passed, contemptuous about the mediocre spell we were then experiencing, and brashly confident that we could not expect any better from what was to come.

I had always thought the Irish a mite pagan in the phrases they used to describe the weather, as if careful to placate Aeolus or Pluvius or whatever other gods had once been deemed to control the elements. A freezing day was no worse than 'hardy' and one of incessant, drenching rain was 'soft'. But this woman was certainly breaking the mould, and was determined that I should not ignore her insistent comments, much less silence her with my unenthusiastic and barely audible monosyllabic replies. She was young-looking, probably about ten years older than me, with a broad, country voice in which the normally musical accent was masked by her grating harshness.

Having delivered her last word on the weather as the train commenced its journey, she began to revile the Great Southern Railway for its inability to get her from Dublin to Cork in less than four and three quarter hours. That was an issue in which, to my weary surprise, she found far more to sustain her litany of complaints than I would have thought possible, but with the matter fully aired, she proceeded to broaden her target, accusing the government of a variety of evildoings. Her progression from the particular to the general was, I suppose, predictable, but as national politics was something in which I had never taken a close interest, I merely occasionally threw in a neutral 'Is that so?' among otherwise noncommittal grunts.

By now the train was passing through the plains of the Curragh in Co. Kildare, headquarters of Irish horseracing.

Some horses were being exercised by their stable lads, cantering smoothly along the grass at a steady, workmanlike pace. As I watched them I was thinking of my father and his 'bob each-way' bets when the woman opposite me suddenly rasped out 'The Curragh', with clearly hostile emphasis.

'Yes,' I said, tonelessly, anxious not to stir up whatever bizarre prejudice she could have against such an inoffensive, picturesque tract of countryside.

'When I think of the boys there . . . behind bars . . .' she moaned bitterly.

What boys, I wondered. I knew there was a military prison on the Curragh, but she looked impossibly young to have any sons confined there. Brothers perhaps?

'Boys?' I couldn't help asking.

'Our boys. The IRA.'

Now I understood what she was on about. The papers had been full of the news when the government interned a number of IRA suspects without trial, locking them up in the Curragh prison.

'And do you know who put them there?' She leaned forward until I could almost see myself in the glare of her eyes.

'It was the government, wasn't it?' I said. 'de Valera.'

'Ach, nonsense,' she spat, recoiling and shaking her head vigorously as if at the naïvety of my reply.

'It was the Jews, them Satan divils. They're behind everything in the country.'

I was stunned into silence, too astonished to halt the tirade that followed.

'It's the same everywhere, all over the world. They want to own everything. They have so much money, you see. They steal and scheme until they get their way. Monsters. Horrible, ugly creatures, with black, oily hair and hooky noses and cruel, divilish eyes. That's how you'd recognise them. Oh I'd know a Jew anywhere!'

At that I found my voice.

'You'd know a Jew anywhere?'

'Of course I would. They can't fool me.'

'Well, here's one who *has* fooled you,' I said, calmly and coldly. 'You see, I'm a Jew.'

Her face flushed scarlet but she made no sound. I turned away from her and resumed looking out the window. The now distant horses were still in my sight but I was no longer seeing them. My feelings had taken over, elation at having been able to downface the silly woman, but anger at her naked, arrogant anti-Semitism. And then sheer relief when she jumped up, took her suitcase from the rack, and left the carriage.

I remember again now what I remembered then, how, long ago and very much more dramatically, a train had figured in the life of my grandfather, my mother's father. He was in his teens, living with his parents and siblings in the Jewish community of Ackmeyan in Lithuania, then Russian-controlled. He and three or four of his friends were near conscription age for the Russian army, the most terrifying fate faced by young Orthodox Jewish males. In the army they would be stripped of their religion, forbidden their Jewish prayers, forced to eat non-kosher food, and they could expect constant bullying and persecution. The only way to avoid conscription was to flee by boarding a train to a neighbouring country and trust to luck that the Russian military police might not bother to board the train at the border in search of conscription fugitives, as occasionally happened. My grandfather and his friends decided to take the risk.

When the train stopped at the border, the Russian police did come on board and commenced checking every carriage.

The distraught group of young Jews could do nothing but await capture. Identification papers did not exist at the time, so the police always removed any adolescent males they thought looked Jewish. When they entered my grandfather's compartment, they asked no questions, just took his friends, but ignored him. Why? Because his hair was blond, and clearly they had never come across a Jew with blond hair or believed such a creature existed. Strangely, my grandfather never produced a blond-haired child in all his nine children. Perhaps his hair had turned black with fright – or with relief at his escape.

And as to my erstwhile fellow-passenger lamenting her IRA heroes behind bars, her bizarre victims of Jewish designs for world domination, what would she have said or thought if, after revealing to her that I was one of her hated Jews, I had also revealed that my mother, before she married, had been a member of Cumann na mBan, the women's political wing of the IRA? Would it have changed her mind, or would she have much preferred to learn that that Cumann na mBan member had in her teens been one of the Jewish community driven out of Limerick in the 'pogrom' of 1904, while her father, my grandfather, had escaped Russian anti-Semitism only to settle in Limerick, be hit in the head by a stone and carried to hospital by a fellow-Jew when none of the citizens watching would help him? 'Forgive and forget'? Really an ill-thought-out piece of advice, unworkable short of a lobotomy. Perhaps a wiser, more effective counsel, surprisingly not brought down from the Mount, might be 'Seek not revenge.'

I had expected to spend the journey from Dublin to Cork worrying about *Irish Writing* and its future, but by the time the train was approaching the long tunnel into Cork station which always in the past had made me glad to be getting home, I was buoyed up with relief when I felt its magic beginning to work again. I was ready to dismiss from my mind the problem of anti-Semitism; it had no immediate relevance. What was bringing me home was my future, and what *I* was bringing home was the Board of Trade agreement. It was not anything like enough, my grandiose plans were in ruins, but at least it gave *Irish Writing* some sort of chance, however indeterminate. So I would regard it as a partial victory, would report it as such, and would look forward to the actual launch of the periodical in November and to building on plans already made for the second issue. I remembered a phrase from Virgil's *Aeneid*, 'They can do all because they think they can.' That would do for me. There was no alternative.

CHAPTER TWELVE

Cheques and Balances

Before I went to London Terence suggested that he write to B.G. McCarthy, lecturer in English at University College, Cork, of whom he thought highly, to tell her about *Irish Writing* and ask if she would contribute a critical article to one of our future issues. She, it appeared, had replied declining the invitation. When I asked him why, he only reluctantly showed me her letter. Her reason was that she did not think I could be a suitable person to have a part in editing the sort of periodical he had outlined. I was in no way upset by her refusal – I did not know her and her name meant nothing to me. I presumed, however, that she had known or ascertained that I was Jewish, as it seemed clear that, basically, her objection to me was that I was not an Irish Catholic.

Around that time another incident proved to me that, but for Terence, I would have been guilty of an indiscretion an Irish Catholic would very likely have avoided. It involved Sean O'Casey, who had agreed to review a book for us – he had already contributed a characteristic article to *Irish Writing No. 2* about adverse criticism of his plays – and to me his review appeared in no way objectionable. However,

Terence alerted me to the description in it of the confessional being the Catholic Church's method of spying on the people. Had I, he asked, considered the offence this might give to many of our readers, with consequent damage to our circulation, still at the time restricted to Ireland because of the British embargo? My answer was that the thought never struck me, but accepting his *caveat*, I wrote to O'Casey explaining our difficulty and asking if he would agree to drop or suitably alter the relevant passage. He refused, saying the review must be printed as written or else returned, so I returned it. Fortunately he did not hold this against us, and in fact about three years later he gave *Irish Writing* an extract from the volume of autobiography he was currently working on. By a very lucky coincidence, an invitation at about the same time to Denis Johnston – then considered in some quarters to be Ireland's leading playwright – to contribute a critical article on a subject of his choice, was rewarded with an essay on O'Casey's later plays which cogently outlined what he saw as the fallacies in the widespread adverse judgements these plays had met with from the Irish critics.

Irish Writing No. 1 was duly published in November, 1946. There was no launch – a launch was virtually an unknown phenomenon in Ireland in that era – but *No. 1* was well received by the press. Patrick Campbell, whose *Irish Times* 'Quidnunc' column was one of the paper's most popular items, had interviewed me before publication and raised anticipatory interest with his amusing account of our conversation. It took place in his Irish Times office about the size of a small cloakroom, inhabited by a table, two chairs and a snowstorm of paper littering most of the floor. I do not recall that he noticeably stammered, though in later years the stammer and his inimitable humour made him one of Britain's most popular TV stars. He became almost certainly the best comic writer Ireland ever produced, and his collections of short stories, rivalling those of the great US humorists Damon Runyon and James Thurber, contain many evergreen classics. Once when browsing in Eason's, I happened to take up one of his collections and, casually starting to read the first story, I laughed so much that I had to return the book to the shelves and hurriedly leave the premises.

In 1963 he had inherited the title Baron Glenavy, and on his death it passed to his then nineteen-year-old brother, Michael. The death of Michael Campbell at an early age took from Ireland one of its best young writers. *Irish Writing* published his first short story (under the pseudonym Peter Hill) in 1970, and in its pages his next three stories, now under his own name, also appeared. These stories were in a serious vein, but later he produced some every bit as funny as his brother's had been. One was an hilarious account of his efforts, at the behest of the Irish Times when he was working in their London office, to collect and take care of Brendan Behan on one of the latter's visits, and another, which was published in the *New Yorker*, was a richly-recounted morsel of ludicrousness about how his first novel barely avoided being withdrawn on publication day by his London publishers because of a threatened writ for libel by Jimmy O'Dea, Ireland's most popular comedian of the time. In the novel, based on Haggie, the author's eccentric elderly aunt who used take a box for every one of O'Dea's Dublin shows, it was alleged that the comedian drank on stage. In fact he used drink a pint of Guinness in one go, the audience would cheer, and he always got an encore. In desperation Michael Campbell sent him a wire: 'Book stopped. What on earth is wrong? Please give permission. Michael.' The reply was swift: 'Congratulations. Only objection: nowhere do you describe your aunt and myself going to bed together. All the best. Jimmy.' The novel was duly published. Michael Campbell went on to write five further novels, by far the most important being *Lord Dismiss Us*, about the homosexual activities of masters and boys at an Eton-style college – reputed to be St Columba's, which he had attended – and one of the best on that subject ever written.

My first estimate of the financial damage that would be caused by the restriction of British sales of *Irish Writing No. 1* proved to be accurate. Over half the bank overdraft had been expended, and while what still remained was sufficient to guarantee publication of the second issue, albeit with rigorous cutting of overheads, the total embargo on further British sales meant that at very best only break-even could be expected. Thus was confirmed how totally ruinous that embargo was to all my dreams of becoming a big-name publisher and a global impresario of the short story. Had normal trading conditions prevailed, all costs of the first two issues would have been recovered and I would have been in a position to chase the rainbow. As it was, there was no knowing how long the embargo would last or whether, while it did last, further losses on top of bank interest payments would bury the periodical. How, then, would I be able to repay what I owed? Having given up the Bar, I could not contemplate returning to it, and having no apparent earning capacity, I was being kept by my father. Many black years were in prospect.

At least, however, the contents list for *No.* 2 had been building up most encouragingly. There was Sean O'Casey's own defence of his later plays, a short story by Mary Lavin, a poem by Oliver St John Gogarty and an article on Yeats by

Padraic Colum. I had met Padraic and Mary Colum more than once in Dublin, and to my great surprise I received, some time later, a letter from the publishers, Macmillan, saying that Padraic Colum had suggested that they commission me to write a biography of James Stephens. Was I interested? Ah, if only I had been an academic I might have taken it on, but Alfie O'Rahilly's broad hint not to try to do a BA along with a Law degree had already left me unequipped for such a task. But *De mortuis nihil nisi* bones! Coincidentally, around the same time one of the English Societies at Trinity invited me to give a talk on Stephens's work. I offered them instead a talk about the American poet e.e. cummings, an offer that they accepted, to my great surprise.

I was still awaiting the promised works from Shaw and Dylan Thomas. The time had come to send polite letters to both of them, reminding them of the imminent copy date and telling them how much I was looking forward to their manuscripts.

From neither was there any reply. I wrote again. Still only silence. Two more appeals, impressing on them the importance to the periodical's survival of their appearance in its pages. From Shaw came another of his postcards. His reply, in red capitals, was written with the card on its narrow side to allow for the largest possible letters and emphasis. Just one word: 'NO!' signed G. Bernard Shaw. This was so firm and total a rejection that I had no alternative but to accept it. My minuscule consolation was that at least I had not received it before the *volte-face* of the Shavian from the British Board of Trade! To amuse myself now I speculate on what the latter's attitude might have been had I had the full story to disclose of how his so highly admired great Irish playwright had gone back on his word to an Irish editor. Would he have given the periodical a full licence to show that British civil servants were not as hard-hearted as reputed or indeed as unreliable as Shaw had been? Ah well, daydreams always have a built-in happy ending.

Unfortunately, setbacks are commonly serial rather than single. There was still no word from Dylan Thomas, and despite my further efforts through various intermediaries to get him to reply, he remained silent. Then I had an idea I thought might do the trick. Thomas already had gained his reputation of being constantly short of money, so I decided that if I paid him the fee in advance, he could not but deliver. I sent him a cheque, along with a further appeal, but when this, too, met with no response, I had to write-off the money and hope that readers of the second issue would not be too disappointed at the non-appearance of the already announced new Dylan Thomas poem. Reputations, however, whether good or bad, are not always lived up to or down to. Over a year later I received from the poet a most apologetic letter, explaining that it is sometimes not possible to produce a poem good enough for publication even when one most wants to. Attached to the letter was a cheque, stained, grubby, and with many fold-lines – the very cheque I had sent him with my final appeal.

A pity I had not sent Shaw a cheque in advance. After all, he always complained he was a poor man, did he not?

CHAPTER THIRTEEN

---✇✇✇---

The Exhilaration Elixir

During these weeks and months of worries and pressure – and for some nine previous and twenty-five subsequent years – I had two very contrasting forms of relaxation: playing the piano and sport.

From the beginning both had the capacity to release an essence, a compound of the immaterial and the physical. Activity alone was no promoter: at the piano, not the arm scurries or finger frenzy or prayer-like forward- and backward-leaning body movements; in sport neither the muzzle velocity of limb, nor the head jerks and neck swerves, not even the miracle synchronisation of instinct, eye and action. It was the nothing and everything of the visceral brain waiting, like 007's, to trigger the transmission of the secret message: exhilaration.

I am not and never have been even a competent pianist. I make far too many mistakes, so every time I play the piano it always wins, usually by an oxymoronic cricket score of own goals. Consequently I can never play for family or stranger, or even for myself. I just sit at the keyboard and practise in unlonely isolation. Had it ever been halfway possible I would have given up everything at an early age to become a piano virtuoso. But key-basher though I be, not very often but sometimes – especially immediately after I have listened to some of my recordings of great pianists – I succeed in bringing off one of my favourite pieces better than ever before, and then I want to stand up and cheer, punch the air and surrender to tears with the indescribable onset of that essence which has inspired perhaps my thousandth attempt at a Beethoven movement. Like the millionth passenger to board a company's plane, I have been given a free trip: exhilaration.

In sport the result has been the same, but minus the tears. My favourite sports were cricket, soccer, and table tennis. Cricket I played for Pres, mostly on the Mardyke grounds opposite my home. I fancied myself as a batsman, my idol being the Australian Don Bradman who, as far as I was concerned, was the greatest of all time. The most painful disappointment of my youth was when, in 1938, Australia was touring Britain and was scheduled to play in Dublin against Ireland – were we then still known as the Gentlemen of Ireland? It was the first time I was allowed make the journey to the capital alone. Bradman was, of course, the big attraction, the god I had never in my life expected to see in action, but shortly beforehand in an attempt to prevent England's Len Hutton breaking Bradman's own world Test Match innings record of 336 runs, he put himself on to bowl and succeeded only in twisting his ankle. Hutton scored 364 and Bradman could not come to Dublin.

However, I myself achieved something so unique in cricket that I always regret not having applied to have it included in the *Guinness Book of Records*. I scored a boundary with my head! For those who may not know what a boundary is, it is the four runs added to a batsman's score if he succeeds in propelling the ball to the perimeter of the playing area. I went in to bat for Pres against our deadly rivals, Christians – this was long before the days when batsmen wore helmets for protection – and in some trepidation I faced up to Christians' fast bowler. He was well over six feet and ran up like a rocket to deliver the ball which, like a second rocket, flew from his hand at over sixty miles an hour. It was his first ball to me and my eyes had not yet had a chance to get used to the light – well, I am entitled to some excuse for not picking up the ball's flight. It hit me on the head, flying up and over all the way to the boundary. The crazy part was that I felt nothing. Not knowing where the ball had gone I started to run down the pitch so as to open my score, but I was prevented by the fielders who, thinking I must be poleaxed, crowded around me. They couldn't believe that I hadn't been killed and couldn't begin to imagine how I hadn't even been hurt. The only explanation is that the ball, travelling at a furious speed on an upward trajectory, merely glanced off the top of my forehead sufficiently for the contact to be seen by them but not felt by me. I have to record that the bowler was in no way put off his stroke by having nearly killed me. His next ball was even faster than the first and took my leg stump out of the ground.

I cannot say that I was in the slightest bit exhilarated by the incident. Having felt nothing out of the ordinary, how could I be? However, some years later I did experience the real thing, though only for a split second before fate dowsed its flame. It happened in one of the occasional soccer matches arranged each year, but this one was special. It was the annual meeting between a motley eleven varying in ages from sixteen to forty-five conscripted from the Cork Jews, against the tough, experienced players of Dublin's Carlisle Jewish Club.

To say that we in Cork ever trained would be a ludicrous euphemism. On Sundays, as long as the weather was not too inclement or a sufficient quota hadn't slept late or the older members didn't have the much more exciting attraction of an official Jewish Congregation meeting, we would drive or cycle or walk out to the Lee fields and kick a ball around, with a few jackets thrown on the ground to do duty as goalposts.

Even such an apparently unexacting kick-about had a curious effect on me that always forced me, after the first five or ten minutes, to remove myself temporarily from the playing area. On the first occasion it caused consternation, but as soon as my brother Louis, who was one of the 'team', explained the reason and assured them I was perfectly all right, my 'affliction' never again caused them to hold up play. In a newspaper article many years later Louis had occasion to describe the phenomenon, and as his account perfectly recreates the almost farcical, variety stage element, let him tell it as it was:

> The only game we played together on a regular basis was soccer, on the Cork Jewish Youth Club team. I played in any position, depending on who didn't turn up for the match. But David was a centre-forward pure and simple, the most glamorous position in those days before the game deteriorated into an incongruous imitation of chess.
>
> He had the slightly Mediterranean good looks that went with star centre-forwards, like Tommy Lawton of Chelsea or our local Paddy O'Leary of Cork United. But he had one unnerving habit as a soccer player. After five minutes of every game he would walk to the side-line with stately resignation to get sick in cavernous

retchings that made me clap my hands to my ears.
Then, he would resume his position and play uncon-
cernedly for the rest of the game.

But his real sport was table tennis . . .

I have quoted the opening of my brother's paragraph about
my long love affair with table tennis because that was what
caused my regular sideline upheavals on the soccer pitch. I
had been playing table tennis – serious table tennis – for two
to three hour sessions virtually every night of the week
excepting Sundays, winter and summer through, since I was
fourteen. Table tennis was rated the second fastest indoor
game in the world after ice hockey, and with a table only
nine feet by five from which one often had to retreat up to
some twenty or more feet to defend an attack and then in an
instant scorch all the way back to collect a drop shot, the
speed and energy required was of a very high order. It was
therefore hardly surprising that three hundred or so nights a
year for many years at this regimen would have a noticeable
effect on one's internal body rhythms. In my case, when
these rhythms were suddenly required to change gear over
much greater distances and in the open air, it was my wind
supply that registered the shock and precipitated an attack of
nausea. With that over, however, my second wind was able
to accommodate itself to the new tempo and I could go on
for hours.

I had some moments of exhilaration on the soccer field in
the odd friendly match, but for me the most important one
could not have been more epiphanic, for it happened during
one of the annual clashes with the Dublin Jewish team. The
ball was swiftly delivered from our full back to centre half to
right wing, who crisply volleyed it towards me. I was caught

with my back to the goal, but I deftly trapped the ball, pivoting in the same movement, and struck it firm and true into the corner of the net. It was the most inspired, artistic, skilful goal I ever scored, and the exhilaration factor I experienced had to wait many years before being properly christened: lift-off. That we were at that stage already three goals down with only five minutes to go hardly mattered. Nor did it greatly matter to me that the referee whistled me up for off-side and disallowed the goal, though his deplorable *faux pas* rather dampened my team mates' shouts of *mazeltov*. I had done what I had done and I had known what I had known – the quintessential moment of exhilaration!

But table tennis was a completely different sort of experience – and a different sort of psychological test. I started playing at home with my two older brothers on a table in the room we always called 'the nursery' when I was about eleven or twelve. Not to put a tooth in it, I soon became a very good player. Of course sporting grades are only relative, and Ireland, being only in its table tennis infancy, was easily gobbled up by almost any other country. The best in those days were the middle-Europeans led by the Hungarians, whose Viktor Barna, inventor of the famous backhand flick shot, was World Singles Champion year after year.

As regularly as Barna was World Champion, Cyril Kemp was Irish Champion. He was a very tall, very graceful player, bespectacled, handsome, and at his best quite unbeatable in Ireland. In my teens it was my misfortune to be drawn against him in the first round of a tournament in Cork. My reputation, such as it was, was purely local, so no doubt he was not expecting to have the slightest difficulty in disposing of me. However, he found his progress not quite plain sailing. Clearly he was not deigning to take my opposition seriously and that he did not need to was borne out by the fact that although I led in the first game by 20-15, he won it 22-20. Had I been experienced enough to remain calm, I might have fluked a sensational one game lead, but over-excitement made things easy for him.

At that stage I had the satisfaction of seeing that he thought it advisable to take off his sweater for the second game and make sure to put me in my place. He did win of course, but only 21-15, so although he had knocked me out of the tournament, the applause of the spectators showed that I had come through with honour. Perhaps his comment as we shook hands was not meant as an added put-down but I never forgot it: 'That was a nice little knock.' Years later, before his home crowd in the annual Munster v. Leinster Interprovincial, on the only other occasion I met him in singles, I gave him another 'nice little knock'. I won in straight games and the headline next day in the sports pages was 'Marcus Beats Kemp'. Exhilaration!

The war provided me with one of the most imperishable, if bizarre, memories of my table tennis career. It was the year the Munster Championships were held in Waterford, eighty miles from Cork. Normally the trip would have presented no problem, especially as the distance involved meant that Bertie Levinge, who held the singles title, and I were exempted until Friday, when we would have to play all our rounds of the singles and doubles up to the semi-final and finals – provided we got that far – which were played on the Saturday night. Petrol being rigorously rationed, we could find no enthusiast driving to Waterford, but that did not discommode Bertie. All his life from early youth he cycled everywhere near and far, but I never possessed a bicycle and seldom rode one. However, I was young, strong and keen, and Bertie, who could get the loan of a good bike, assured me that the trip, as he put it, 'won't take a tack out of you'. Never having won the singles title and knowing I had a good chance, I blithely agreed. On Friday morning we cycled the eighty miles non-stop, played all our games in the afternoon and evening, reaching the semi-finals of all events – both of us pairing up with local girls for the mixed doubles. On Saturday night we played our semi-finals, which we won, and our finals, winning these also, Bertie and I the men's doubles, Bertie the singles (yet again) and one of us – I forget which – the mixed doubles. Afterwards there was a party and dance in which I took part until the small hours, but Bertie, being an observant Methodist, retired to bed once the tournament was over. Next morning we rose early, breakfasted, and set out on the return trip.

Again we planned to do the journey without stopping. Did we manage it? Bertie did, of course; as he said next time we met, 'It didn't take a tack out of me.' But well before halfway I had felt that many tacks had been taken out of me, and Bertie's relentless pace meant that keeping up with him took another tack or two with every mile. So how far did I get? About two miles from home I had, metaphorically speaking, reached the end of the road. Arriving at Tivoli, opposite the picturesque Marina and the Lee drawling out into Cork Harbour, I knew I had no more energy left, not an ounce. Fortunately there were some inviting riverside benches along the adjoining path which discouraged me from pushing the bicycle and my luck any further. I dismounted and collapsed onto one of them. Bertie stopped to ask if I was alright. I hadn't even the breath to answer him, so taking my silence for an affirmative answer, he said that as there was no point in waiting, he would go home. I don't know how long I had to rest to make it possible for me to muster enough energy to get back on the saddle, or even to want to do so. Eventually I managed to reach home at a pace that would have won for me any slow bicycle race. I struggled off the machine, threw it against the garden wall, opened the front door and went straight to bed. When my mother found me comatose some hours later, she could not be certain if I was breathing or not, so she immediately summoned the family doctor, my appendix extractor. It didn't take him very long to pronounce his verdict, not that I was in any state to hear it, but I believe that when he was told of my trip to Waterford and back, he said, 'The young fool is just exhausted. Keep him in bed for a couple of days and sell the bike.' Of course I was up the next day, and although I cannot say that the saga inspired any moments of exhilaration, I still recall it with something of the sort of satisfaction that Hillary must have felt on reaching the summit of Everest.

Since the rise of the Irish short story from the 1920s onwards, Irish practitioners have recognised the possibilities offered by sport as a story backdrop. Apart from the excitement and tension of the contest itself, whatever the particular code, there is the effect on participants and spectators, and the stimulation, for good or ill, of hitherto hidden character traits in those more intimately connected. In treatment there is often the incidental licence for a more colourful descriptive style than would be apt in a social or domestic setting, a licence that most Irish writers are exuberantly able to exploit.

Gaelic football and hurling provide ideal material for sporting stories in which an anecdotal core is both bracing and embracing. Of the former, Patrick Kavanagh's 'Gut Yer Man' is not as well known as it should be, and of the latter John B. Keane's 'You're On Next Sunday' is a classic example, with the added advantage of being an inspired ghost story. With so much water in and around Ireland, the sea and river have been popular settings, though whether fishing can be ranked as a sport rather than just an out-of-doors activity can be questioned. Whether or which, however, one cannot disqualify Padraic O'Conaire's 'The Trout in the Big River', while Daniel Corkery's rowing story, 'The Lartys', shows how much readers continue to miss since his four collections went out of print. The rugby story, 'The Wing Three-Quarter', reveals an unexpected side to Liam O'Flaherty's genius, and Brian Friel's two collections – sadly only two – surprisingly contain some half-dozen sporting stories on diverse subjects, including greyhound racing, cock fighting and pigeon racing, of which latter his 'The Widowhood System' is an excellent example of his short story phase. Pigeon racing also attracted Seán O'Faoláin in 'The End of a Good Man', while the greyhound racing story 'My Love Has a Long Tail' came from the pen of one of Ireland's most flamboyant and imaginative short story masters, Bryan MacMahon.

Hunting (*pacé* the anti-blood sports lobby) has many gems by Edith Somerville and Martin Ross, while T.P. O'Mahony's 'The Bowlsplayer' is one of the most vivid sporting depictions of all. Readers as well as those who cherish native traditions are fortunate to have this reminder of bowls, now virtually extinct except perhaps in parts of Northern Ireland and Co. Cork. Dermot Somers, one of the Irish team that in 1993 successfully ascended a hitherto unconquered route to the top of Everest, has produced two little-known story collections which include 'Cliff Hanger' among its many climbing stories, and even croquet is not forgotten, not at least by Patrick Campbell, whose madcap humour is at its wildest in 'A Goss on the Potted Meat'.

Some of these stories, and many others I have not mentioned, succeed in word-snaring the exhilaration elixir for anyone ever gifted with sporting enthusiasm and proficiency. *Elixir vitae*, the elixir of life, was once thought to be a drug capable of prolonging life indefinitely. We are not so gullible now. Life, no; but memories, the next best thing, definitely yes.

CHAPTER FOURTEEN

Endgames

Irish Writing had been planned to appear quarterly but the delayed traumatic birth of *No. 1* caused a lapse of six months between it and *No. 2* and a similar period between *Nos. 2* and *3* while I monitored progress and assessed whether life could be sustained on Irish circulation alone without further losses. In fact, after *No. 1* only two issues, *No. 4* and, strangely, a much later one, *No. 16*, failed to at least break even. The profit earned by the twenty-seven issues after the catastrophic loss sustained by *No. 1* at least confirmed that *Irish Writing* was keeping its head above water, if only for an average of £25 per issue, but such exiguous returns could make no inroad on the standing debt plus the additional bank interest payments. The British Board of Trade embargo remained for some three years but its removal was of no help because, as I had feared, the lapse of time and the increasing supply of books and magazines coming on stream in Britain after the return of normalcy meant that the interest readers there had shown in the first issue had completely melted away.

Yet I persevered for another four years until 1954. Why? Certainly the principal reason was that I simply had no alternative. But I was also growing increasingly aware that the editorial seed that had awakened me in the middle 1940s had burgeoned into flower before the end of that decade, by which time I was fully committed to nurturing it. As each issue appeared, the search for new writers and for new work from the many distinguished Irish writers living at home as well as abroad, was a continuing challenge. The need to maintain a high standard as well as an accompanying anticipatory what-next feeling among readers was, of course, vital, but I began to feel that it was doing nothing to assuage my expansionist itch. My global ambitions might have been buried, but nationally were there not still gaps to be filled? Financially they were totally without prospect, but in that era in Ireland cultural endeavour, like virtue, had to be its own sufficient reward. One gap in particular seemed to me to be most urgently in need of attention, and as my enquiries suggested it could be tackled inexpensively and on a likely break-even basis, I followed my nose and my need. In 1948 I founded and edited the quarterly *Poetry Ireland*.

It did, as I had hoped, break even – indeed, to give it credit, its nineteen issues showed an overall profit of £15! At that point, however, I had to accept that the technical and commercial burdens involved in continuing to produce it as a separate periodical were just too onerous to bear. But kill it off I wouldn't. Instead, under the title of *Poetry Ireland Supplement* I gave it what I amused myself by regarding as a mythical Irish Board of Trade licence to import it into *Irish Writing* with a quota of six pages per issue filched from the main quarterly, though not dropping from the latter its usual three or four poems. This supplement commenced in March 1953, in *Irish Writing No. 22*, and ended only with the publication, in September 1954, of the latter's twenty-eighth and final issue under the co-editorship of myself and Terence Smith. *Poetry Ireland*, however, proved to have the longevity of a cultural oak – perhaps not surprising in view of the country's standing army of poets – and was soon reborn as a separate periodical by Liam Miller's Dolmen Press, as, too, was *Irish Writing*, the latter surviving for some half-dozen further issues under Seán J. White, and the former being constantly reincarnated right up to the present time under a succession of distinguished editors.

Poetry Ireland had accomplished what it set out to do, that is, provide space for the established poets as well as dis-covering the best new talents, notably Anthony Cronin and Thomas Kinsella. It also featured a number of special issues, including an Irish Translation Issue followed by the publi-cation of Lord Longford's 'Midnight Court' translation, then an American Poets Issue, an Ulster Poets Issue, and an Easter Rising Memorial Issue guest-edited by M.J. MacManus.

Irish Writing, once it had been able to resume a quarterly schedule, also continued to seek out the best poetry, the most interesting stories, the most informative and provocative criticism. In the latter category Patrick Kavanagh's 'The Gallivanting Poet', an attack on the poetry of F.R. Higgins, caused quite a furore in the press, and among other stimulat-ing critical essays were 'Irish-American Literature and Why There Isn't Any' by John V. Kelleher, Professor of Irish History and Literature at Harvard University, 'The Parnellism of Seán O'Faoláin' by Donat O'Donnell, then the pseudonym of Conor Cruise O'Brien, Padraic Colum on O'Casey, on Ibsen in Irish Writing, and on Swift's poetry, and Diarmuid Russell on his father, AE.

The most frequent contributors of short stories from among the country's leading writers were Benedict Kiely,

Mary Lavin, Bryan MacMahon, Frank O'Connor, Seán O'Faoláin, Liam O'Flaherty and James Plunkett, while two writers who contributed a single story each proved, for very different reasons, more distinguished than I could have known at the time. One, William Walsh, previously unpublished, I much later learned was the husband of Mary Lavin; the other, then almost unknown but later world-renowned, was that most intriguing non-Irish Irishman, Patrick O'Brian. The American-Armenian William Saroyan, whose sensational debut story collection had, in 1939, set aflame my growing interest in the form, was a guest-writer who sent me a char-acteristically titled 'Four Hours for *Irish Writing*', but the periodical's first guest-writer was Jean-Paul Sartre, whose short story, 'Herostratus', was translated by A.J. Leventhal of Trinity College, one of Samuel Beckett's closest friends.

To celebrate *Irish Writing*'s twenty-first birthday a double issue was published which included stories, poetry and articles by, among others, Seán O'Faoláin, Frank O'Connor, Liam O'Flaherty, Francis Stuart, Austin Clarke and Lord Dunsany, and this was followed by a Tóstal issue. *An Tóstal* was the Government-sponsored 'Festival to reflect the spirit of Ireland at home to its friends and exiles' and the issue was introduced by Cecil Ffrench Salkeld, Executive Officer in charge of the Festival. Its contents included short stories by Chicago-born, Irish-descended James T. Farrell, author of the acclaimed *Studs Lonigan* trilogy, Dublin's Paul Vincent Carroll, whose play, *Shadow and Substance*, won him a world-wide reputation during the first half of the twentieth century, and James Hanley, one of Ireland's forgotten great short story writers. A 176-line poem by Oliver St John Gogarty bristled with that author's celebrated wit, and Francis Russell contributed an article on Finley Peter Dunne, the American humorist who, under the pseudonym Mr Dooley wrote eight volumes of Mr Dooley speaking his mind in a voice in which, as the author himself said, 'one can hear all the various accents of Ireland from the awkward brogue of the "far-downer" to the mild and aisy Elizabethan English of the southern Irishman, and all the exquisite variations to be heard between Armagh and Bantry Bay, with the difference that would naturally arise from substituting cinders and sulphuretted hydrogen for soft misty air and peat smoke.'

In 1953 Dublin held the Twenty-fifth International Congress of the PEN, and to record the occasion *Irish Writing* published an International Issue with work by many of the most distinguished European writers of the time. There were stories by, among others, Arturo Barea, author of a celebrated trilogy about the Spanish civil war; Italian Ignazio Silone, whose novel *Fontamara* is his most famous work; Georges Simenon, whose detective, Maigret, is one of the favourite characters of the reading and viewing public. The issue's critical section was particularly strong. One of the most widely-acclaimed and prolific French authors, André Maurois, wrote about the main causes when, in literature, 'certain events impose a break with tradition, a revolution in modes of expression and in ideas'; German novelist Lion Feuchtwanger, whose *Jew Suss* made him famous, contributed 'Notes on the Historical Novel', and the British author Storm Jameson wrote a trenchant response to commentators who predicted that film and television would precipitate the death of the novel.

However, certainly the most famous writer to figure in the quarterly's pages was the then very obscure, Paris-based, pre-*Waiting for Godot* Samuel Beckett. I had read his startling story collection, *More Pricks Than Kicks*, wrote to him care of his French publishers, told him about *Irish Writing* and asked him if he would contribute. He sent me an extract from the novel he was then working on, *Watt*, and later, unasked, sent me a further extract which I used in the Tóstal issue.

A recollection of which I have no reason to be proud arises out of an exchange with Stanislaus Joyce. He sent me a poem he had translated from the Italian nineteenth-century poet Giovanni Pascoli. It did not seem to be of any particular interest or distinction, but his accompanying letter was such as to make me accept and publish it without hesitation. He told me that he was working on a biography of his brother, James, and was extremely anxious to trace a report which he believed was published in a local paper of an appearance by his father in a play produced by the UCC Drama Society. He promised that if I could unearth this and send him a copy, he would reward me with previously unpublished translations of four biographical essays written in Italian by James Joyce on celebrated Irish personages. My memory of the four he named is, unfortunately, uncertain, but I seem to recall that Parnell and Wilde were two of them. I of course willingly and assiduously trawled through all available papers and was elated to turn up exactly what he had been seeking. I sent it off to him, but he failed to respond to my excited anticipation of the four essays. What a *coup* it would have been! What it would have done for the sales of *Irish Writing* can only be guessed at. Spread over four issues, it would surely have made the quarterly world famous. Ah well, on such ingratitude one's fortune sometimes rests. Stanislaus Joyce fobbed me off with his brother's Italian translation of James Stephens's poem, 'The Wind' – perhaps as some sort of celebration of the coincidence that James Joyce and Stephens were supposed to have been born on the same day. I published it as no more than a curiosity and was in no way appeased to find that when Stanislaus's biography appeared I had been listed in the acknowledgements!

Of course the craziest, most bizarre, most cockeyed and almost most sensational episode during my *Irish Writing* days was the period during which I was editor of *The Bell*! After Seán O'Faoláin retired from it in 1946, Peadar O'Donnell had two spells as editor, from 1946 to April 1948, and after a break of two and a half years during which the monthly did not appear, Peadar announced what he called its Second Coming and revived it from November, 1950, until it disappeared finally at the end of 1954. It was early in the second of these two spells that he phoned me and said, 'How about you editing *The Bell*?'

I thought he must have taken leave of his senses. I had never met him, never been in touch with him, so had no idea what sort of person I was dealing with. Surely he must have known of *Irish Writing* and my involvement.

'What do you mean?' I asked him. 'How could I edit *The Bell*? I'd have to give up *Irish Writing* and live in Dublin.'

'Not at all. You could handle the literary stuff. I'd send it down to you by post, and I'd handle all the rest.'

Clearly this appeared to be a different proposition from what his opening question had implied. However, I did not see how I could seriously consider the suggestion without hearing a full job-description and having time to think about it. While I was hesitating, Peadar put in, 'Why don't you come up to Dublin and we can talk it over?'

That made sense, so up to Dublin I went.

I found Peadar O'Donnell to be a jovial, bonhomous individual who quickly put me at my ease. He took me to lunch at the Gresham Hotel, and when we took our seats I told him about my only previous visit there when I had called on Liam O'Flaherty. But when I read the à la carte menu the waiter handed me I felt distinctly unhappy. Although I presumed Peadar would be paying, I was still appalled at the prices of the various dishes. Peadar, however, being of the same mind, was equal to the occasion. Closing the menu quite firmly, he took my copy from me, ceremoniously handed them both back to the stiff-looking waiter, and with a naughty twinkle in his eye, said, 'I think we'll have the pass paper.' Having successfully passed that examination, the meal was taken to the accompaniment of an easygoing, discursive, but not particularly informative outline of what he expected me to do for *The Bell*. In fact it boiled down to a repetition in various different ways of what had been the gist of our brief telephone talk. The only phrase that did not change was his repeated statement that I would be editor. I couldn't see how handling only the 'literary matters' qualified me for such a title, but as I wouldn't, anyway, have wanted to take on 'the rest', I wasn't worried about what title I had or hadn't. When Peadar eventually offered me what would be an extremely helpful monthly payment, I was more than happy to agree. We shook hands on it, Peadar saying, 'I'll be in touch', and we parted. He wasn't in touch. That was the last I heard of the matter, the beginning and end of my reign as 'editor' of *The Bell*. A somewhat dotty episode on which to reflect, especially in view of the freak coincidence it gave birth to – Seán O'Faoláin being invited to edit *Irish Writing* and I being invited to edit *The Bell*!

The game of life is often like the first game I fell in love with when I used watch it from my parents' bedroom windows – cricket. You can make a stunning catch or be caught out yourself or stumped or have to change your position on a sudden change of circumstances or sit frettingly waiting for conditions to improve so that you can get on with the course of your life. When the last issue of *Irish Writing* with its papoose-borne *Poetry Ireland Supplement* passed into other hands, I presumed that my innings as an editor had come to an end. However, I had forgotten the best thing about the classic game of cricket: there is always a second innings. Mine came later, much later. But it was all the sweeter for that.

CHAPTER FIFTEEN

Coming Back for More

At the dawn of 1954 there had not been the slightest hope, much less prospect, of any development that might enable me to bring my first editorial innings to an end in September of that year. But come an end there did, and what made it so unexpectedly possible to pay off the bank – thus ensuring that my father would not be called on to make any contribution – and give me the chance to emigrate to London and seek my future there, all happened in a sudden rush.

Although we sometimes can legitimately take credit as the authors of our own good fortune, how often can we claim to have planned it exactly as it came about? When, towards the end of 1952, I decided to write a novel, the only objective I had was just that – to write a novel. No strings were attached to it, no pecuniary aims shaped it. It was the result of an inquisitiveness, as a test for myself to ascertain whether, having written only poetry and short stories, and not having been a particularly dedicated novel reader, I could get down on paper a story in enough words to qualify, lengthwise, as a novel.

I do not remember how long it took me to write – probably about six months – but there it was, finished, with a title, *To Next Year in Jerusalem*, under which I could type the first appearance of the words 'A Novel by David Marcus'. The title was the exilic mantra of the Jews, repeated annually for centuries at the Passover *Seder*, glass of wine and eyes raised to heaven. The novel was of course Jewish, more accurately Irish-Jewish, set in a mythical town in the west of Ireland with a barely viable Jewish community, and involving the hopeless romance of a young Jew and his Catholic girlfriend. There had never been, so far as I knew, an Irish-Jewish novel, excepting of course *Ulysses* which I had not read or ever come across, not because it was banned – in fact, contrary to general belief, it was never banned in Ireland, but given its reputation and the traditional Irish susceptibilities, it was not stocked by any Irish bookseller – and so mine was the first Irish-Jewish novel by a real Irish-Jewish writer, with a real Irish-Jewish main character which Bloom, being born of a non-Jewish mother, was strictly not.

And that, the unchallengeable Jewish parentage of its author and central character, I thought was all that was original about *To Next Year in Jerusalem*. Not that this made it worthwhile – indeed I could not imagine that, merit apart, any British publisher would be interested in such a hybrid, the Jewish novel not yet having arrived in Britain. Yes, but apart from 'merit apart' was merit a part? That I reacted with more than a touch of flippancy to my own verdict on it after I read the completed opus tells quite bluntly the opinion I had formed. Quite simply, it appalled me. The only flash of pride I momentarily felt was at having proved I had the *zitzfleisch* to write a full-length novel, albeit an execrable one. I showed it to no one and just wanted to forget it.

Which is what I did, promptly locking it in a drawer and metaphorically throwing away the key. Daily life resumed its normal routine.

Then came the day early in September 1953 when I received a letter from the American magazine *New World Writing* – a blueprint of which I had seven years earlier conceived as the cornerstone of my burst bubble dream of global publishing – informing me that they were happy to accept the short story 'The Religion of Love', which I had submitted, and that the fee would be $315! To use one of James Stephens's phrases, I was flabbered and I was gasted. Any short story I had previously sold had never realised more than ten guineas, usually less, sometimes no fee at all, so what amounted to over £100 was for me a not so small fortune.

It took me a few days to get used to feeling affluent and to succeed in containing my delight sufficiently to re-read the story, having already read the letter countless times. It was a good story, yes, of course it must have been a good story if *New World Writing* were publishing it. But what was this? I had forgotten it was an Irish-Jewish story, or not exactly forgotten that, but because the majority of my stories were habitually Irish-Jewish, I was no longer attaching any significance to this trend in my writing. At that sudden realisation my mind ceased to function. It was as if I was afraid to allow entry to the thought struggling to surface. But the thought forced itself on me. My reviled, worthless, banished novel, *To Next Year in Jerusalem*, that was Irish-Jewish too. Had I been right about it? Could it . . .? Might it . . .? Should I? After all, it could only be rejected. And having already been rejected by me, its author, it could hardly be offended if it should be rejected by a stranger. It could only say to me, 'Serves you right. You told me I was no good. If you send me off to a publisher and he sends me back, then don't blame me, blame yourself. *You* can bear the disappointment. I'll be happy to go back into my little drawer and be forgotten again.'

Thus did my mind play around, screwing up courage to convince myself that thinking of trying to get the poor thing published was part of the game, just as having it declined was also part of the game, only to be expected and so nothing to be upset about. Without further thought – indeed to get rid of further thought – I parcelled it up and sent it to Macmillan. They were the London publishers of many Irish writers, including such as Yeats, O'Casey, O'Connor and James Stephens. I picked them because of that, and because of being that they would know how to deal with my alleged novel. They would put it in its place.

About a month later I received a letter dated 27th October, 1953, from Lovat Dickson, director and publishing editor of Macmillan. It read as follows:

Dear Sir,

We have been giving careful consideration to your novel *To Next Year in Jerusalem* and have been considerably impressed by the qualities it shows. It is an unusual and promising book, and we should like you to know at this stage of our genuine interest in it.

We are writing to you now because our readers have made certain suggestions which we think you might be ready to consider. The most important of these deals with the question of the love affair.

Our chief adviser on this novel has been Sir John Squire, whose name you will know as an eminent literary critic, and whose opinion we feel you will value. He has told us that he would like to write to you about it himself, but before he does so we feel that we should tell you of this suggestion and ask if you would be ready to consider and work on the changes he would recommend. If you would do so, we should be prepared to make an offer for the publication of the book.

Perhaps you will let us know how you feel about this. We are attracted by the work, even in its present form, and are only anxious to do what we can to make it as good as possible.

Looking forward with great interest to your reply,
Yours faithfully,
Lovat Dickson

What day of the week was it? What was the weather like? I had no idea, because my mind was blank, or perhaps too crowded to think. I distinctly remember feeling suddenly cold, not with shock, but with fright. I sat down and stared at the letter until full control returned. Then, deciding that I must have been wrong, wildly wrong, in my estimation of the novel, that I was very lucky in my choice of publishers, that they had to know what they were doing and that my job was just to mind my own business, i.e. just write, I immediately put a page in my now proud-looking Olivetti and typed a letter expressing my deep gratitude and my eagerness to have the benefit of Sir John Squire's advice and recommendations. With the letter posted I waited in suspended animation, marvelling at how in exactly other than the way I had expected they had put *To Next Year in Jerusalem* in its place. And me too, perhaps. And me too.

On 6 November Lovat Dickson wrote to tell me that Sir John Squire was moving house but hoped to be in touch with me 'by the middle of next week'.

On 19 November another communication to the effect that Sir John 'would be writing you, via us, in a few days time'. However, what was far more important to me was the news that Macmillan were sending a copy of my manuscript to Ian MacKenzie, vice president of St Martin's Press, their US imprint.

By 30 November there was still no word from Sir John Squire. 'I know', was Lovat Dickson's comment, 'that literary critics are not always good correspondents.' He went on to say, 'I think I must tell you the point which he was going to put although I do not like to anticipate anything he may write. He thinks that the end of the book should be rewritten. I am attaching on a sheet of paper that part of his report which deals with this matter. You may like to be thinking it over in advance of hearing from him. I should add that you must not feel constrained to follow his advice. You are the author, and you know what you were trying to do.'

The 'sheet of paper' attached read as follows:

. . . the author, who has shown such unusual understanding of the Gentiles and Jews and the antagonism (though he is unaware of our reaction against the Chosen People doctrine), funks his last fence. He doesn't tell us what is going to happen to the love-affair of the hero and his girlfriend, in whom and in whose lives he makes us believe from the start.

Frankly I think it is because he couldn't work out the end himself. But the book is so good that the end should be written; it is no good leaving the problem in the air.

It is not for me to say what would or should happen to these two, tragically or otherwise, in Palestine or Ireland. It's his business to face it; and not to fake it.

In other words, the book is unfinished. But it is a superbly honest affair by one who is (he must take it from me) *animal naturalitas Christiana*, and I can't help thinking that if the author is *made* to bring his book to a conclusion, bitter, sweet, or bitter-sweet, he has the brain and the guts to do it.

I should like to write him to this effect; but I feel I should ask permission. The book has stirred me.

I replied to Lovat Dickson to the effect that 'the chances of my changing the ending are almost non-existent . . . I think Sir John is wrong when he says that I don't tell what happens to the love affair. I certainly do (the ending of the novel took months of thought and heart-searching). I make it quite clear that the hero will continue to go with his girlfriend for a little while longer, and then cut the association with her and go to Israel to make his life there. Sir John may not consider that a satisfactory ending – that is an entirely different question; but it is the only ending which could emanate from the characters as I have drawn them.'

Lovat Dickson's response came on 4 December:

May I say now what I did not like to say before, that I am entirely of your point of view about the end of the book which seemed to me perfectly clear.

My stand against the points made in the extract from Sir John Squire's report had had me in two minds. To oppose the opinion of an eminent critic who was also Macmillan's chief reader was not a step I could take without some hesitation. But the text clearly showed him to have been wrong, and I also felt most disinclined to take it from him that I was *animal naturalitas Christiana.* Lovat Dickson's disclosure that he, too, had not agreed with the report's conclusion gave an invaluable boost to my self-belief, but in truth, what had decided me to stand by my guns in taking on Sir John Squire was the final paragraph of Lovat Dickson's letter of 30 November accompanying the crucial report. It said, 'I think we should not wait any longer to make an agreement,' and went on to offer me a contract to publish *To Next Year in Jerusalem.* If he had had doubts about the book's ending, I reasoned that he would hardly have offered me a contract before having the doubts resolved. It was comforting to know that I had not been wrong. I had learned a valuable lesson: never blink when reading between the lines.

I went to London on 18 December to meet Lovat Dickson, who had with him Ian MacKenzie on a visit from St Martin's Press. I was glad we were three rather than two. Meeting my publisher – even the phrase had brought back all my antici-patory nervousness of first encounters with important people – was much less of a strain with Ian MacKenzie present to keep the conversation moving. He told me he had received my novel and would let me have the St Martin's Press deci-sion by the end of January when his readers' reports would be to hand.

We were lunching at the Garrick Club and for the dessert course Lovat Dickson said he had something special, where-upon he drew from his briefcase the contract for *To Next Year in Jerusalem* for me to take home, read and sign.

I had already received a note of the important clauses from the Contracts Department, so I saw no reason to put off the ceremony. We both signed it, Ian MacKenzie acting as witness, and on 2 January 1954 St Martin's Press also sent me an offer to publish the novel in the US. The

Macmillan edition came out on 3 July and the St Martin's Press edition on 3 September. The former sold 2,000 copies by September and the *New York Times* included the US edition in their annual list of the best three hundred books of the year.

Perhaps I should have been pleased, but I soon had misgivings. I think both publishers expected better sales than they had, and while there were many reviews, few were especially enthusiastic, the majority being rather routine notices composed more of clichéd responses than considered reactions. For me the important ones were from the Irish papers, all but two of which were supportive. The two exceptions were *The Irish Times*, where Bruce Williamson was not impressed but helpfully gave cogent and convincing reasons for his opposition, and an even more critical and very much fuller review by Owen Sheehy Skeffington. Ironically, this was a review I had commissioned myself for *Irish Writing*, where it duly appeared. I had known the reviewer only by reputation, and was glad not to have received the sort of review readers could conceivably have regarded as in any way sycophantic. In fact, that it and Bruce Williamson's were particularly critical, carefully giving chapter and verse for the faults to which they drew attention, made me return to my original opinion of *To Next Year in Jerusalem* and decide that its first home, the locked drawer, should also have been its last. Of course that left me with the problem of accounting for the praise frequently expressed by Lovat Dickson in his letters and by Sir John Squire in his report. They were, of course, sincere, but I wondered to what extent the novelty of the theme might have so intrigued and attracted them that their wanting to approve of what they were reading helped them to gloss over its weaknesses. The advertisement

Macmillan placed in the June 1954 issue of *Irish Writing* announcing the novel's forthcoming publication had one particular sentence that made me all but certain of the accuracy of my assessment. '. . . [the novel's] theme is one which we can confidently say has never previously been that of a work of fiction in the English language'. That such a statement was factually correct did not, of itself, make the novel worth publishing or prove I was a good novelist. I had, however, a further test.

For about a year I had been working on a second novel. It was set in Cork, and dealt with the relationship between the young members of a classical music string quartet, one of whom was Jewish. I finished it before the end of 1954 and sent it to Lovat Dickson. He rejected it – with the most sympathetic of letters – as being not at all as convincing or impressive as the first novel, and advised that I should put it aside, but if I wished to try it with another publisher of my choice, he would be happy to forward it for me. I accepted his kind offer and asked him to send it to a particular editor in Rupert Hart-Davis with whom I had once been in contact. Once again the new novel was rejected, but this time with the suggestion that if I would agree to change the classical quartet to a jazz quartet, they would be most interested in making an offer to publish. They even offered to recommend someone to help me rewrite the music content if I so required. I refused their offer, realising that changing the nature of the quartet would entail rewriting far more than just the music content, but mainly because I had no interest in a jazz quartet.

There was also another, and more fundamental, more important reason. I accepted that the performance of *To Next Year in Jerusalem* was, at best, only mediocre, and that the rejection of the second novel by two publishers was proof that I was not a novelist and would be well advised to give up trying. The self-belief I had developed on the enthusiastic acceptance of *To Next Year in Jerusalem* had dissipated. I abandoned all ambition of becoming a novelist, mentally inscribing 'He closed the book' as the epitaph on ambition's grave.

Life, however, or fate – call it what you will – still had a trick up its sleeve. When writing the foregoing account I searched for and found the Macmillan correspondence, which I had not read since 1955. The final letter in the file was one from Lovat Dickson dated 4 March 1955, rejecting my third novel after reading the first seven chapters that I had sent him. The title of the projected novel was not named, the file contained no copy of my letter of submission, and nowhere in the papers I had kept from these years was there any trace of the seven chapters in question. To complete the total blackout, I had not, and still have not the slightest recollection of any such manuscript. It has been wiped from my memory as if it never existed. But it did exist, as Lovat Dickson's letter proves – though why I retained the letter is a mystery to me. My most likely explanation is that it represented for me the incontestable proof I would never make a novelist, that I thereupon put into operation an act of willed amnesia to forget all such ambition, destroying all textual evidence of the third novel in symbolic confirmation of my determination, but keeping the letter as a warning in case I should ever be so foolish as to back-slide. This is a somewhat tortuous explanation, suggestive perhaps of a Rabbinical attempt to interpret a difficult Talmudic injunction. The ironic flaw in all this is, of course, the total success of my amnesia, for my loss of memory was so complete that it also included the warning letter and so could not prevent me from exhuming the bones of my old ambition and backsliding into another novel all of thirty years later.

CHAPTER SIXTEEN

Where and Wen

Not that Cork was a wen, certainly not compared to the uncharming megalopolis that was London in the eyes of one who had lived in Cork, child, youth and man for thirty years. So it was hardly surprising that after only a month of exile, I was already missing it.

It was a felt absence, a permanently lost property of my emotional DNA far more than the cityscape that Joyce, using words for bricks and phrases for architecture, modelled on the responses to his Dublin enquiries. Hampstead, where I had settled, was treeless, but the Mardyke elms had offered free-gift embraces. In Cork there had been companionable, if cacophonous trams, superseded by buses onto which conductors routinely help-lifted child-filled buggys, but London's buses were pramless, and in its Underground's daily offering of scrabbling insectman life my mind was early scored with the rush hour sight of a rabbi struggling to get out at his stop but unable to push his way through the press of people fighting to board – a small horror perhaps, but its recollection is still fused with images of other rabbis failing to escape from other carriages at other times in other lands. Near my new abode was a Jewish delicatessen, like nothing of which Cork's Jewtown could ever boast, but once every year Mrs Silverstein's small front room would become the community's eight-day Passover commissariat from where she traded specially imported matzo, matzo meal, kosher chocolate, biscuits, wine and other annual exotica in exchange for gossip-warmed coinage, and twice in the week my brothers and I would journey to our milkman's farm on Cork's rural edge where we watched the excretion of the milk hissing straight from udder into the scoured, made-kosher cans we had brought with us. And in London one heard no bells, Big Ben being but a musically unalliterated bong-beater, while in Cork Angelus bells rang twice a day with Shandon pealing over all.

But even if in the first few months separation from the sights, sounds and scents of home was a deprivation of the freedom I had enjoyed, that did not mean London was a prison in which I was confined. Or if it was, it was very much an open prison, and like open prisons it offered many privileges, the earliest one of which I availed being visits to the Royal Festival Hall to hear my idols of the piano and violin, Artur Rubinstein and Jascha Heifetz. Listening to these two gods made me forget what I was and where I was – a failed writer whose real prison was one into which I had locked myself and thrown away its only key, my disgraced pen. But I would not recant or retreat back into any literary *cul-de-sac*. That was the route to verbal dipsomania. There had to be another way to earn – I could not exist indefinitely on the little savings I had. And there was, with a word for it too, a four-letter word: WORK. Recognising it brought me to the Jewish Sabbath Day Observance Employment Bureau.

Why there? Why not some leading, well-known exchange with wider, more varied possibilities, or why not the job offers in the daily newspapers? But what work could any of these offer me that I would be fit for? I was merely a barrister whose practical experience was minimal and the remnants of my legal knowledge by now exiguous. In any event, to practise as a barrister in London would have meant a further year's study followed by a qualifying examination and a virtually certain long period of unemployment even then. The Jewish Sabbath Day Observance Employment Bureau promised to be a godsend. It would be recommending only Jewish businesses, where I could expect to be among my own, and where, into the bargain, employees would get many days off for religious duties. If the Bureau could find some post for me that I might be able to handle and that would not be too uncongenial, it would give me time to find my feet, perhaps make one or two Jewish friends who shared my interests, and, most important, build up the nest egg I would be likely to need when launching myself in whatever direction I might eventually want to follow. With no further hesitation I decided to take the plunge.

The Bureau was a small office with a few chairs, none holding any hopefuls, and a counter from behind which a heavily bespectacled, bouncingly bosomy, no longer young-looking woman rose and eyed me.

'I'm looking for a job,' I said, feeling somewhat intimidated.

Wordlessly she handed me a card and a pen. I filled out my name, address, age, place of birth, and left the Special Qualifications question unanswered.

She scanned the card, read it a second time, then looked closely at me for so long that I blushed. I knew the question she was on the point of asking and I guessed from the way she carried her big bust that she would not be worried about offending me. As if in some doubt she reluctantly drew a

card from a box on the counter. Then, briskly, in a no-
nonsense voice, she accused: 'You're sure you *are* Jewish?'

I wondered how I could prove my authenticity to her –
apart from one particular way that would hardly further my
cause (though one never knew).

'I mean,' she grated on, 'we never had an *Irish* Jew before.
And you don't *sound* Jewish.'

Perhaps I should tell her the joke about the two Chinese
Jews. One Chinese Jew met another Chinese Jew. Dialogue:
'You Jlewish?' 'Yes, I'm Jlewish. And you?' 'Yes, I'm Jlewish
too.' 'Funny – you don't look Jlewish.' For God's sake, what
would I be doing in the Jewish Sabbath Day Observance
Employment Bureau if I were a *goy*?

But she was as sharp at combating questions – even
unspoken ones – as at asking them.

'We *do* get a few non-Jews here, you know. It's quite an
attraction to them to pretend to be Jewish if it means a job in an
orthodox Jewish business house – no Saturday work, early closing on Fridays in the winter and all the Jewish holidays off. As
well as *all* the national holidays too. We *do* have to be careful.'

'Of course,' I submissively agreed.

She allowed herself a wintry smile which she tried to hide
by examining a non-existent speck of dust on her bosom.
Then it was back to business.

'How is your maths?' Tonelessly, eyes riveted on the filing
card in her hand.

'Oh, very good,' I assured her. 'I got a hundred and five
per cent in the Intermediate Examination for maths.'

She raised a slow stare and I knew I had said something
wrong.

'Sorry. I should have explained,' I quickly added. 'The
Inter is a big, national exam. All the Irish schools do it.'

There was a solid pause. What now?

'One hundred and *five* per cent? In maths?'

She seemed shaken. Obviously *all* my credentials were suspect. I was about to tell her that the extra five per cent was for answering the paper in Irish but she waved me aside.

'Go to these people,' she said, writing out an address for me. 'They're looking for an accounts clerk.'

I thanked her.

'You may just suit them,' she added. She suppressed the hint of sarcasm in her tone, but that expressive bosom jerked up like two massive eyebrows raised in doubt. Small wonder – as I left the office I suddenly realised that I was not wearing a hat. Imagine! An orthodox Jew with his head uncovered! I could guess what she was thinking: What can you expect from the Irish?

Baron's, four storeys high, was a wholesale distributor of ladies-wear in a lane behind London's teeming Oxford Street. It was owned by three brothers, Sid, Manny and Abie Baron. Sid was the boss, the boss of everything, sharp-voiced, terse, a small, well-dressed, smartly groomed controller who wielded authority with a Napoleonic confidence and composure. His brothers appeared to be merely sleeping partners, for though they were always present, they seemed to have no specific functions. Manny, tall and in appearance the eldest of the three, would be more accurately described as a sleepwalking rather than a sleeping partner, for all he did, hour after hour every day, was patrol all areas of the premises, never uttering a word, hands clasped behind his back. With a helmet and a uniform he would have passed for Policeman Plod. Not so Abie, who was big, brawny, with a shock of unruly black hair, who also patrolled the different floors, his path designedly avoiding Manny's. But in contrast to Manny, he frequently stopped to entertain the workers with stories and small talk. And entertain he did, though not quite in the way he intended, for his English was not so much broken as rearranged almost to the point of genius. His information always came 'from the horse's neck'; there were people he wouldn't trust 'as high as he could throw them' because what they told him were only 'cock and hen stories'. Unfortunately, I was never the direct recipient of such gems. As an accounts clerk I spent my working hours ensconced in a top floor room with the two other accounts clerks and the firm's typist, and so I heard Abie's latest classics only in secondhand reports from the floorworkers on days I got together with them at lunch breaks.

The nine months I gave to Baron's just totting up invoices were the most unexacting nine months of my life. They were, however, anything but a bore, for in our quiet little office in which the only noise, apart from our chatter, was the clicking of the typewriter keys, we made a congenial and international Jewish quartet. The typist, Hilda, was German; Joe was born in India but had been brought to London when he was only three; Saul was an Eastender whose family had come from Poland in the late nineteenth century; and I, second generation Irishman, father Dublin-born and mother from Limerick, was jocularly referred to by Saul, who had read about the Black and Tans, as a mad Republican whose President had mourned Hitler's death. I did not explain to him de Valera's reason for his visit to the German Embassy because I knew he had only been trying to take a rise out of me. The four of us got on too well to quarrel. We often disagreed on general and religious issues and sometimes these disagreements were passionate, but the passion was that of four Jews, not young, not old, who whether for long or short periods and under different degrees of stress, had seen ourselves as sojourning in the valley of death. Being spared enabled us to feel not just life, but the immediacy of being alive, of the force that drove our blood. But we had not yet followed through on that. We had not yet discovered where to go from there. I certainly hadn't, and I knew why. But what about the others? What kept them – three intelligent, alert people – in such dead-end jobs? Extrapolating from my own experience I suspected that in each case there must lurk some memory, or some situation, that held them in its web. What they had gone through in the war? That was now almost a decade past, but perhaps they had lost loved ones in the Holocaust. Hilda was from Germany – she might have. As delicately as I could, I asked her. In her accented, very Germanic voice, slowly, tonelessly, with many pauses, as if repeating a statement she had made many times before, she told us.

'There isn't very much. It was something . . . *schnell* . . . you know, quick. We were born in Berlin, my father, my mother too, and I. I had no brothers or sisters, *Gott sa danken*. When my parents married my father was a teacher. He taught history. German history. He became a Professor of German history. He wrote a book . . .'

She paused, tapped some of the typewriter keys. She went on.

'It was 1938. I was fifteen. One day in the street – it was raining – my mother saw a young Nazi soldier make an old Jew go down on his knees on the wet stones and dry the soldier's boots with his beard. The people laughed. They all laughed. My mother didn't laugh. She went to the old Jew and lifted him to his feet. Then she bent down and spat on the soldier's boots. Before she could get up, he crashed the butt of his rifle down on her head. Then he shot her. Through the heart. I thought he would shoot me too. I ran away.'

She looked at her notes, typed a line, stopped, pulled the page from the machine, balled it up in her fist and threw it in the wastepaper basket.

'We left, my father and I. He wouldn't stay in Germany. We had enough money to get out. His friends, his Jewish friends, helped. We brought nothing with us. I put a book in my bag, a copy of the German history book he wrote. He took it from me and threw it away.'

She stopped again, then turned from her desk to face us.

'Do you know how I live now?' she asked.

None of us answered. We waited.

'I live every day with my suitcase packed.'

The next day Joe did not turn up for work. He phoned in that he wasn't well. I wondered. Could Hilda's awful revelation have reawakened some memory he would prefer to forget but never could?

Whatever about Joe, perhaps his absence that day and Hilda's willingness to respond to my tentative enquiry were what Saul had needed to unburden himself. We were munching our sandwiches – it was lunchtime, Hilda had gone out for hers but we, as we sometimes did, had brought in sandwiches and flasks of tea or milk – when he looked at me for a steady moment, straight into my eyes, then turned away and asked, 'Have you ever been in love?'

The question startled me, and without taking the time to think, I answered, 'I don't know.'

'If you were,' he said, in a tone of morose regret as of one who knew what he was talking about, 'you'd know.'

'Then I take it you have been.'

Usually Saul was voluble, but now he did not reply. I felt that if he hadn't wanted to talk, he would not have made the approach. He needed help.

'Tell me about it. I'm interested.'

He still held back, then suddenly shot out the words, like someone hesitating on the edge of a diving board before making a deliberate plunge into the cold water.

'Her name was Rebecca.'

'Snap,' I said. 'My mother's name is Rebecca too.'

He turned his stare on me once more.

'So is mine,' he said.

He put his sandwich, unfinished, into its bag and closed up his flask.

I laughed. 'That's quite a coincidence. I mean your mother and the girl you were in love with having the same name.'

'A coincidence? I suppose you could call it that.'

'What would you call it?'

He re-opened his flask, shook it to see if there was anything left, then closed and tightened it again.

'I call it a curse.'

I looked at him sharply, but he wasn't joking.

'I don't understand,' I said. 'How could that be a curse?'

'You're not an orthodox Jew, are you? I mean one hundred per cent orthodox.'

'No,' I acknowledged. 'We keep a kosher home, things like that. But I suppose we couldn't claim to be more than about eighty per cent orthodox. Are you a hundred per cent then?'

Saul gave a mocking, derisive laugh.

'No, we're not one hundred per cent. We're about one hundred and ten per cent. My father is a rabbi. Oh, I respect him of course. I believe in my religion. It can be very inconvenient at times, extremely strict. But if you believe, you must perform. Fully. That includes not only God's laws.'

'What else are there but God's laws? His Ten Commandments.'

'They're only the beginning,' Saul explained. 'There are more laws, a lot more, laws that are capable of different interpretations, depending on which rabbi you follow.'

'And you follow your own rabbi, your father?'

'Of course. I told you, I respect him. Besides, he didn't make the interpretations. They were made by other rabbis who preceded him. And their interpretation of one very obscure law was that a Jew may not take as his wife anyone who bears the same name as his mother.'

I was stunned. I could hardly believe it. I had never heard of such a law, but then I wouldn't have.

'Oh, Saul, I'm sorry. Very, very sorry. I can see why you called it a curse, the girl having the same name as your mother.'

'I shouldn't have called it that. It's a sin to call any of God's laws a curse, even if the interpretation is the word of rabbis, not God's. I must accept that. I can't pick and choose. End of story.'

There was no more to be said – by either of us.

That afternoon there was little or no talk in the office. Hilda's return was the signal for us to get back to our work and the three of us behaved as if we had so much to do that there was no time for conversation. The truth of course was that small talk would have been an embarrassment. Silence was the only fallback.

It proved to be a beneficial fallback for me, for it made me realise that the time had come to review my situation. Saul and Hilda, and possibly Joe too, had had the sort of experiences that might well have been what had brought their lives to a stop and driven them into their present dead-end jobs. But I had no remotely comparable excuse to be in Baron's any longer. I had thought I would be best off among my own people, where I would meet no unfamiliar challenges, where I could sit back a while trying to work out how I might make a worthwhile future for myself. But now I could see I had been wrong. Returning to what was only another version of my Cork ghetto world would lead nowhere, and every day I stayed would make it that much harder to break out and find my identity. I had to look for another job, a better one, with more responsibility. I was no longer a barrister, or an editor, or a publisher, or even a scribbler. But I did at least have the experience gained from these occupations. If I wanted to regain my self-respect, I would never do so as an accounts clerk, in Baron's or anywhere else. I had to get out – the sooner the better. So after nine months I gave in my notice, and a week later I said goodbye to Hilda, Joe and Saul.

On the way out at the end of my last day I bumped into Abie Baron. He had never spoken to me before, but this time he stopped.

'You're leaving us, Mr Markey,' he said, typically getting my name wrong.

'Yes, Mr Baron, I'm afraid so.'

'Well, son,' he said, putting a hand on my shoulder, 'let me wish you *mazel tov*.'

'*Mazel tov*!' I laughed, thinking he had got his words mangled again. When a Jew wishes another Jew '*Mazel tov*', what he is saying is 'Congratulations.'

'Yes, *Mazel tov*,' he repeated. 'You know what the words really mean?'

'Of course. They're Hebrew. *Mazel tov*. They mean "Good Luck".'

'That's right, Mr Markey. Good luck!'

He turned and resumed his patrolling. I left, going out once again into the great wen of London, a smile on my face.

Whatever about mangling his English, Abie had got his Hebrew right.

CHAPTER SEVENTEEN

Work and Play

I spent that weekend thinking over the best way to go about finding a new job. One thing was now clear: this time I would have to make use of the only worthwhile qualification I had, my legal degree. Not practical use – I had no intention of trying to get work in a solicitor's office – but making it known that I had BL after my name made sense. It was surely likely to give me a considerable advantage over applicants with no qualifications at all.

I then poured over the job advertisements in the news-paper heavies. The result was not hopeful. There seemed to be plenty of openings, but one way or another the stated specifications or requirements ruled me out. And then in the Insurance column I came on one that advertised vacancies 'in many departments'. The scope of its offer was mildly encouraging, but what really struck a response was the com-pany's name: The London Assurance. 'London Assurance', I remembered, was the title of the first play by the eighteenth-century Irish playwright Boucicault, the most successful one of the many he wrote. Might be an omen, I thought. Why not try it? I had nothing to lose.

The London Assurance was in the City, the centre of the
insurance and banking world, in a building named Chetwynd
House on the corner of Lombard Street, a building that
bulked large. I was in and out in under ten minutes. I told the
front desk why I had come, I filled in the card handed to me –
this time including my degree. I was asked to wait while it
was taken away and soon brought back with a request to go
to the Guildhall Insurance Company just around the corner
where they were expecting me. Things, I thought, seemed to
be looking up, and look up they did. I was interviewed, surprisingly cursorily, by someone with an Irish-sounding
name, Mr Toomey, who turned out to be the manager. He
informed me that the hours were from nine to four-thirty, no
Saturday work, the salary was mentioned, and could I start
the next day? I could and did.

The deputy manager, a Mr Gordon, was waiting for me
when I arrived. He was very friendly and welcoming, telling
me that I would be in the claims department, and explained
that the Guildhall was a reinsurance company, which meant
that they did not deal with the public but with other insurance companies all over the world which did not want to
carry the full liability for some of the risks they had taken on.
The Guildhall would accept a certain proportion of the risk,
receiving that proportion of the premium and incurring a like
share of any loss. He took me up to the first floor where the
claims department was located. There were about a dozen
large desks there, but in fact the claims department itself was
just two of them, nearest the door, one of which was occupied
by a gangly youth who looked to be hardly out of his teens,
while the other one, unoccupied, was to be mine.

The desks were joined together face to face, so that I
could the more easily be shown what I had to do by my

intended colleague, Robert Allen. Immediately we were introduced and I had taken up my place, Robert instructed me that he was to be addressed as Robert, not Bob, to which I was able to respond that I was David, not Dave. It was abundantly clear that he needed an assistant, for his desk was covered with many piles of neatly stacked files. To my consternation, however, he did not remove from my desk any of the further stacks of files there, although they proved to be no part of my immediate tasks, so before the week was out I explained to him that I was unhappy to have my desk used as a parking lot – it might give the impression that I was not keeping up with my work. I think it was the shock of being taken to task by his assistant, however tactfully, that made him transfer the files with all alacrity to his own desk. A minute later, however, I was amused, and a little admiring, to see him shift them again, this time depositing them on the floor, as if the gesture should illustrate that he was still the boss. Nevertheless, I was satisfied that I had won the battle of the files.

During the first week I had spent a few lunch hours reconnoitring the area in the immediate vicinity of the Guildhall Company and was intrigued to discover a vegetarian restaurant. Not that I was a vegetarian myself or had ever been in such a restaurant – I had never even seen one in Cork – but feeling that it would be *infra dig* to bring lunchtime sandwiches to the Guildhall, I was anxious to find a place to eat that would be more attractive and less noisy and rushed than the many snack bars in the area. I still preferred to avoid non-kosher meat, not because of the religious prohibition, but because my stomach, having a mind and habitude of its own, was far less tolerant than my principles. I also found that luncheon vouchers – standard additions to one's salary –

were far better expended on a proper meal than on cellophane-wrapped conveyor-belt sandwiches.

Another discovery, even nearer to my base of work than the vegetarian restaurant, was St Paul's Cathedral. I remembered how overwhelmingly impressive it had appeared on the only occasion I had seen it. That was in the television relay of Winston Churchill's funeral, and apart from the approach to the entrance, the various views and vistas provided by the cameras saw the building, particularly the dome, to far greater effect than I could when trying to take in its majesty with my perspective reduced to nil from a standpoint within touching distance of the walls. I thought of Cork's St Fin Barre's Cathedral, one of the places of worship nearest my home, with its triple spires, one tall flanked by two not so tall, like a father and two children, eyes raised in search of God, hands raised in prayer. I had never been in a place of worship apart from a synagogue, so was curious to see what St Paul's was like inside. I did not find God – anyone's God – there, nor did I think I might, but I beheld the awesomeness of the roof above me and sensed the dome's long intake of breath as it drew up every merest whisper, leaving only a noiseless reverberation below. When I emerged into the air to return to my work, I searched for what was missing; I knew something was. Unconsciously I looked up, to find myself surrounded by high buildings with tall, inscribed windows like sheets of headed glass notepaper. I could see no spires. At home in Cork I could not have gone five hundred yards in almost any direction without coming on a church spire – 'making its point', was the phrase that occurred to me, as if I was still dealing in words. It was hardly surprising that in the City of London's Mammondom centre there was little room for a house of holy worship, and I thought of the low roof and dun-coloured walls of my box-small synagogue on South Terrace, barely holding on between its incongruously matched neighbours – run-down tenements on one side and Denny's bacon factory on the other.

It did not take me very long to become acclimatised in the Guildhall though I felt that I would never be really comfortable there. I got on very well with my colleagues in every department without actually fraternising with any of them, except for one. He was the statistics manager, about my own age, also unmarried, and also a very keen follower of horse racing. Together we went to all the London courses for the Saturday meetings and to many of the evening meetings when they were introduced. Only once did I agree to join the group going for their monthly after-work outing to a pub, and my refusal to take anything but a soft drink caused hilarity which soon turned to disbelief. They seemed to think that I was having them on, for to them an Irishman who didn't drink was a contradiction in terms. Consequently, as the night wore on and spirits rose – in more senses than one – efforts on some of their parts to overcome my resistance became almost annoyingly insistent. Not that I was really worried. If there is no hope of breaking down an Irish 'pioneer', what chance could there be with an Irish-Jewish one!

However, as the months began to pass I had increasing doubts about the likelihood of my wanting to stay in the Guildhall for any extended period. The reason, quite simply, was the nature of the work. I did not find much difficulty in what Robert was giving me to do, but I felt that he was in no great hurry to add to my knowledge. Perhaps he could not spare the time, perhaps he was not a good teacher, perhaps he was deliberately holding me back. To compound my problem, while reinsurance was no more to my liking than law had been, employment conditions were very comfortable and there were possibilities for considerable advancement. So once again I had to apply myself to plotting the next step or steps in my future path. I had moved from being a lowly accounts clerk in a ladies wear store with no prospects, to being a claims clerk in a reinsurance company with . . .? With what? I had to make a positive effort to find out whether, if it came to it, I could bear to spend the rest of my life in the profession in which I found myself, and how worthwhile such a career might be.

I learned that there was a Chartered Insurance Institute of which, after passing the requisite examinations, one could become an Associate and then try for a Fellowship. Obtaining these degrees would bring an increase in salary as well as an accompanying step-up in one's status, and presumably one could also then expect some more important doors to open. That I decided to enrol forthwith for the Associateship course was not due to any burst of enthusiasm, but mainly as a way of staving off boredom and of half fooling myself into believing that I was seriously addressing my future.

In due course my relationship with Robert developed on a more friendly footing rather than on a teacher/pupil basis, and I was being allocated work of greater importance and difficulty. Proof of this advance came one day when the deputy manager gave me some special files to examine, analyse and provide a written report. I stayed back late to start working on them when, after about an hour, the caretaker came down from his flat to investigate the noise I was making, opening and closing filing cabinets. Mr Newman – Dickie to all of us – was a small, ruddy-faced, friendly man not very far short of sixty.

'Oh, it's you, Mr Marcus,' he said. 'You're working late then?'

'Yes, I have some things I'd like to get through before morning, if I can,' I explained. 'I'm not interfering with you, Dickie, am I?'

'Far from it. Wait, I won't be a tick.'

He left me, but returned within five minutes carrying a tray on which was a cup of tea and a plate of biscuits.

'Take a break,' he said. 'You probably need one.'

'That's very kind of you, Dickie. But you shouldn't have troubled.'

'No trouble. Anyway, the wife would have had my balls for buttons if I'd let you work with nothing inside you since lunch. Tell me, how do you like it here? They're a good company, aren't they?'

'They are indeed,' I said. 'I'm very happy here.'

'And what about the rest of the men? Do you get on O.K. with them?'

He sat up on an adjoining desk as if eager for a chat.

'They're a good crowd,' I said. 'I've no complaints at all.'

Dickie hesitated before taking a biscuit and munching on it. He looked at me, a puzzled, almost fatherly smile on his face.

'You're Jewish, aren't you,' he suddenly said. It was a statement, not a question.

Startled by the turn in the conversation, I nodded.

'Yes, I am.'

'Welcome aboard,' he said. 'So am I.'

His smile broadened. I was dumbfounded.

'You're Jewish, Dickie!' I exclaimed.

'Yes, but they don't know it here, so keep it under your hat. The wife isn't, but I am. Not that religion means a tosser to me. Born in Manchester. Served all through the war. In the navy, I was. Was sunk once. Got a medal for it. A great bit of luck. I don't mean getting the medal – what good are medals? I mean coming out alive and landing this soft berth.'

'How did you know I was Jewish?' I queried.

'Oh, it gets around.'

He picked up the tray and turned to go.

'I'll let you get on with it, Mr Marcus. Glad I had the chance for these few words with you. Had to let you know you weren't alone.'

'I'm glad too, Dickie. Thank you for telling me. And thank your missus for the tea.'

He winked and left.

Dickie's startling revelation brought an end to any further concentration on the deputy manager's files.

Back at my flat that night I fell to thinking about the complete unexpectedness of the meeting with Dickie, and one thought buying another, I recalled an earlier, even more unexpected and certainly more life-enhancing meeting that living in London had brought about. It was with a lady I had known during my late teens in Cork. A member of the Cork Jewish community, she was the first aesthete I had ever met, and she had, so to speak, taken me under her wing when she heard I wrote poetry. However, she soon moved to London and indeed had long dropped out of both my thoughts and memories. Yet learning that I, too, was living in London, she sent me a brief, terse letter instructing me to meet her on a certain date, at a certain time, in a certain place. As my main cultural sustenance up to then – I was still an accounts clerk at Baron's – had been provided by frequent attendances at the Royal Festival Hall concerts, I guessed that she would have planned for me something of an artistic nature.

The occasion was the first British production of Samuel Beckett's *Waiting for Godot*. The play had already been acclaimed both in France and Germany, so its premiere in Britain had been eagerly awaited and was attended by a full house, including all the leading drama critics.

Peter Bull, who played Pozzo, afterwards reported that 'Waves of hostility came whirling over the footlights, and the mass exodus, which was to form such a feature of the run of the piece, started quite soon after the curtain had risen.' In fact, at the interval about half the audience left the theatre, and the reviews next day were so unfavourable that it was thought unlikely the play would last the week. However, in the Sunday 'heavies' the two most powerful and highly regarded critics, Kenneth Tynan of *The Observer* and Harold Hobson of *The Sunday Times* were particularly supportive, with the result that by the afternoon the play was booked out and thereafter became the rage of London. Harold Hobson's verdict was, 'Go and see *Waiting for Godot*. At the worst you will discover a curiosity, a four-leafed clover, a black tulip; at the best something that will securely lodge in your mind for as long as you live.'

My own reaction was that, barring Shakespeare's, it was the greatest play I had ever seen or read, and since then I have never had reason to change that opinion. Indeed, as far as I was concerned Harold Hobson's comment was prophetic, excepting that *Waiting for Godot* took up permanent residence not just in a corner of my mind, but in its ground floor living room.

I did not, at the time, intend to grapple with the play, but its 'waiting for something to happen' theme gradually began to occupy my thoughts. Having taken a step that seemed to represent a firm commitment to a career in insurance, my mind may have suddenly been freed for the confrontation with the awful challenge that always lurked in my subconscious:

mortality, life's inevitable obliteration. As I believed in neither Heaven nor Hell, the prospect of my own non-existence was something I had little trouble dismissing in daylight, and though in darkness it occasionally frightened the daylights out of me, waking from sleep was a certain antidote. Thus was *Carpe diem* silenced. But it could not be silenced indefinitely.

And that, I now realised, was when my Godot had arrived in the comradely person of Dickie Newman, bringing renewed awareness of what for quite a while I had not been conscious – my Jewishness. Dickie, for his own reasons, had kept the secret of his Jewishness from the Guildhall, but I doubted that he revealed it to me simply because I, too, was Jewish. He revealed it for his own sake, otherwise he would hardly have bothered. Being a Jew gave him his identity, and my fortuitous presence was the chance to establish that identity. Identity is existence, what makes existence important. My existence may – will – end, but my identity will outlive it, if only in the thoughts and memories of those I leave behind. The stronger it is established, the longer it will live. What was the identity of each of Godot's tramps, how strong was its establishment, how long was its shelf-life? The comparative rarity of an Irish-Jewish heritage was the quiddity on which my identity was founded, a golem I had to breathe on and bring to life as mortality's denier.

Macbeth's 'There's nothing serious in mortality' could never have a place in my *vade-macum*.

CHAPTER EIGHTEEN

Ups, Downs, and a Family See-Saw

My progress at the Guildhall continued to be not only satisfactory, but more satisfying, and in due course I was successful in obtaining my ACII degree, to mark which I was promoted to claims manager. I was already handling more important claims than before, involving far bigger liabilities than had previously landed on my desk.

There were the natural disasters – that raging climatic quartet of cyclones, hurricanes, tornadoes and whirlwinds – which were usually filed under the place-names of where they struck, except for hurricanes, which were always misogynistically called by female names. There were also claims with unique features or those involving a celebrity. When the celebrity was a world-renowned film star in the process of making a film, insurance cover to recoup loss caused by interruption of filming due to the star's illness was usually very expensively rated. On two occasions Elizabeth Taylor was the star involved in claims of which the Guildhall had insured part of the risk. The first was of a minor nature, but the second was much more serious. At one stage the medical experts feared her illness might be life-threatening, especially as they were having great difficulty making a definite diagnosis, but fortunately whatever it was cured itself.

Coincidentally, it was Elizabeth Taylor who was at the centre of one of the most shocking scenes it was ever my misfortune to witness. I attended a gala premier of a new ballet at which the guests of honour were Miss Taylor and her then husband, Eddie Fisher. When the show ended, it took quite a while for the theatre to empty and I happened to be among the last to leave. Outside the doors I found that the foyer, the footpath and the road were completely packed with hundreds of people waiting for Elizabeth Taylor to emerge. The police had somehow managed to clear a narrow channel for her, and as I did not want to be held up I tried to force myself along its edge. I was only halfway through when a volley of screams and cheers broke out and the pressure of the crowd almost bowled the police over. I turned and saw Elizabeth Taylor approaching with her husband behind her, his arms enveloping her as protectively as possible to save her from being mobbed. She struggled past, right next to me, shaking visibly, her mouth gasping in fear. Never before or since did I see such a look of terror in a person's eyes. It was a look that I can never forget, and whenever I see on television today's pop stars trapped in similar situations, I think of Elizabeth Taylor and deplore the unreal craziness of the modern pop fan's behaviour. It is one of the most reprehensible of social curses which was started by impresarios and publicists hiring adolescent females to scream and faint at Frank Sinatra's concerts, and it continues to be fomented by media hype. As a crooner, Sinatra, probably the most gifted of them all, was best enjoyed and appreciated in conditions in which one could close one's eyes and imagine him singing for oneself alone.

At the Guildhall, having gone on to add the Fellowship degree to my ACII, I had little thought other than remaining where I was for the foreseeable future. My feeling of contentment was, however, rudely shattered when, without warning, London Assurance and the Guildhall Reinsurance Company were taken over by Sun Alliance, whose first decision was to move the Guildhall Claims Department to Horsham, some distance from London. That was a move I had no intention of making, especially since only a few years earlier my parents had come to live in London. What would I do now? Start once again the whole unmerry-go-round search for a new job, or contemplate returning to Ireland to test out the ground there and thus risk once again living across the sea from my parents so soon after we had been re-united? That reunion had meant a great deal to me. It had made it possible not only for me to get to know them again, but to be with them now as a new version of their son – secure, mature, no longer their dependant – and I had begun to see them as a father and mother whose lives and sacrifices I had never before fully appreciated. Their move to London, following the path their first three sons and their daughter had previously taken, meant that only their youngest son, my brother Louis, was left in Ireland, living in Dublin, and the name of Marcus had disappeared from Cork after over half a century.

In the eighteen hundreds it had been the practice for young Jewish men who had fled persecution in eastern Europe and settled in Britain, to rescue their parents as soon as they could. My parents' departure from Cork was a reversal of the process. It was their emancipation not from persecution, but from loneliness, and it was paid for not by their children, but from the earnings of my father's life of labour which had also prepared his children for what he knew would be their own eventual emigration. Yet to attribute the move just to loneliness is too simplistic. Before the cohesiveness of society started to crumble, what bound together a Jewish family was more than blood. Parents' love for their children – and this of course applied too to most Western non-Jewish families before materialism and the greed of bloated capitalism debased us – included the duties and responsibilities of child-rearing until the children were ready to take over at home or to go out into the wider world. Jewish children did not often take over at home, for the family business would be unlikely to become prosperous enough to support them and their hoped-for progeny, but when they moved away or emigrated, their parents' deontological corpuscle continued to operate within the cell of loneliness. I believe that was subconsciously the main force that drove my parents to London. The telephone did not bring them and their children together. It was the technological lie that kept them apart. But they still had the responsibility to be on hand. Their need was to be there whether they were needed or not. Their job was not done, merely changed.

For my father it had, of course, changed utterly. 'With the sweat of thy brow shalt thou earn thy bread', and from his early twenties when he started a picture-framing factory, that was how he had to work. The strong-arm element involved was to help lift the approximately twenty-four feet long packing cases of mouldings that came from Europe to be unloaded from horse-drawn floats onto the footpath, then carry them indoors, break them open and strain to heave out the armfuls of similar length thin, swaying mouldings and stagger with them to the back of the factory. There he would plant them against its high walls like some bald, exotically-hued saplings. It did not take many years of this repeated exertion to give him a hernia, for which he wore a truss the rest of his life, and which in the end led to his death. Every morning he would rise at eight, shave, don his phylacteries to say his prayers – Sabbath excepted, when phylacteries were not worn and prayers were said in *shul* – make his boiled-egg-and-cup-of-tea breakfast, and walk nearly a mile to his factory.

How it came to be called a factory or why, we never asked and so never learned. It was really only a long shed with a concrete floor wildly lawned like a stable with straw from the packing cases, and a flat roof over thirty feet high. There were two large work-tables at which Christy and John made the frames and fitted the pictures. Christy was the younger, married, with a family; John was much older, a bachelor, one of the most knowledgeable of self-educated mortals in sociology, history, philosophy and kindred subjects that one could ever meet. However, because he had a bad stammer that greatly embarrassed him, the only person he discussed his interests with was my father. The latter listened, commented, asked questions, while John cut the mouldings into the required lengths on a machine with the sort of handle now found, if at all, on a rural wayside water-pump. Lever the handle up and down and a stream of sparkling, spring-cold water gushed out. Lever my father's cutting machine handle up and down, and the moulding was severed cleanly and crisply – which was what happened to the little finger of his right hand one day when he himself was doing the cutting. The finger was left dangling by a thread of skin from the knuckle joint. He went straight off to hospital where immediate surgery sewed the finger back on, but nothing could be done about re-joining the nerves and tendons. My father went back to work, returning home that evening with the finger standing straight out from his hand, in which position it remained ever after. He boasted that in future whenever he raised a cup of tea to his lips he would be seen as possessing the best social graces in the community.

His whole behaviour throughout the accident and his acceptance of it was fully in keeping with his temperament. Never once did I see him display the slightest sign of panic; he was calmness personified. Calmness is often accompanied by wisdom, and my father was probably regarded as the wisest man in the community. He never took risks, as witness his reaction immediately the very first report of a possible connection between smoking and cancer was made known – he gave up cigarettes, permanently, even though his consumption had been only some five a day and he never inhaled! He was completely open-minded and trusting, the only person he did not trust being the weatherman, a not unreasonable attitude to adopt in Ireland so long before the advent of satellite weather forecasting. Not only did he never display panic, indeed the one time he showed what for him was a degree of excitement was when, after fathering three sons, my mother was at last delivered of a daughter. Nella inherited the best of her parental genes by growing up to play in the first violins of the Cork Symphony Orchestra as well as gaining a diploma as a piano teacher, and later in life taking up her pen to write *Careers in Classical Music*.

One of my father's most admired qualities was his scrupulous honesty. I don't think he was ever aware of it himself, just as one normally is not aware of the flow of one's blood or the rise and fall of one's chest. It was part of his nature, his code, as was also his sense of dignity. He came home one evening –

his time for recounting to my mother and anyone else present the news and gossip of the day – and said, matter-of-factly, 'When I went back this afternoon, there was a message from the bank manager that he wanted to see me. Urgently.'

'Urgently?' my mother repeated, half-startled. 'What did he want?'

'Oh, he accused me of doing something in my account that I should not have done. He had some ridiculous *mishegoss* that was absolute nonsense. He had his facts all wrong.'

'Well, I suppose you explained it to him.'

'He didn't give me a chance. He got very angry about it. Warned me never to try anything like that on him again. He was quite insulting.'

'You didn't let him get away with it, did you?'

'No. I told him he was talking through his hat and to check his facts.'

'Is that all you said?' My mother's anger was now threatening to show.

'I got up and gave him a warning of my own. I told him never to talk to me like that again. I told him that the only man who was ever allowed talk to me like that was my father. That shut him up.'

My mother gave a snort of satisfaction as she poured my father's second cup of tea.

She was very different from him, and they appeared to have little in common apart from their love of Grand Opera. She had two younger married sisters, but as neither of them lived in Cork, she had no one in whom she could confide, though I doubt that she ever felt such a need. She never sought company and her relationships with the other women of the community were made up of little more than polite exchanges of conventional pleasantries. Day by day she was fully occupied being a wife and mother, with little time from cooking and housework for any serious, extended conversation. Once a week, always on Monday evening, she and my father went to a cinema, and that was her only regular source of entertainment until the war of 1939-1945 broke out, when my father bought a wireless, as the radio was then known. He would not allow one in the house before that because he insisted that schoolwork was more important, but of course the need for the very latest daily news on the fight against Nazi Germany overrode all other considerations.

One thing my mother appeared to treasure was letters from her children when they were away from home and it was she, never my father, who answered every letter. She was an expressive correspondent, and as English had always been her favourite subject, I suspect that our being away also gave her time to read. Not only to read, but to write too in her later years, when to her great delight *The Irish Times* published her article 'On Becoming Sixty' and Radio Éireann broadcast other contributions. During her last years, when she was a widow living in London, she wrote a long memoir of her early life in Limerick, including an account of the 1904 'pogrom' in which her father was injured. No doubt it was from her that I inherited the writing bug she displayed early in life. I have a letter Daniel Corkery wrote her from his home, 9 Ophelia Place, The Lough, Cork, dated Nov 29, 1913.

It runs:

Dear Miss Goldberg,

I have kept your play too long, I'm afraid. The Cork Dramatic Society is no longer in existence. Cork, I'm inclined to think, didn't want us.

As for your little play: Before sending it anywhere

else you would want to shorten very much the long speeches. And soliloquy is hardly ever used in modern plays. Of course it may be used, but it is dangerous. Also I think you would want to tone down the whole thing – I think that it is too wild and melodramatic as it is. Many thanks for sending me the play; and sorry that I'm not able to help you further than by this useless criticism.

I remain,
Very sincerely yours,
Daniel Corkery

My parents' departure from Cork had, for me, one unfortunate consequence that did not surface in my mind until long afterwards. When I founded the *Irish Writing* quarterly in 1946, I used my father's factory as the editorial address but did all the work from a very small storeroom in my home on the Mardyke. When I disposed of the magazine in 1954 and emigrated to London, I made a bonfire in the back garden of the mountain of accumulated correspondence, having first extracted all the letters that had passed between me and the many celebrated authors I had been in touch with at home and abroad. This pile I put on a shelf in the little 'office'. When my parents sold the house, they either destroyed it or left it to the new owners to get rid of, not knowing that it was of any importance and naturally believing that if I had wanted it, I would have taken it with me or asked them to send it to me later on. When, not long after I settled in London, I gave up writing, and – as I thought, permanently – all idea of a life in literature, the very existence of that treasure trove became buried in my mind until very many years had passed. Fortunately, when in 1967 I once again became involved in editing, I remembered the lost *Irish Writing* correspondence and found to my surprise that I was able to recall and record the details of some of the most noteworthy letters.

Certainly the, to me, most important letter arising out of my *Irish Writing* years was also the most exceptional in that it was not written until some twelve years after I had left the quarterly.

One evening in 1963 in my flat in London I was listening to the BBC's Third Programme. A playwright was talking about his plays, the first of which was written in 1957. In the early 1950s he was a repertory actor – Anew McMaster returned from Australia to Dublin in 1951 and was probably the actor-manager – moving from place to place through small parish halls in Ireland. Waiting one day at a station he noticed in a railway bookstall a literary periodical called *Irish Writing*, bought it, read an extract by a writer of whom he had never heard. The extract was from a novel, *Watt*, by the author Samuel Beckett, published in *Irish Writing No 17* in December 1951. The genius of Beckett, unknown in Britain, was discovered by the actor, Harold Pinter.

His revelation made me almost combust with delight at the growing realisation of what *Irish Writing* had accomplished. To know that I had introduced the work of Beckett to one of the most important and influential of contemporary playwrights, and I wrote him a letter, care of the BBC, telling him what his debt to *Irish Writing* meant to me. By return I had a reply.

Dear Mr Marcus,
     I was extremely glad to hear from you. It took me back to other days. I remember your name, of course,

very well. I regarded it with great admiration, since you were the editor of such a damn good magazine.

Irish Writing meant a great deal to me in those days while I was wandering from Ballybunion to Carrickmacross. Beckett was certainly unknown in England, at that time. I returned to England with the great tidings. You, of course, had discovered them before me. For this, I must always remain thankful to you.

I do hope things are well with you now. Those days were certainly other days. With very best wishes,
Yours sincerely,
Harold Pinter

CHAPTER NINETEEN

∞∞∞

Not so Eine Kleine Nachtmusik

The decision to leave London and come back to Ireland was not really a decision; it evolved from the collision between the avoidance of a decision and the logic of my brother, Louis, by then married and living in Dublin. Logic's best message was brief, cool and reasonable. 'Try it for a year,' he said. 'If it doesn't work, you can go back to London. After only a year away, you wouldn't have been forgotten in insurance there and you'd probably walk back into a job as good as the one you left.'

Perhaps, I thought. But perhaps not, too. In that sort of situation, before one makes the leap one is riven with doubt. And it did not help when I remembered Graham Greene's description of Dublin: 'Like that most nightmarish of dreams, when one finds oneself in some ordinary and accustomed place, yet with a constant fear at the heart that something terrible, unknown and unpreventable is about to happen.' But that had been 1923; this was 1967. And I had Louis and his wife, Chookie, without whom I would not have lasted a week, to ease me back. They put me up until I found a suitable flat, and Louis introduced me to a friend of his, a Radio Éireann

producer, Seán MacRéamoinn. With this introduction he set
in motion the process that led to my re-entry into the world
and its traffic that had been my milieu in Cork. Before we
parted Seán invited me to write a short piece about coming
back to Ireland after thirteen years in London. He said that if
I could do it by five o'clock that day I should bring it in to him
at Radio Éireann, then based in Henry Street. The weather
was fine, the sun was shining, I went straight into Stephen's
Green, wrote the piece, brought it in to Seán, and he had me
record it for next day's Radio Éireann regular mid-morning
miscellany. From then on he and his co-producers gave me frequent airtime, and in so doing did more for me than they ever
realised. The payment I received, most welcome though it
was, was the least of the benefits their kindness and support
conferred. They proved to me that I was not unemployable,
they refurbished for me the shards of a literary identity I had
cherished, and they made me hear again the humming wheel
of words that had been stilled in me for so long.

Only recently I learned from my brother that after I had
left for Stephen's Green to write my piece, he had asked Seán if
he had suggested I do it so as to give me a start or because he
needed another contribution for the next day's programme.
Louis, being a very old friend of Seán's, was sufficiently
familiar with his way of working to ask the question with a
twinkle in his eye.

'A bit of both, Louis, a bit of both,' Seán twinkled back.

Liam Miller, who under his Dolmen Press imprint had
first published my 'Midnight Court' translation, was another
who frequently helped me by sending me manuscripts for a
reader's report. They were a very varied lot, but they did
include one that I can still recall. It was a first novel, *The
Gates*, by an unknown writer, Jennifer Johnston. Because of

what seemed to me some structural and plot problems, I did not think it was ready for publication, but the writing was rich in promise and I recommended that Dolmen Press should ask to see any other novel Jennifer Johnston might write. I don't know whether they did or not, but in any event Jennifer Johnston went on to produce her second novel, the widely-acclaimed *The Captains and the Kings*, which was published by Hamish Hamilton, who followed with the publication of *The Gates*.

My first Dublin flat was on the second floor of a four-storey house opposite Huband Bridge on the Grand Canal. The bedroom was in the front, and while at night there was always the intermittent noise of cars stopping to pick up ladies of the streets – the canal was a noted 'beat' – the canal itself provided my most comforting and pleasurable lights-out bedtime sounds. In London I had found it difficult to fall asleep and so had taken to listening to cassette music while lying in bed. But this proved to be a frustrating exercise. Music I particularly liked and to which I could listen with total concentration when awake and sitting up, would set me nodding off within minutes when stretched out in a warm bed in the dark. But wasn't it sleep I was chasing, so wherein lay the frustration? That was double-barrelled: firstly, the music was always a favourite piece, the opening bars of which would make me want to hear it through to the end, a desire that was never satisfied; and secondly, the click of the machine turning itself off often woke me up, thus rendering sleep even more elusive. I had found, however, that strong wind rattling the window and/or rain pattering or battering it was the ideal *nachtmusik*. That was London, but Dublin was better, for whatever the weather, there was night after night the music of the canal waters, joycefully babbling under quiet skies or squalling Wagnerian protests against high-gusting winds. For me, clearly, nature's noise was the most satisfying and effective soporific.

One evening, however, when I was contemplating an early night, I heard startling but clearly recognisable noises from the room below mine – the sound of quite heartrending, female sobs. No other voice, male or female, was audible, so whoever was suffering was not under physical assault, nor, I thought, in any pain that might require medical attention. Who could she be, I wondered. I did not yet know any of the other tenants. Most of the post, I noticed when I glanced at the letters in the hall, was addressed to female occupants, all with Irish names except for one whose name was foreign, Swedish or Finnish I guessed, though I had not given it more than a glance.

The sobbing continued for at least half-an-hour, sometimes indrawn gulping breaths, sometimes anguished, inconsolable laments. By now I was worried. It seemed that I was the only other person in the house and I felt I should investigate, see what was wrong, find out if I could help. Certainly any thought of an early night in bed was out of the question, for if the sobbing continued I would have no alternative but to dress again and go down.

Very wearily I descended and listened outside the room from which the sobs were coming. There wasn't any doubt so I knocked on the door. The crying stopped immediately. I waited. The silence from inside was as if laden with fear or shame, or both. I knocked again. After a moment the door was opened very slightly. Dominating all I could see of the face in the gap were the swollen, red-rimmed eyes, the wet cheeks, and the crown of fair hair.

'Are you all right?' I asked, somewhat foolishly. 'Can I help?'

'No, no, I'm all right.' The door was swiftly closed and I went back to my room.

For a short while, not as long as ten minutes, all was silent, and then the crying resumed. This time I didn't wait.

The door was opened immediately I knocked.

'Look,' I said, 'you can't go on like this. You'll only make yourself ill. Let me in. Talk to me.'

She shook her head.

'Please,' I insisted. 'You need help. You can trust me. Come up to my flat and I'll make you a cup of tea. Do you drink tea?'

The direct, innocuous question did the trick. She nodded and even whispered, 'Yes.'

'Right then. Lock up and follow me.'

Surprised at my own decisiveness, I just turned and led the way, leaving her no alternative but to follow.

'My name is David,' I told her as I motioned her to one of the two armchairs. I did not ask her hers.

'I know,' she said. 'I've seen letters to you downstairs.' She smiled shamefacedly, as if the knowledge had been the result of inquisitiveness.

'What's yours?' I asked, to even things up.

'Ingrid.'

'Right, Ingrid. Tea or coffee?'

'Tea, please.'

While I made the tea, she leaned back in the armchair and closed her eyes. She was petite, long-haired, with a pale, oval face now disfigured by the red, swollen eye-sockets. She looked to me no more than about twenty, and vulnerable.

She opened her eyes only when she heard me shake some biscuits onto a plate.

'Now,' I said as I took the other armchair, 'I don't mean to pry, but when one is in trouble, it's always good just to talk about it, preferably to an outsider, an outsider who is a fair bit older than you. Which I think I am.'

Ingrid didn't answer, but she did blush.

'All right,' I said. 'Let me make a guess. Man trouble?'

She started to dab at her eyes so I knew I was right. When she did not deny my suggestion, I felt I could go on.

'Well, your boyfriend has broken up with you.'

'No, it's not a boyfriend.'

There was only one other category.

'A married man, then.'

Once more she broke into tears. I waited for the spasm to pass.

'Tell me about it,' I urged. 'I'm sure talking will help.'

Her story was predictable. He was in his middle forties, married, with children. She had known him for six months. She was in love with him and he said he was in love with her. But he and his wife were Catholics, so could never get divorced, and anyway he did not want to lose his children.

Here we go again, I said to myself. Back again in dear, old Ireland, where sin, soil and sex were always the three tyrannous S words. So I talked to the poor girl, but cautiously. She would have to disentangle herself if she was ever to make anything of her life. He would never do it for her unless one of three things happened – either his wife would find out, or he'd fall for someone else, or he'd eventually get fed-up and break her heart. And in the nature of things one of these three events would come to pass, I told her. I talked to her for an hour, saying everything I had already said in as many different ways as I could invent. She said little herself, never agreed or disagreed. She knew I was right. Her tears had probably been as much for her future as for her present.

In the end there was nothing more I could say, so I fell

silent and hoped she might soon go. I hadn't talked as much
as this for ages. My throat was dry.

Suddenly she said, 'You shouldn't be helping me.'

'What do you mean? Why shouldn't I?'

'But you're Jewish.'

I was so startled that it never occurred to me to ask how
she knew.

'What in the world has that got to do with it?'

'I'm German,' she replied. 'After what we did to your
people, you should be cursing me.'

I had to laugh.

'And how many Jews did you kill, Ingrid?'

She jumped up from her chair.

'But I wasn't even born then.'

'Exactly. I didn't think you were. And even if I had known
you were German, it wouldn't have made any difference,
believe me. Now I think you should go to bed and try to forget
your worries.'

She went to the door and with a wan smile said, 'I'll try, but
. . . Anyway, thank you for helping me. I'm really grateful.'

'Don't mention it. Goodnight, Ingrid.'

She needed a good night and I hoped she would have one.
I knew I wouldn't, not because I'd be thinking about her
predicament, but because she had been surprised that I, a
Jew, had helped her, a German. If I had known, would I have
helped her? I upbraided myself for even asking such a question. Of course I would, and I'd help her again if I could. Yes,
but now you've got yourself involved, my mind answered, so
the situation is different.

I lay in bed for a long time, thinking. Not about German
anti-Semitism, but about its aftermath, Jewish anti-
Germanism. I remembered the German who in the years

before the war used pay an annual visit to my father as the traveller for a prominent German mouldings factory. I remembered him as very friendly, a bringer of presents when he came to dinner at our home, a happy talker whose strange accent amused me. I didn't just enjoy his visits, I looked forward to them. He was the only German I had ever met. I could not imagine him killing a Jew. But supposing I were to meet him again, if he were still alive, how would I react? It was a reaction I could not predict to a situation I could not contemplate. I had tried to help Ingrid, but had I known she was German, would I really have bothered? It was easy for me to assure myself that I would, but how could I be certain? I had only to ask myself if I would ever want to go to Germany, have a holiday there, see its famous sights, walk down the Unter den Linden, visit its museums, hear the Berlin Philharmonic. No, I knew I wouldn't. Uncomfortable with that self-admission, I eventually fell asleep.

The dilemma continued to trouble me off and on for weeks, being reminded of it every day when I passed Ingrid's room. I hadn't heard her sobs any more – or perhaps she had successfully stifled them – but her words kept echoing in my mind. 'You shouldn't be helping me. You're Jewish. I'm German.' Yes, I was Jewish, I had survived the Holocaust without having had to suffer it, nor had I lost any friends or relations in it. But considering it from this more probing angle, I realised that it had affected me even more deeply than I had known. Nothing like as deeply or as everlastingly as it had those who came out of the concentration camps as living skeletons, some of whom later committed suicide, unable to carry the burden of shame they felt that millions of their co-religionists had perished simply because they were members of the Chosen People, while they had survived only because they had been random members of another chosen people. Discrimination wields a double-edged sword.

I knew that there was now a growing number of Jews, all over the world, who advocated reconciliation with the new Germany, some Jewish musicians, for instance, who performed there despite the opposition of Jews in the Diaspora and of still active neo-Nazi groups. I believed, sincerely believed, that this was the right course, the only course, but I doubted my ability, or even desire, to pursue it actively. I was back in Ireland, where anti-Semitism had no expression, where I should have been aware of being a Jew only by not being conscious of that awareness. It was the last place I expected to have to face a unique, deeply personal, historical-ethical question. Only months later, when I moved to another flat and no longer saw, every day, Ingrid's name over a doorbell, did that question at last disappear from my mind – but it disappeared without an answer.

CHAPTER TWENTY

The Midnight Courtship

'I'll see you in The Mucky Duck at about eleven.'

The Mucky Duck, I guessed, was a pub, but before I could ask him where it was, he had put the phone down. He had called me early that morning, introduced himself as Sean McCann, features editor of the *Evening Press*, said he had heard I was back in Dublin and suggested I might meet him and talk about doing some writing for the paper.

'A gang of us have our morning coffee at The Mucky Duck. You'll meet all the boys there and then we can go up to my office.'

It was a warm, encouraging invitation that I very much welcomed, promising to continue the good start Radio Éireann and Liam Miller had provided and give me another string to my bow. But where was The Mucky Duck? It stood to reason that it wouldn't be more than a stone's throw from the paper's offices in Burgh Quay, and when I came upon, only a few doors away, a pub called The Silver Swan, guessing The Mucky Duck to be a typical example of send-up, journalistic persiflage, I had little doubt that I had made harbour.

In a corner inside the door was gathered a group of some six or seven, and immediately I appeared one of them rose.

'David, Sean,' drawing me in and introducing me all round. None of the names meant anything to me, nor did those of others who looked in and joined the circle. I gathered that the majority were from the *Evening Press* editorial desk, but some were connected with the Irish print and book world. Here was a clerisy of the kind that presumably had existed during my years in Cork but which I had lacked both the confidence and courage to seek out. But as I so often reflected after returning to Ireland, these had been different times and different circumstances. The past was another country, for me two other countries with two very contrasting worlds, in both of which I had survived and, I felt, left some sort of mark. Since then, too, I had grown up, even if not as much as I had grown older. With a bite already taken out of my forties, I knew I had to plant some lasting roots. Sean McCann helped to dig the soil.

I quickly recognised him as someone with flair, ever on the ball, as indeed the features editor of a national paper has to be. People with flair are easy to get on with if you can adjust to their tempo and then let their enthusiasm fire you. I, however, had never been very dry tinder for a quick response to ideas involving any major development or change of direction. Sean suggested I do six articles for the paper based on interviews with up-and-coming young women from different walks of life. That was the sort of 'in' to print journalism that I was anxious to gain. It certainly did not need thinking over and I readily agreed to it. It would be another unfamiliar world, one I would have to get used to and exploit if I was to make a reasonable living. I took a note of the interview arrangements, and happily thought that was that.

The offer in itself had no strings attached. If I did good interviews the result would benefit both myself and the features page, and perhaps more commissions would follow. But Sean did have something else in mind, something he clearly had been mulling over before our meeting.

'Remember your "Midnight Court" translation?' he asked in a rising, more-to-come tone.

'Yes, of course, even though it's about twenty years since I did it. Why do you ask?'

'Do you know, it would make a great stage show, with music, songs, an expanded text using all your lines but with additional scenes. I think it could be a hit. Did that ever strike you?'

'No, it never did,' I immediately answered, adding, 'And to be honest, Sean, I can't see myself being able to tackle something like that. I wouldn't even know how to start.'

'Then how about the two of us collaborating on it? I'm certain there's a smash-hit in it. No one else has ever done it. Will you think about it?'

I said I would, but in truth the suggestion seemed to me a non-starter, and when I left his office what fully occupied my mind was not Brian Merriman's famously infamous poem about eighteenth-century Irishwomen looking for husbands, but the interviews I had to produce about twentieth-century Irishwomen looking for a career in life.

The interviews presented no difficulty. Interviewees who are keen to be written about are easy, co-operative subjects, and writing the articles themselves revived the sort of problems I had met with years earlier in my prentice novel-writing days – making the person I was interviewing audible to the reader and in this case filling out the photograph that would accompany the feature, being clear and concise while trying to get everything of importance down in a style that was controlled, fluid, and with a personality of its own. I was happy with the result, and Sean McCann was happy with the articles too when I brought them in to him.

'Well, what about the "Midnight Court"? Did you think over my idea? We'd have great fun doing it. And I know a producer who's interested.'

The last, almost casually dropped touch, aroused my interest.

'You do? Who?'

'Phyllis Ryan, Gemini Productions. I know Phyllis well, so I sounded her out.'

'And?'

'And she's keen to see it. All we have to do is write it. It's up to you.'

It would have been stupid to turn it down. The interviews had been new territory and they had been successful. The 'Midnight Court' on stage was even newer and stranger territory, but even if it never got that far, it would certainly, as Sean had said, be fun writing it. And instructive too. And if it did make it . . .

'Let's have a go, Sean,' I said. 'We can only make a balls of it.'

'Not a balls, David. A ball, we'll have a ball.'

That we did.

Sean came to my flat two or three evenings a week, where over cups of coffee we discussed, plotted and planned, scribbled, crossed out and re-scribbled, driving our imagination to even higher flights of fancy with loud, self-congratulatory laughter. Sean was full of ideas for special scenes set in an Ireland brought up-to-date, ripe with songs for which we wrote topical lyrics, the storyline weaving cheekily through the infrastructure and scaffolding of my deliberately racily-rendered Brian Merriman couplets. In the Introduction to the publication of my translation I had said it was '. . . an attempt at presenting the poem as Merriman might have written it were he alive now and composing in English'. Once Sean and I finished, I realised that what we had done was to give my version flesh. I wasn't unhappy with the result, but I was very fearful of the result's result were it ever to be produced.

Sean gave the finished script to Phyllis Ryan, we awaited her verdict, and very soon it came. Acceptance. We were *en route* to the stage. It was a heady moment.

From then on the pace of events accelerated. Shay Healy was commissioned to write the music. The cast engaged included some of the leading Irish actors and actresses of the day – Eamonn Keane, Maureen Toal, Bill Golding, May Cluskey, Frank Kelly and Eoin Ó Súilleabháin. The director chosen was Michael Bogdanov, then studying at Trinity College, who had put on plays for the Trinity Players and was later to achieve a distinguished reputation in London's theatre world.

'The Midnight Court' opened at the Gate Theatre on 3 June, 1968. It was a full house, including my parents who had come over for it from London, and the applause was loud and long. It was a very happy, very encouraging start. The theatre had been booked for a six-week run, with an option to be exercised after two weeks for a follow-on run of a further six weeks. During the first week Ireland was bathed in a heat wave and theatre attendances were low. A very different atmosphere enveloped the country for the second week when Robert Kennedy was assassinated and theatres continued to be poorly supported. Understandably, the option on a second six-week run was declined. Immediately afterwards the entertainment world quickly came back to life and 'The Midnight Court' played the rest of its six weeks to full houses.

It is likely that but for the unhappy and unpredictable events of the first two weeks, the show would have lasted a full three months, but Sean and I were not complaining. The experience of living through its presentation for what, over-all, was a successful run forestalled any possibility of down-cast spirits. The feeling of an almost otherworldly buoyancy engendered by the knowledge, day after day for six weeks, that something one had created – albeit as merely a translator and co-fabricator – was being performed before an audience and being enjoyed and applauded, left its imperishable memory. To remember that it had all started with a Jewish schoolboy falling under the spell of twenty-two lines of Irish poetry written by an eighteenth-century teacher of mathematics in a village in Co. Clare seemed the sort of bizarre accident only the most extreme quirk of fate could bring about.

Yet that was not the last of my 1968 'Midnight Court' memories, for a few months later I was invited as one of two speakers on translating from the Irish at the opening night of the Merriman Summer School in Ennis, Co. Clare, graced by President de Valera, whose Dáil constituency Clare had been. If I was ever to intuit the spirit of Brian Merriman this was surely the occasion, for the other speaker was Arland Ussher, the first translator of 'The Midnight Court'. Years earlier I had read his version, which I discovered in the Cork Public Library. It had been published in London in 1926, the first translation to appear in print, and I remembered it as being a somewhat restrained rendition. We did have a brief conversation about the poem, but as over forty years had elapsed since he had produced his translation and as he clearly hadn't read mine, a few general comments sufficed us. However, to shake hands on the one night with both President de Valera and the first translator of 'The Midnight Court' was, I thought, as unlikely an occurrence as my having become one of the poem's later translators. Only the materialisation of Brian Merriman's spirit could have topped that.

CHAPTER TWENTY-ONE

Annus Mirabilis

It cannot be said that I had returned from London with any course in mind apart from an ill-defined intention of scouting in the field of Irish journalism, for it was in that field rather than in the world of literature that I hoped I might find a footing. It was, however, in the Dublin bookshops that my acclimatisation strolls took place, and I suppose it was natural that I should seek out the shelves of the Irish literary periodical, like an ex-soldier revisiting his old battalion. What I found appalled me. *Irish Writing* was gone. Gone also, or rarely in evidence, were *The Bell*, *The Irish Bookman*, *The Dublin Magazine*, *Envoy*, *The Kilkenny Magazine*. It seemed that what I had been fighting was now a lost cause.

I had started *Irish Writing* out of a passionate concern for and love of the Irish short story. Without it and the other periodicals which had also published stories, how could we hope to nurture successors to such masters as Moore, Joyce, O'Faoláin, O'Connor, Corkery, O'Flaherty, Bowen and others who had given the Irish short story its world-wide twentieth-century reputation? What had been a great tradition was, it appeared, approaching literal and literary extinction.

But what could be done about it? Ireland was not the only country in which the circulation of literary periodicals had declined below survival point, and greatly increased printing costs meant that anyone attempting to launch a new story magazine would quickly find the financial loss intolerable. Not that even the slightest thought in that direction crossed my mind. I felt like a mourner at the wake looking towards the bourne from which no traveller returns. Even if the miracle of a sponsor were to turn up, it would require an even bigger miracle to attract a core of committed readers numerous enough to pay the inflated price such a periodical would cost. And the reluctance of bookshops and newsagents to give precious shelf space to such unpopular, minuscule sellers would, anyway, render any such venture pointless. Time to move on. Besides, I had a more pressing and personal agenda.

And then, shortly afterwards, *The Irish Times* published within weeks of each other two letters from readers deploring the decline in the fortunes of the Irish short story. At first I was merely glad to find that there were others around who shared my feelings, but then I wondered why *The Irish Times* had thought it worthwhile to give the subject space twice. Could they possibly be flying a kite, or was that just wishful thinking on my part? Perhaps it was, subconsciously, but as my work schedule was as yet hardly exacting, I had the time and sufficient room in my mind to become engaged with the problem – just as an economic conundrum, I told myself.

Question 1: If short stories were too expensive to print and too costly for readers to buy, how does one eliminate both these difficulties?

Answer 1: Produce them for little or nothing and price them at little or nothing.

Question 2: How can this be done?

Answer 2: A page in a newspaper. The paper would be using the space anyway, and the cost to the reader would be as little as pence, or even nothing if the newspaper was the one he or she normally bought or that normally came into the home.

Lateral thinking? Lateral, vertical, horizontal – it didn't matter to me. If there was a kite in the sky, I wasn't too old or too busy to chase it. So, one morning early in 1968 I set out to call, unannounced, on the editor of *The Irish Times* and put my crazy idea to him. On the way I realised that it was somewhat early to expect the editor of a morning paper to be at his desk, and that even if he were there, it might not be as easy to get an unarranged audience with *The Irish Times* editor in 1968 as it had been for me to see its literary editor in 1945. With time to kill I changed course to kill it in The Mucky Duck, it being just about time for the *Evening Press* coffee break.

As I expected, Sean McCann and his colleagues were there, and after a while Sean asked how things were going for me. I made some inconsequential reply, adding that I was thinking of dropping in to the Irish Times.

'What for?'

I explained my idea. It drew an almost horrified expostulation.

'My God, don't do that. Go home and sit tight until you hear from me.'

I did so, wondering how long I'd have to wait and what exactly I was waiting for. I knew that at that particular time Sean happened to have the post of acting features editor of the *Irish Press* added to his other duties, the morning paper having unexpectedly found itself without one. But I did not have to be patient for long. That evening Sean phoned me, asking if I could come in immediately and see Tim Pat Coogan. I knew nothing about Tim Pat Coogan except that he was the recently-appointed *Irish Press* editor. I couldn't imagine why he wanted to see me. Some talk about doing the odd feature article perhaps? That would be very welcome, I thought, trying to restrain myself from offering a hostage to fortune by wondering if his invitation could be connected with what I had disclosed to Sean. If it should be that, I wished the call hadn't come so quickly, because I had impulsively rushed ahead with my idea without first thinking through how it might be organised and executed. It had been my abject failure to do some proper research when founding *Irish Writing* that had led to the demolition of its exciting prospects by the Board of Trade embargo, and now here I was again, perhaps on the brink of crippling a second chance with woeful, inexcusable, slapdash impetuosity. There is an anonymous saying: 'The only lesson history has taught us is that man has not yet learned anything from history.' Ditto when the history is your own. I held my breath all the way to the Irish Press building.

When I got there Sean was on hand to introduce me and Tim Pat immediately took me out for a chat over a drink. I felt very comfortable with a cup of coffee in my hand in a social rather than an office setting, and Tim Pat's down-to-earth impact, a ready laugh accompanying his person-to-person manner, banished my initial nervousness. As I had hoped, Sean McCann had already told him what I had in mind, and almost certainly had sharpened his interest by adding that I had at first intended to approach the Irish Times. In any event, the basic details were quickly agreed. I suggested a full page every week, containing a short story with poetry to fill any space left over. I would aim to find and develop good new writers, and to encourage them I would frequently include work from the then leading Irish writers. I felt on safe ground in committing myself to obtaining the support of the latter, confident that such as Seán O'Faoláin, Frank O'Connor, Benedict Kiely, Bryan MacMahon, Michael McLaverty, and others who had frequently contributed to *Irish Writing* would welcome the new venture. Tim Pat's unhesitating approval of my outline encouraged me to make one further request – that as the page was for the writers and their work, it should carry no advertising. Tim Pat nodded, as if that went without saying.

'And what'll we call it?' he queried.

I felt that to establish the connection with the past would be a fitting symbolic gesture, so I suggested, 'Why not "New Irish Writing"?'

'"The *Irish Press* New Irish Writing",' Tim Pat amended, the one and only stipulation he made, adding, 'Every Saturday. With the book page it'll make a solid literary section.' Sean McCann would take care of page make-up and all the technical details and I would prepare the stories, editing wherever necessary. I would be paid ten pounds a page, payable monthly. I explained that the page would have to commence with a succession of well-known writers to establish both its presence and its standards, and to cover the two to three months until such time as publishable stories and poetry by new writers would begin to come in.

'That's fine. I'll arrange for you to be paid from next week. Just keep me informed of progress.'

Tim Pat rose, we shook hands, and it was over.

I walked back to my flat. It was a fine night, but even had a storm been raging I believe I would have walked. I felt the need of exercise, open air, people around, so as to re-enter the normal world. And as I walked I suddenly realised that I was back, back in my own normal world of the Irish short story, with a national medium, a huge readership, and a weekly platform. My idea might have been crazy, but what was even crazier was my good fortune in finding an editor ready on the spot to take on a unique experiment as if it was the most natural thing in the world and give its control to someone he had never met and had heard about only a few hours earlier. As it happens, he knew more about me than I thought. Many years later I learned that he had, in fact, been a reader of *Irish Writing*! Fate had dealt me the right cards. After all, even if the editor of *The Irish Times* had been my first call, is it likely that he, too, would have been a reader of *Irish Writing*?

I set to work the next day, telling the leading Irish story writers and poets about New Irish Writing and soliciting work from them or their agents. The first one I wrote to was Samuel Beckett, hoping he would remember his appearances in *Irish Writing* and have something with which I could launch its successor. He replied immediately, his clear hand-writing slanting over two sides of a postcard. It read:

Dear Mr Marcus
    Thank you for your letter.
    I should like nothing better than to contribute to the revival of *Irish Writing*, but at the moment have literally nothing. I have been writing very little, and that little in French, and though there is a certain amount of old jettisoned material in English, there is nothing that I would wish published. However I shall look through it again. I promise you however that the first presentable

text in English I succeed in writing will be yours. The fee is neither here nor there.

With all good wishes for the success of this new venture.

Yours sincerely

Sam. Beckett

The fact that I never did receive a 'presentable text' from him was in one respect a relief to me. With the *Irish Press* seeing itself as a 'family newspaper', there were, I felt, some constraints I would have to bear in mind, at least until the page was well established – though Tim Pat had not mentioned any – and I did not relish the obloquy of having to reject something by Samuel Beckett because of *risqué* words or passages. To have rejected Brendan Behan in the early days of *Irish Writing* on some such grounds I could regard as a misfortune; to compound it by rejecting Beckett would look like something far worse than mere carelessness!

Indeed, the need to be able to see around corners even when the road ahead seemed dead straight was brought home to me when I told Tim Pat two weeks beforehand that the first page would be ready to go on 20 April.

'What have you got for it?' he asked.

Proudly I told him. 'A new story by Edna O'Brien.'

'God Almighty, no! You can't start with that!'

'But it's a completely innocent story, absolutely nothing the slightest bit objectionable in it.'

'No matter. The management won't wear Edna. Many of the readers still won't either. It could kill off the page before it starts. Find something else and keep Edna's story for later.'

I found something else. There was a touch of irony in my choice, and perhaps, too, a squeak of independence, for the story I substituted was by John McGahern, whose banned novel, *The Dark*, had become a *cause célèbre* when the banning led to his being dismissed without explanation from his teaching post. I allowed only two weeks to pass before publishing the Edna O'Brien story.

Tim Pat's intervention was the only time he queried, much less objected to, anything I put in the page. Indeed – and this was another late discovery of mine – any readers' letters protesting about the 'New Irish Writing' contents went into his drawer or wastepaper basket without even being brought to my attention. I gathered that stories involving the treatment of pupils by Christian Brothers teachers were the likeliest to draw the ire of readers. Then there was the elderly executive who now and again admonished me not to allow certain words to be used – 'arse' was, unbelievably, one of them – and there was also the occasion he insisted that the Holy Name as an expletive was banned. After a short while I began to overlook a few examples of 'Jaysus' where I felt the dialogue required the authenticity they provided, but when necessary I did not hesitate to cull objectionable expressions, for literary reasons rather than any other. Young, inexperienced writers often failed to realise that the overuse of strong words only served to weaken their effect.

My prediction at the outset that it might take two to three months before I would have a publishable story by a new writer proved to be right on target. On the tenth week the story was by sixteen-year-old Desmond Hogan from Ballinasloe, Co. Galway. He went on to have thirteen further stories in the page, win many prestigious literary awards and have his story collections published by Hamish Hamilton, one of the leading British imprints. Novelist and travel writer, he has remained since his debut one of the most highly regarded writers to have emerged from the 'New Irish Writing' page. I often wonder whether he, and so many other well-known Irish fiction writers and poets to whom it gave their first opportunity, would have written at all if it hadn't existed. Certainly Desmond Hogan might not have. When he came to see me shortly after I had accepted his first story and I encouraged him to write more, he told me that he had just won a nation-wide art prize awarded by a major oil company and had not yet decided if he wanted to be an artist or a writer.

Before long Sean McCann returned full time to his post in the *Evening Press*, having first taught me all I needed to know about the technical side of my job. This meant that I had not only to edit what was going into the page each week, but to copy edit it too, have the make-up prepared and see the page through the press. What I found most enjoyable about all this was that I spent a lot of time in the caseroom, where I soon formed warm friendships with the overseers, linotype operators and the men on the stone. They regarded the 'New Irish Writing' page with the respect to be accorded a very special feature, they were proud of it, and often under great deadline pressure went to endless trouble to get things right, something that in the days of hot metal printing was not always easy. In the caseroom I felt I was one of them, one of a team. I shared their interests, particularly sport and the trading of horse racing tips, and eventually I was able to reach a highly irregular nod-and-wink arrangement with the proofreaders which allowed me correct my own proofs once they realised how important it was to me that the page should be as free of errors as possible.

In 1970 the prestige of the 'New Irish Writing' page and its appeal to new writers was greatly enhanced by the establishment of the annual Hennessy Literary Awards for short stories by unpublished writers appearing in the page during the previous twelve-month period. In the region of sixteen stories qualified for consideration each year, the best four being chosen by two eminent authors, one Irish, one non-Irish. Apart from a cash award, each winner had the opportunity of having his or her work read and commented on by the judges and of meeting them when they came to Dublin for the presentation of the Awards. It was my practice to invite as judges writers of international renown, most of whom also agreed to attend the Awards dinner as guests of Edward Dillon & Co., the Irish agents for Hennessy Cognac. Elizabeth Bowen, William Trevor, Kingsley Amis, Seán O'Faoláin, V.S. Pritchett, Edna O'Brien, William Saroyan, Brian Moore, John Wain, D.M. Thomas, Julia O'Faolain, Heinrich Böll, John Mortimer and Frank Delaney are some of those whose names established the status and importance of the Hennessy Awards. On only one occasion did I make what turned out to be an unfortunate choice. Roald Dahl, upon reading the year's qualifying stories, complained somewhat testily that none of them was funny and too many did not have a beginning, a middle and an end. I thought the latter criticism quite incomprehensible and the former rather perverse from one whose own stories could hardly be regarded as 'funny'. In any event, I suggested as politely as I could that perhaps he would be happier to be released from his task. He agreed that he would be, thereby making both of us happy.

The 'New Irish Writing' page soon gained a reputation far beyond these shores, both for itself and for the *Irish Press* as the only English-language newspaper in the world to devote a regular weekly page, untrammelled by advertising, to creative writing.

Inevitably, the page was not completely free of setbacks. The savage recession of the early 1970s meant that for a few years it had to share its space with book reviews, and in the year before my early retirement at the end of 1986 it was frequently moved – without notice to readers or editor – from Saturday to Thursday, then back to Saturday, and latterly to Friday. Nevertheless, its popularity and its readership remained constant, as indeed did the volume of manuscripts received, a monthly average of sixty stories and over two hundred poems.

There were, however, some new excitements ahead of me before that early retirement was reached, and not all of them were of a literary nature.

CHAPTER TWENTY-TWO

Getting to Know Me

It was Sunday afternoon.

I was in my flat.

The phone rang.

'Hello?'

'Is that David Marcus?'

A female voice.

'Yes.'

'Don't open your post in the morning. There's a bomb in it.'

I didn't panic. I wasn't flustered. Perhaps at the back of my mind the first stir of thought was this must be a joke. But my first conscious thought was to keep her talking. Find out more.

'What post? Do you mean my post here or in the office?'

She began to reply, but said only two words which I didn't catch when she was suddenly cut off as if someone else had aborted the call.

A hoax, yes, must be a hoax. What would be the point of warning me if it was serious? Who was she? And why me? I still felt completely calm. Perhaps I was numbed without even knowing it. It was before the spate of explosions in the

North, but for years there had been terrorist attacks and bomb assassinations of Jews by Arabs in Israel. I decided to call the police. Just in case.

They arrived within minutes. Two Special Branch men, looking very much the part. Short, stocky, in their thirties, tough. Very tough.

They took all my details and got me to repeat everything I could that had taken place. They asked me if I had recognised the voice or had any idea or suspicion of who it might have been.

'No.'

They asked me was there any reason I should be singled out for a bomb threat.

I hesitated momentarily. If I hadn't hesitated I'd have said 'No', but they had noticed so there was no point in holding back.

'Well, I'm a Jew,' I said. 'But it's probably someone playing a joke.'

They stood up to go.

'What time do you get in in the morning?'

'I go in early. About eight.'

'Well, on no account open your post. We'll be there before you. What about your post here?'

'I never get any letters here apart from my parents or my sister in London and I'd recognise their writing.'

'If you get anything else, don't touch it and call us.'

And they left.

I settled down without worry. It was probably two girls from the office having a joke and one put an end to it before it went too far or they gave themselves away.

Next morning, and every morning for the next few weeks, the Special Branch were on the spot early, down in the post room, checking my letters. Before the two weeks were up they told me I was being taken out of the phone book.

'What are you doing that for?'

They told me why. It was the first bomb threat by phone that had ever been received so the file had been sent straight up to the Taoiseach. He ordered that I be immediately put 'ex-directory'.

The Taoiseach was Jack Lynch. I had had no contact with him since I returned to Ireland, but when he had first been elected Taoiseach I had sent him a letter of congratulations from London and received a warm letter of thanks in reply.

I did not need the confirmation that nothing untoward had been found in my post to set my mind at rest. I had forgotten about the incident even before the Special Branch had disappeared from the scene. It hadn't been long since 'New Irish Writing' was launched and I was still decorously drunk with the excitement of my new situation. I'd have thought that was enough and more than enough to be getting on with, but out of the blue a bombshell of a very different nature suddenly burst. Tim Pat asked me to become literary editor.

True to form and just as I had reacted when Sean McCann first suggested we collaborate on a stage version of 'The Midnight Court', I shied off like a startled pony.

'Why not?' Tim Pat asked.

I offered the first excuse that came into my mind.

'I'm much too taken up with the page. I've not got used to it yet.'

'Fair enough. Think about it anyway. I'll come back to it.'

If Tim Pat said he'd come back to it, he'd come back to it, so when he did, I had my arguments ready.

'Look,' I said, 'I was thirteen years away in London and I'm only a year back. I'm out of touch with Ireland. I haven't followed developments. I don't know anyone any more, who's who in so many areas, politics, current affairs, history. A literary editor needs names so as to give out the books to the right people, academics in so many different fields, things like that.'

Tim Pat was sitting back comfortably. When I paused, he jumped in.

'You'd get used to it in no time. And if you have any queries, just ask me. I'll give you all the help you need. Now, anything else?'

He sounded as if he wasn't taking no for an answer, so I brought out what I thought would put an end to the discussion, something on which I wouldn't give in.

'Well, I'm afraid I couldn't be literary editor of a morning paper because I definitely wouldn't work at night.'

'I don't care when you work as long as you put in the same number of hours as the rest of the staff. Just get the job done.'

It was so unexpected an answer that although cornered I kept clutching at straws.

'I don't want to review books.'

'Who reviews the books is your own choice.'

'I won't write leaders.'

'I won't ask you to. Anything else?'

I was silenced. I knew I had shot my bolt.

'Look, come in to me tomorrow and let me know how much you want. I have a meeting with the Board tomorrow night, so I can fix it up quickly. Now, unless you can think of anything else you won't do . . .'

I had to smile. I had never before dealt with anyone as cutely persuasive as Tim Pat. When I refused his first offer of the literary editor's chair, he let the idea settle in my mind before bringing it up again, and there he was, waiting to accommodate whatever objections I might have before administering the *coup de grâce* of salary and security. When I found myself leaving his office with the same lightness of heart as I had felt after we had shaken hands on the 'New Irish Writing' arrangement, I realised that he had taught me the value of self-analysis. 'New Irish Writing' had been my own idea, something I had wanted because I knew from previous experience that I could do it. But being literary editor of a national daily newspaper was a new challenge, unlike anything I had done before. When, after the First World War, Siegfried Sassoon was appointed literary editor of the *Daily Herald*, the first piece he wrote for it said:

> The life of a literary editor is like a fairytale. He gets up at a not unreasonable hour; on his way to work he pops in to see a few eminent and sympathetic publishers. Finally he drifts down Fleet Street like a ray of sunshine and arrives at the office, where he finds that people have sent him presents of lovely books. After glancing at a few of these, he writes some literary notes and goes away to spend his salary.

I knew that being literary editor of the *Irish Press* wouldn't be anything like that, but it was for another reason that my press-button reaction had been to run scared. Automatically I had raked up from my subconscious the recollection of the mess I had got myself into by starting *Irish Writing* without the slightest conception of what it entailed, but just as automatically I had blotted out the memory of how I had fought to keep *Irish Writing* going until I could get out from under with honour and credit. So why had I tried to reject Tim Pat's offer with negative after negative and yet welcome the delight I felt when my excuses melted away one by one? The answer was clear. I had a deep, psychological fault-line: I was afraid of failure. And deeper than that was its cause: pride. And even deeper still was my pride's particular underlay, the ancient ghetto instinct that warned me not to venture outside the walls of self-preservation unless I could be certain that I wouldn't have to scuttle back in. In other words: *Don't Fail.* At long last I was forced to face it. At long last I was coming of age. Never again would I turn down a challenge because of fear of failure. Not everything one tries in life is destined to succeed. There is the old saying, 'If at first you don't succeed . . .' Beckett knew it well. In his wisdom he divined the full-frontal secret of its message: next time fail better.

So all I was now required to tell Tim Pat was what salary I wanted as literary editor. I had nothing relevant to guide me, no idea what the going rate was or what *Irish Press* salaries were like. I knew only that when I had left the Guildhall Insurance Company as claims manager only a year earlier I had been earning £2,000. But insurance was considered to be a well-paid occupation, and of course London salaries were higher than anywhere else. So I asked for £1,500.

When I went in to Tim Pat to hear the answer, he looked at me rather dolefully.

'I'm afraid I didn't get you fifteen hundred.'

Before I even had time to feel any disappointment, he smiled broadly.

'But I got you sixteen-fifty.'

Not bad, not bad at all. Back in Ireland, a weekly short story page, the title and status of literary editor, and sixteen fifty a year. If I were to fail at that, I'd just have to make sure that next time I'd fail better.

CHAPTER TWENTY-THREE

God Above?

Nobody likes being interrupted when making a point. The only time one can be sure of avoiding such a nuisance is to talk to oneself or to be asked to give a talk on radio. I don't know if that had anything to do with the satisfaction I felt whenever RTÉ invited me to do the latter, but I was very glad that such invitations continued for some time after I became literary editor of the *Irish Press*.

The preparation of a radio talk requires thought, and since my work entailed far more reading than thinking, I was happy to be given something to think about that was completely different from my daily consideration of manuscripts and books. In fact the path my thoughts took in fulfilling some of these occasional commissions eventually led to my having to crystallise for myself a question that had obsessed me for very many years.

But not at first, for the first series of talks arose out of a chance comment I made in a casual conversation with an RTÉ producer. I happened to say that I was fed-up waiting for something or other I expected to happen and he riposted, 'Patience is a virtue', going on to remind me of a jingle I hadn't heard since my schooldays:

Patience is a virtue,
Possess it if you can.
It's seldom in a woman,
And never in a man.

'Not likely,' I came back.

'You mean that men are just as patient as women?'

'Not that. I'm referring to the assertion that patience is a virtue. If it is, it's a damned awkward one. Like all virtues.'

My own assertion wasn't made too seriously but I was quickly picked up on it.

'That's an idea. Wouldn't it make a good subject for a series of talks? "The awkward virtues." How about it? Like to take it on?'

I could hardly refuse, not that I wanted to.

When I got down to it I immediately realised that the first problem was not the choice of virtues, but the general treatment to adopt for a series suggesting that certain virtues can be awkward. The answer seemed clear: it was a fun subject, so the talks – though hardly the delivery – should be tongue-in-cheek. Even at that preliminary stage I was enjoying myself, in the mood. Debating which virtues to send up – no, better still, turn inside-out – was troublesome only because I found that almost any of the best-known ones could be accused, ever so lightly, of having something about them that often proved uncomfortable.

Ever so lightly? A light blow can be a knock-out punch if delivered where it is least expected. 'Modesty' was the virtue that seemed to be asking for the *coup de grâce*: that it had no existence! Proof? Ask anyone you meet one question: 'Are you modest?' The answer must be 'Yes' or 'No'. The truthfully brash will answer 'No', thus leaving only the foolishly self-contradictory to answer 'Yes'. So if nobody is modest, then modesty doesn't even exist. Awkward, isn't it?

The next virtue I targeted had to be 'Patience', since the whole series had arisen out of the jingle that the producer had quoted. The awkwardness of patience wasn't so easy to uncover. The Irish were well endowed with the virtue because for centuries they lived off the land, at the tempo of nature's unfolding and the vagaries of the weather, processes that made the cultivation of patience essential. Then, too, their history had held them back for seven centuries before they won the right to govern themselves. But that was yesterday. Today's pace is that of the go-getter, and patience in this age is often a cover-up, perhaps for indecision, or lethargy, or indifference. There was once an Indian fakir who held his arm aloft for years until a bird came and built its nest in his hand. For all those years he had waited patiently. If he did that today without first arranging for TV and picture rights, serialisation in the tabloids, and copyright on models of himself and his bird, his patience would be poor compensation for his lack of foresight. And when we fall ill and have to lie in bed unable to do anything, we become a patient, suffering patiently. There it was, the awkwardness in patience, the indecision it imposes, the risk of loss it courts. Nowadays little or nothing comes to him who waits, not even a bird in the hand.

Other of my awkward virtues included 'Sobriety'. Being a non-drinker I seldom had occasion to enter a pub, but any time I did, I found myself in one with a group of friends and was caused much embarrassment by not being allowed buy my round, so my sobriety proved to be a mixed potion of a small dash of virtue and a liberal chaser of awkwardness.

I also waxed indignant over 'Righteous Indignation', risked being tactless about 'Tact', and ended the series with

an *amende honorable* to the family of virtues by going to the
aid of 'Punctuality', which someone had substituted for 'pro-
crastination' in the observation of the eighteenth-century
poet Edward Young, that it was 'the thief of time'. Time is
continuous, stretching into infinity, always there. Supposing
then – to use that delightfully devastating Euclidean hypoth-
esis of my schooldays whereby to prove that a proposition
was palpably absurd, you merely supposed it to be true –
supposing you *could* steal time, wouldn't there still be as
much left as if you hadn't taken any at all? Therefore time
just cannot be stolen. Punctuality a thief? Certainly not,
though in these frenetic times we are all so busy that striving
to honour it can be awkward.

Later RTÉ invited me to do another talks series, the
preparation of which renewed recollections of the question I
had been dodging for a very long time. The subject was
mooted in a phone call, complete with its title, 'Thought For
The Day'. As the title suggested, it was of a broadly religious
nature, early morning through the week, soft-sell, very brief.
The producer didn't know whether RTÉ had ever chosen a
Jew for this long-running series, but he didn't think they had
and felt it was time they corrected the omission.

'You know the kind of thing – serious without being
heavy, Jewish in context but universal in appeal. You may
have listened to it now and again.'

I hadn't. Drinking in anything in the nature of spiritual
guidance was never my early morning brew, besides which I
was always in the Irish Press by the time it was broadcast.
But I agreed it would be interesting to have a Jew spread the
Jewish word, so to speak – never mind that the one they
chose wasn't a religious Jew. I did not disqualify myself by
revealing that; after all, I could remember enough of the Old

Testament not to let myself down, or disappoint my venerable ancestors, Abraham, Isaac and Jacob.

I had not anticipated that the fashioning of the first talk of the series would cause me any aggravation. But it did. The idea for it came from a phone call I had made a few days earlier to a theatre to book tickets. I was putting the phone down when I heard the parting words of the lady in the box-office: 'Goodbye now and God bless.' The unexpectedness of that 'God bless' over the phone from a perfect stranger had made me stop for a moment and think. Now it came back to me and made me think again. It seemed to be just what I needed to start on the right note – 'God bless' used not only as a benediction but as a farewell, anywhere, at any time, and to anyone. That would lead me into the Jewish particu-larisation of God's blessing. Jews have one for everything – for seeing a rainbow, for fruit growing on trees, a different one for fruit in the ground, one for smelling fragrant flowers and another for smelling fragrant wood. Even one for seeing a King and his court – not that that ever got much use. I would not be able to quote any of the blessings on air because it was a sin to speak a blessing in vain – I'd be sure to tell listeners that – but I'd be able to end the talk with 'Goodbye now, and God bless.'

I wrote it out, it gelled, it left me with the feeling that I had done a good and fitting job. But the sense of satisfaction was subverted when I thought about what seemed the sheer humbug of having a different, custom-built blessing for everything, no matter what. What sort of a God would insist on being first on the scene on every occasion? Was that His idea, His word, when giving Moses the commandments on Sinai? If so, no wonder Moses had to spend forty days and forty nights on the mountain. Or was it the result of the ancient Rabbis' passion for detail and hair-splitting, their insistence on as much separate billing as possible. There was a showbiz element about it, God's blessing in lights outside every theatre.

Fortunately, for subsequent talks I managed to come up with ideas that, as well as appealing to listeners, steered me away from further fits of cantankerousness. There was the instruction in Deuteronomy: 'It is well to give an ample weight and measure. That is, one should give somewhat more than the exact quantity required, as it is written – "A perfect and just measure shalt thou have" and by "just" is meant: give him a little of your own.' That brought me back – and no doubt many listeners too – to childhood memories, when the morning milk was delivered by a milkman driving a horse and chariot, with two or three tall, gleaming milk churns surrounding him like a bodyguard of Roman warriors. He would 'whoa there' the horse to a stop and stride up to our door with a large, covered can in one hand and a pint measure in the other, and if my mother asked for a pint, he'd fill his measure as full as he could and then pour it into the jug she was holding. Then, from the can he'd give her some more, and it was always far more than the top of the pint measure that hadn't been filled. He was 'giving a bit of his own'. It was known as 'the tilly'. Later, when I started going to school, I learned that 'tilly' was from the Irish *tuille*, meaning 'a little extra'. Later still, reading about Cleopatra performing her ablutions in a bath of milk, I remembered our milkman and thought it was lucky for him that she wasn't one of his customers expecting a tilly every morning.

By that point I was in full and comfortable flight with my 'Thought For The Day' series and was made happier by the one that suggested itself for the final talk.

I was going to start with a story about my late grandparents who had come to Ireland as refugees from Lithuania in the 1880s. A group of them found a haven in Cork and naturally they tended to crowd together in the same district, which soon became known as 'Jewtown'. When I was a youngster that appellation was regarded by the community as unpleasant, even derogatory. But that I, a Jew, could speak it over the radio without a trace of embarrassment would be witness to a social and spiritual revolution. Time, sense, familiarity, had made the word 'Jewtown' a part of local history, the equivalent of no more than a street-sign, the place where the Jews had lived. The fairytale ending would be implied: 'And they all lived happily ever after.'

I knew it was a bit pulpity, the upbeat note, the party line emollient. But wasn't that what the whole series was about? Surely there couldn't be anything wrong in that?

So I thought, until I listened to the broadcast of my initial talk, the one about the different Jewish blessings. I knew then what was wrong about the series. *I* was. There I'd been, standing up for God. It was like voting in an election that was already rigged, an election in which there was only one candidate whom you had to obey, or else. Wasn't that what I had felt from way, way back? Aged ten, Hebrew class, Genesis, God, the Garden of Eden, Adam and Eve, the Tree of Knowledge, banishment: DEATH. Because they had disobeyed God. Adam and Eve – who knew no better and could know no better – in their ignorance and innocence had disobeyed God and because of that, I would die. Eventually *I* would die. I was only ten then and the knowledge never left me. It was no use telling myself that the Garden of Eden was all probably only a myth. Maybe it was, but I could see what was supposed to have resulted from it. And it had. Nobody, ever, had lived for ever.

Then soon afterwards I learned that the innocent had to suffer with the guilty. Why? No one could tell me. The usual answer was that it was part of God's plan which it isn't ours to question. But what about the phrase thrown around by so many professional religious: 'A just God'? Oh yes, the after-life would take care of that. The afterlife, heaven and hell, all that jazz. Trouble was that in the Jewish religion the afterlife, heaven and hell, such as they were, had all been invented by interpreting Scripture with Talmudic speculation based on metaphors and parables. Rabbis had nothing else to do, so, being Rabbis, they rabbited on and on. A messiah? Oh yes, they invented that too. The irony was that they did produce one, or at least an alleged one who to them was just another Jew, not their Messiah. And I knew what all that had started.

At that point I gave up believing in religion. I worked out that I could have a religion of my own without a God, or maybe even a God of my own without religion. I didn't at that time try to work out which to choose. It was all too baffling, and I was too young and angry to grapple with it. But it taught me one lesson that I have tried to steer by ever since: if you come up against something about which you can do absolutely nothing, then stop worrying and get on with something else. So I got on with something else, but only something else in a manner of speaking, in that it included Hebrew class, Barmitzvah, synagogue, Hebrew prayers – all because I could hardly do otherwise. Hypocrisy? At that age? I didn't even know the word.

As I progressed through the teen years other diversions kept God very much in the back stalls, though he was still around. But by now I was seventeen, about to enter university, and in the interval had come upon three things that had helped dispel some of the fog in my mind about my attitude to God and religion. The first was a concept, 'faith', and the other two were the words 'atheist' and 'agnostic'.

Faith I learned about not from the Catholics who were my classmates in school – we never talked about religion – but from becoming aware that Catholicism was referred to as the Catholic faith. I wondered about 'faith', about what it was. It seemed to me that it wasn't belief, but that it was interchangeable with belief, and so if you had faith, you didn't need to question whether you believed or not. Self-examination just did not arise. That discovery told me what I lacked, what I needed to solve my problem. But of course it could not tell me how or where I might come by faith. In Hebrew school belief in God had been axiomatic, but I had no recollection that any need had been felt to pay it special attention. After all, wasn't God ours? Hadn't we founded monotheism? And hadn't God chosen the Jews – or the Israelites, as they were then – to carry His word to the world? Fortunately for me – for understanding it all was difficult enough as it was – I hadn't at the time known that God had chosen the Jews because every other tribe had turned Him down. There being no one else He could ask, the Jews became His chosen people. Perhaps that was the first example of being made an offer you couldn't refuse.

Clearly then, I just did not have faith. But at least discovery of atheism and agnosticism gave me some succour. As an atheist I would have to believe that God just didn't exist, but as an agnostic I could keep an open mind. I hadn't the courage, nor anything near the required certainty, to be the former, so I could take refuge in the latter.

Nevertheless, that did not satisfy me. On the threshold of university I told myself that it was time I knew my mind. Which drove me back into the *cul-de-sac* of faith. Like an apprentice Rabbi composing a new Talmudic argument, I applied my own logic to the problem. If God exists, He made me. But not only did He make me without faith, He left me without even the intellectual or emotional or spiritual capacity to develop faith. I was incomplete, unfinished. How then could He justifiably expect me to believe in Him? Wasn't it up to Him to do something about it? Wasn't it up to Him to make it possible for me to believe?

What I sought was certitude. I desperately wanted not to have to go through the rest of my life in a spiritual vacuum. Actually, what I was experiencing was a major trauma. That is the only explanation of the absurd means I chose to put an end to my dilemma. If God existed, I was His responsibility, so I would leave it up to Him.

I said to God: 'I don't know if You're there. I need to know. Tell me. Perform a miracle for me, a very small miracle, of no material benefit whatever.'

I took a candle, stood it on the table, sat in front of it, and lit it. Then I said: 'God, if You exist, blow it out.' Nothing happened. Nothing whatever. The small flame swayed happily from side to side, until I blew it out myself.

For quite a while afterwards I sat in thought. I cannot say I was surprised. In truth, I felt rather foolish. I told myself that at seventeen I should have known better. So I was back to square one. Back to the state of indeterminate ignorance in which I had struggled before my failed challenge to God, still unable to say a categorical 'yea' or 'nay' to Him. All I had left were the two words 'atheist' and 'agnostic'. All I had learned was that I was one or the other. I was just too tired to keep on digging for the answer, but too chary of closing any doors. I remained in limbo for almost the next thirty years until RTÉ, all unwittingly, precipitated the moment of illumination that gave me the answer I had been seeking.

They were preparing a series of TV programmes in which they would interview people of different denominations about their life, with special emphasis on their religious belief. Would I be the Jewish interviewee? asked the voice on the phone.

'I'm very sorry,' I answered without thinking. 'I wouldn't be any good for that.'

'Why not?'

'Well, I'm an atheist.'

However surprised the producer may have been by my answer, he couldn't have been as surprised as I was. The statement had absolutely no basis. It just came out and I didn't know why. But before I had a chance to withdraw it, its reception stymied me.

'Great! A Jewish atheist! That'll make a smashing programme.'

Almost every day during the run-up to the interview I thought of making some excuse, any excuse, to get out of it. But I knew that wasn't really an option. It would be letting myself down, and it would be letting down RTÉ who had helped me so much. The problem was of my own making and it had to be faced. Anyway, it probably wouldn't be at all as bad as I feared. As the producer had later explained, it would be about my literary career – he asked me to lend him some copies of *Irish Writing* to show on camera – as well as my Judaism, so the question of atheism could hardly be much more than a small part of it. If I kept my wits about me I should be able to take care of that without actually declaring that I was an atheist. I knew I wasn't one, not yet anyway, though I still didn't know why I had said I was.

In the event, much of the interview did deal with my career, leading to a fairly general and quite innocuous discussion about the Jewish religion and my own experience as an Irish Jew. I don't remember the exact form of the exchange that brought up the question of God, but I do recall that my response was to explain my early puzzlement and unhappiness over the Garden of Eden story and some other Old Testament passages.

'Did you come to any conclusion about them? How did they affect your relationship to the Deity?'

I confessed to my teenage difficulty with that problem and my eventual realisation that the lack of faith was the barrier between me and God.

'And where did that discovery lead you?'

The question made me hesitate. It left me nowhere to hide the story of my naïvety. So I told it straight, as I had told it to God, that it was His fault if I couldn't believe in Him, and that it was up to Him to help me.

'I got a candle, I lit it, and I said to God, "Now if You exist, blow it out." It wasn't much to ask.'

'And did God blow it out?'

The rest of the interview is a blur in my mind. I remember only that as I answered 'No', I had a sudden vision of the candle in front of me with its flame extinguished. It *had* been blown out, not by a God in heaven, but by me, a God in me, my own God. Perhaps there *was* a God in heaven, and perhaps He *had* helped me by giving me the breath to blow out the candle. But there is still a lot about Him I cannot absorb, a lot that no one can explain.

The poet Denis O'Driscoll has pointed out that 'I' and 'God' are the only words capitalised in the language, and that penetrating comment suggests an equivalence I find reassuring. Since my inner revelation on Radio Damascus, I have followed the way of my own God, the God in me, and can only hope that if there is a God in heaven, it will have found acceptance in His eyes. When my time comes, if He does exist I'll find out. And if He doesn't, it won't matter anyway.

CHAPTER TWENTY-FOUR

Getting into the Swing

The first enthusiasm a literary editor must quickly learn to curb is his love of books. An Irish newspaper with a large circulation and a reputable weekly book page is a target for both British and Irish publishers. In the slack publishing seasons, January and the summer months, review copies are not over-plentiful, but in spring, autumn and pre-Christmas, they swell into a flood of hundreds a week. Inevitably they include a considerable number the literary editor will covet, but he would be well advised not to get hooked on dipping too deeply into any he knows must be reviewed or else he may find himself working against the clock when it comes to putting together a balanced page. Unless, of course, he likes to review a book himself, in which case it helps if he is an expert skimmer or speed reader.

As a young teenager I had an inordinate love of books. If the book was fiction, story and voice drew me; if non-fiction, I craved its knowledge and punditry. In Washington Street, not ten minutes from my home, there was a second-hand bookshop run by a delightful character known as Jockey Joe. His flashing smile, sparkling spectacles and quickfire wit drew patrons as much as did his very varied stock. One day when I was flusher than usual, I dropped in and scanned the shelves for some book or books I could feel I had to have. There, on a high shelf I could just about reach, was Ruskin's *Modern Painters*. All I knew about Ruskin was that he was famous, an authority on many subjects. I knew just as little about art but hungered to learn as much as possible about it, and so Ruskin's five volumes of *Modern Painters* offered, I presumed, my first ever chance to plug one huge gap in my knowledge. I eased them down from their shelf, all five volumes, and brought them over to Jockey Joe.

'I'll take these,' I said, even though I knew, having first checked the price inside the covers, that they would clean me out.

Jockey Joe looked sideways at me, and through his spectacles I could see the dubiety in his eyes, but he made no comment.

I took my Ruskin straight home and sat down with the first volume. All I can now recall is my sense of complete bafflement and intense disappointment. Were there any illustrations to help me? If there were, they made no impression, partly perhaps because they would have been in black and white. I looked through some pages of the other volumes – a painter named Turner managed, aptly, to live up to his name by turning up constantly – but I soon realised that my reach was far, far greater than my grasp. I immediately lamented the expenditure of all my hard-saved pocket money and decided to take my purchase straight back to Jockey Joe and hope he might give me a refund.

When he saw me re-enter so soon after I had left, the five volumes under my arm, he smiled and shook his head, saying, 'Jaysus, you're the quickest reader I ever had.' But he took the books and gave me back my money. I hope I returned his kindness by spending it on some other of his wares.

During the first few months as literary editor of the *Irish Press* I stepped very warily, so it is unlikely that my elevation to the position resulted in any significant change to the weekly book page or its cast of reviewers. Certainly it drew no sheaf of congratulatory letters such as those that welcomed the first 'New Irish Writing' page earlier in 1968, one of which had been from Micheál MacLiammóir conveying effusive praise and a suggestion that we meet. I thanked him for his kindness but did not act on his suggestion.

Once I became familiar with the routine involved in getting the book page ready to be put to bed every Friday evening, a routine that entailed watching over the procedure on one stone in the caseroom while having an eye to another stone where the 'New Irish Writing' page was also being made ready, I felt sufficiently comfortable with my new duties to give thought to the sort of book page I wanted.

It needed to establish a broad appeal, willing to risk the Scylla of eclecticism in order to avoid the Charybdis of an unadventurous conservatism in the lee of which a new and inexperienced literary editor might be tempted to anchor. It would have to sound a contemporary note, send out signals that anyone interested in books would want to tune into each week not only for entertaining reading, but to be introduced to themes and interests they had never before thought within their range. At the same time I was determined to give regular support to the work of Irish writers and publishers. To provide such a page would, I fully realised, be a very considerable challenge after the standards set up by such distinguished previous *Irish Press* literary editors as M.J. MacManus and Benedict Kiely.

I saw the introduction of fresh reviewing voices as vital to the success of that challenge. This meant discovering some new Irish reviewers of style and authority, and also avoiding any tendency towards incestuousness – the debilitating danger to a small-country book page – by attracting from time to time established, high-profile critics from Britain and places further afield. My difficulty in this regard was that being back in Ireland only a year after thirteen years away, I not only didn't know people, but didn't know who were the people I would need to know. Liam Miller of Dolmen Press and John Boyd, editor of the Northern Ireland periodical *Threshold*, were, among others, extremely helpful with lists of recommendations, but it was my brother Louis who steered me to Con Houlihan. Con proved to be a highly individual, widely-read literary critic of idiosyncratic but mellifluous phraseology and startling insights. Just as startling was the particular form his reviews took, reaching me from his home in Kerry as a thick bunch of sheets of paper, each sheet about sixteen inches by ten and containing maybe six lines of hand-written, giant-sized letters, four or five words to a line. They were museum pieces, lacking only illuminated capitals to pass as a new-age *Book of Kells* from a hitherto unknown planet. Unfortunately, they also required to be typed before they could be sent down for setting. When in later years Con Houlihan moved to Dublin and was installed as sportswriter for the *Evening Press*, he became a household name, his articles essential reading for followers of every sport in Ireland, and his gigantic frame, visible from any distance on Dublin's streets, supplied the necessary *avoirdupois* to complete the legend.

Of course I augmented the list of supplied names with my own very long list of world-famous VIPs – writers, politicians, industrialists, showbiz stars, economists, athletes, etc., – whom I knew from the media to be highly articulate and who, offered the right choice of book to review, might be persuaded. I was not merely vaultingly ambitious, but outlandishly so on the basis that if you don't ask, you won't get, so my list included scores of luminaries, from Arthur C. Clarke to Germaine Greer, from Graham Greene to Tennessee Williams. I never actually approached any of the above, but other equally famous personalities I did approach, unsuccessfully alas, were Alistair Cooke, J.P. Galbraith, Dirk Bogarde, Dick Francis, Jordan's King Hussein, and Philip Larkin, all of whom sent me kindly-worded letters of refusal. Other much nearer misses whose regrets included explanations were Sir Anthony Eden, who said that the book I offered him was one he would love to review but he was under strict doctor's orders to attempt no work whatsoever, and Saul Bellow, to whom I had offered a critical biography of Isaac Bashevis Singer but who explained that he preferred to keep his 'sword sheathed until the old bugger dies'.

One opportunity I missed and lived to regret was a woman who phoned not very long after I had been appointed, to put herself forward as a reviewer. Her name was unknown to me but the range of her interests, which she reeled out at my request, bowled me over: 'Novels, poetry, literary criticism, biography, history, art history, craftwork, children's books, sport.' When I recovered my breath I explained that I had a surfeit of reviewers on literary subjects but that I would try to send her something. The idea of a woman covering a sports book intrigued me – nowadays there are many who are a delight to read, but at that time, so far as I knew, they did not exist on this side of the Atlantic. I remember that I sent her a book on rugby and she turned in an excellent, knowledgeable review which of course I used. Unfortunately, sports books were seldom sent to the *Irish Press* and so her name didn't occur to me again. She was Eileen Battersby, now of *The Irish Times*, and in my opinion one of the best literary critics in these islands.

Reviews I especially remember were those by two of the leading British poets, Vernon Scannell and Dannie Abse on Irish poetry collections; Thomas Kinsella on W.B. Yeats; Cork's celebrated sculptor, Séamus Murphy, on *My Father's Son*, Frank O'Connor's first volume of autobiography; Cyril Cusack on Charles Laughton and on Sean O'Casey; pianist Denis Matthews on Beethoven; John Wain on Patrick Boyle; Denis Johnston on Amanda McKittrick Ros and on Swift; William Trevor on Picasso; and A.J. Leventhal on Beckett. Francis Stuart frequently reviewed for me, but unfortunately a review I published of one of his own novels greatly displeased him. It was by a not well-known Irish critic who had already contributed to the book page excellent reviews of important new novels. As was my practice, I first phoned him to ascertain whether he was sufficiently familiar with the work of Francis Stuart to be interested in covering his latest novel. He said he was, but explained that as he was critical of the author's reported activities during his wartime years in Germany, perhaps I might prefer to find someone else. Admiring his openness, I asked if he felt his disapproval of Stuart's Nazi associations might prejudice him, to which he replied that he would treat the book solely on its merits. On that basis I decided to let my invitation stand on condition that he would preface the review with a brief, but clear statement of his reservations so that readers could make up their own minds as to whether any possibly adverse criticism of the novel might, in their opinion, seem inspired by prejudice.

In the event the review was followed by a letter from Francis Stuart to Tim Pat Coogan strongly protesting at its tone and bias. Tim Pat passed the letter to me with no comment other than that I should deal with it. I wrote to Francis, drawing his attention to the condition I had imposed on the reviewer which he had scrupulously followed and which I felt was fair to the author and to readers of the review. I pointed out that I had no reason to question the reviewer's ability to distance his views of Francis Stuart, the man, from his reactions to any of the writer's works. Establishing such a distinction in comparable cases was a dilemma that I had to rationalise for myself decades earlier. In the early throes of my lifelong adoration of Beethoven's music I read much about his life and learned that his behaviour was often extremely unpleasant. I was naïvely appalled that such a genius could be such a boor, but it didn't take me long to grow out of my silliness at expecting great artists to be always upright gentlemen. Had I not quickly jettisoned that delusion I would have had to cut out of my life much music and literature that made life worthwhile. Only in recent years did I discover that Brahms was a convinced anti-Semite, and though the discovery momentarily discomposed me, it has never weakened the spell his music weaves or succeeded in arresting the tears the slow movement of his violin concerto brings to my eyes. Fortunately, my disagreement with Francis Stuart did not lead to any rift between us, for even though I did express my disappointment that he had directed his protest to the paper's editor rather than directly to me, he still continued to review for me.

Once the book page had an established reputation I turned to what I saw as two particular drawbacks. The first arose because, like all other national newspaper book coverage confined to one weekly page, fiction could never command anything like as much space as its bookshop popularity merited. In addition, and compounding that drawback, novels by non-Irish authors tended to be squeezed out of Saturday space, so the *Irish Press* was favoured with review copies of few such novels. To plug that hole I instituted a weekday review feature with the self-explanatory title 'Novel A Day', which led to increased patronage by the British publishers, and included among many important notices one that now might be regarded as a collector's item, John Banville reviewing Francoise Sagan.

The other serious book page drawback was one I have already referred to and to which all Irish book coverage was prone. I regarded it as on a par with the amount of nepotism in the complement of Dáil TDs, that is the disease of 'incesticide', being the reviewing of leading Irish novelists and short story writers by Irish critics or writers who, for a variety of reasons, might not have completely open minds or might be inhibited from expressing the whole truth of their reactions. This could easily be avoided by commissioning an eminent, non-Irish writer or critic, or if possible an Irish one nationally recognised as both outspoken and completely unbiased. A further provision was that he or she should be resident critic for a year, covering the most important new Irish fiction of each month.

Having drawn up my blueprint I decided that the most auspicious, attention-catching launch for this innovative feature would be the appointment as its first incumbent arguably the most distinguished Irish writer of his time, Seán O'Faoláin. O'Faoláin enthusiastically supported the project and contributed not twelve, but thirteen monthly reviews, the final, extra one being an unbidden 'Valedictory', a no-holds-barred, cobweb-dispersing, fresh air blast through the state of contemporary Irish fiction. To read these reviews and other literary criticism by O'Faoláin is to be educated by probably the most wide-ranging, penetrating, rambunctious, unshackled, insightful, inspired and inspiring critic Ireland has ever produced. One of his stylistic delights was the frequent adjectival barrage, a characteristic which – as the previous lines reveal – I found irresistibly infectious.

His twelve commissioned reviews included pronouncements on the latest books by John Banville, Samuel Beckett, Patrick Boyle, John Broderick, Michael McLaverty, Conor Cruise O'Brien, Liam O'Flaherty, William Trevor and Terence de Vere White, plus the debut story collections of Neil Jordan and Gillman Noonan. Such a heavyweight inauguration of the new monthly feature meant that the task of finding successors of comparable status – non-Irish, so as to introduce completely independent voices – was not difficult, and with Anthony Burgess, John Fowles, Susan Hill and John Braine among those who followed O'Faoláin, the feature's service both to readers and to the authors whose work it reviewed made it a resounding success.

Among the non-Irish reviewers who occasionally contributed to the book page was one perhaps surprising name, that of the celebrated harmonica player (he hated having it called a mouth-organ) Larry Adler. An American who left the USA in the days of the McCarthy Un-American Activities investigations and settled in London, he on occasion contributed particularly witty reviews, usually on the American scene, to the leading British Sunday newspaper, *The Observer*. So, when among the books I received one week was *The Twenties* (the American Twenties, in fact) by Alan Jenkins, I thought why not, and asked Larry Adler to review it.

He thanked me for the suggestion but declined, saying, 'If I did that review for the fee you offered, my Jewish grandfather would turn in his grave.'

I answered, 'If I offered you any more, *my* Jewish grand-father would turn in *his* grave.'

The review followed, and was as witty as I had hoped. Part of it ran as follows:

> Mr Jenkins writes a lot in the historical present, which is okay for Damon Runyon, but which sits uneasily on Mr Jenkins. 'I am thirteen.' That's the first sentence, to which my reaction was, 'Look, Alan, that's much too young to be writing a book.'

That still gets a laugh out of me, which I hope proves that I am still young too.

Larry Adler did a few more reviews for me, and when later he came on a family visit to Dublin (he had a son studying at Trinity) my wife and I had him to a dinner party in our home. Yes, he was very witty, but the trouble was that he rather dominated the evening's conversation with unending stories and jokes about his early life in the US. All present would, I suspect, have preferred a mouth-organ (sorry, harmonica) solo.

One constant worry I had in relation to choosing reviewers was whether they would deliver copy on time, preferably even before time. Of course I soon got to know which ones I could rely on completely, which hardly at all, and which only for reviews that could be used more or less whenever they came in as long as they were not outrageously out of date. On occasions when I was awaiting a particular review which was already running late, I often recalled the story I had been told of the very first review written by Terence de Vere White, later the *Irish Times* literary editor. Among the literati of Dublin he was known to be a man of letters, an impressive commentator and an entertaining companion. One day he received a phone call from the then *Irish Times* literary editor, who asked if he might be interested in doing a review of a certain book. Terence mentioned that he'd never done any reviewing but he'd be willing to try.

'That's great,' the literary editor said. 'The only trouble, Terence, is that I need it rather in a hurry.'

'Well,' Terence answered, 'I could read it tonight and review it tomorrow, or review it tonight and read it tomorrow.'

The story may be apocryphal, but Terence was extremely witty, so one never knows.

As the 1970s progressed the book page kept well on course. So I believed, but because of the almost total absence of letters from independent readers offering criticism or advice, I could never be sure. Of course friends often expressed opinions of particular reviews they liked or disliked – many of the latter from writers dissatisfied with the skimpiness of the space given to their own books – but it wasn't until August, 1984, when I relinquished the literary editor's chair, that readers and others wrote letters of regret at my departure.

All of these kind letters were extremely gratifying, but there were three in particular from practitioners in the world of literature that afforded me very special satisfaction.

From Steve MacDonogh, publisher of Brandon Books, came:

Congratulations on your years as literary editor of the *Irish Press*. May I wish you the very best in your retirement, and it is very good to know that you will continue to edit the 'New Irish Writing' page. Some time ago I did a little survey of the national newspapers with regard to their proportional coverage of Irish published books and I noticed with considerable interest that the *Irish Press* came out top of the list: a higher percentage of its reviews were of Irish published than was the case with any other national daily. Statistics may be rather cold but they offer a factual underlining of the impression gained from reading the pages you have edited.

The distinguished, British-based writer and critic Neville Braybrooke wrote:

> Many thanks for your nice letter. It, too, has been a pleasure to work for you. I always thought yours one of the best literary pages in the press today – far, far superior to many over here, including the Sundays.

And from one of Ireland's most respected thinkers and writers, the late Hubert Butler, the centenary of whose birth was celebrated in Kilkenny during millennium year, came this revealing message:

> I am so very sorry that you are leaving the *Irish Press*. To me you *are* the *Irish Press* and I wonder will they get anyone like yourself to replace you.
>
> I was very grateful for the kind things you said about me and I showed it proudly to my American family, which was here on its brief annual holiday. I always enjoyed writing for the *Irish Press*. The link up came for me at a particularly happy time, as I had had a semi-falling out with *The Irish Times* or perhaps it was just with its literary editor – I am not quite clear

how this happened but it has meant that I had to offer my wares to them rather than, as of old, have them solicited. And they never send me any books to review. Actually there was a pause when I didn't want them, as I have been collecting material for a book. But I have put it together now – it is mostly old stuff but assembled round a dominant idea. It is called *Escape from the Ant Hill* and will be published by The Lilliput Press in the spring.

I am sending herewith the Chinese review (*The Gang of Four*). Present-day China seems quite inscrutable and planless and even the author, Bonavia, seems bewildered. Perhaps it is the primeval chaos out of which a brand new world will shape itself some generations from now.

I find Russia much more intelligible – this may be because I know it better. And, if your successor is kind enough to think of me for reviews, I would like to write of Russia again.

Thank you again
Yours ever
Hubert

'New Irish Writing' too had, during the preceding years, kept on course. However, writers under the age of twenty seldom appeared in it – one could hardly expect their talent to have sufficiently matured to make the grade, the outstanding exception of course being Desmond Hogan's success at the age of sixteen in providing the page's first story by a previously unpublished writer. Remembering my own teenage years of obsessional writing – I was convinced I was the best unpublished poet in Ireland under twenty-one – I felt sure that if youngsters were given opportunity and encouragement with not too much expected of them, some really promising talent might emerge. Tim Pat Coogan again gave me the go-ahead and provided sufficient space every Wednesday for some poetry and a short-short story in a 'Young Irish Writing' feature. It was well supported by the schools and proved its value by discovering three writers who went on to gain notable success – Deirdre Madden, Dermot Bolger, and Blánaid McKinney.

An earlier experiment was a weekly page, 'Ireland – the Arts', in which I sought to range over every manifestation of Irish life, giving both 'Arts' and 'life' the widest possible interpretation. Among the very contrasting features I particularly recall were articles by David Greene on Máirtín Ó Cadhain, Seán Ó Súilleabháin on The Oral Art of Storytelling, Peter Borodin on Irish writers in Russia, and Brenda Fricker on Educating an Audience. Hugh Leonard wrote three articles on adapting for stage, TV and screen, and in a series under the title of Aspects of Irish Culture Con Houlihan wrote on the Irish Horse. Architecture, art, the environment, dress, sport, and what-have-you, I saw the page as a hand-me-down encyclopaedia, an Open University offering multifarious mini-courses on the Irish heritage. Unfortunately, owing to increasing pressure on space, the page lived for only a few years, but before it had to be abandoned I succeeded in persuading Cyril Cusack to contribute two long, fascinating interpretative descriptions of acting the roles of Hamlet and the Playboy. I subsequently suggested to the publishers, Faber, the idea of a book of similar articles by the actor on famous parts he had played, but their approaches to Cusack failed because the mounting demands on his time by stage, screen and TV made it impossible for him to take on such a commission.

The 1970s had started as in many ways the most fulfilling time of my life. I had the comfort of being back in my own country, the security of a good job, the happiness of working at something I loved, the exhilaration of the pressure it brought me, the family feeling of mixing with congenial colleagues. Above all, of course, was the satisfaction of having succeeded, admittedly not in achieving my early dream of becoming a noted writer, but in a specially rewarding and much less exacting next best, that of finding, and giving their first chances to, others who went well on their way to reaching the top.

The continuing popularity of the 'New Irish Writing' page, however, soon began to face me with a development for which I was totally unprepared, but which, nevertheless, had a highly gratifying result. It had not been practical for me to use more than two stories in any one year by the same contributor, but in due course some of these new writers each had the nucleus of an excellent collection, with little or no chance of finding a publisher in Ireland or Britain to take them on. I happened to mention this to Philip MacDermott, then the distributor for many of the leading London publishers, whom I often met at coffee mornings in The Mucky Duck. It did not need much discussion before we agreed to join forces and set up a publishing company ourselves with the initial aim of promoting the cause of the Irish short story, Philip running the business side and I being the editor. Thus was born Poolbeg Press, which in its early years reissued in paperback long out-of-print celebrated collections, such as Frank O'Connor's *Guests of the Nation* and Mary Lavin's *Tales from Bective Bridge*, but also published the debut collections of many new writers discovered by the 'New Irish Writing' page. Whenever in recent years I have had to rid my shelves of many books I would have liked to keep, so as to make room for later arrivals, one gradually increasing category has remained sacrosanct. That is the specially inscribed first books – poetry, stories, novels – of authors whose debut in print was in 'New Irish Writing'. At the head of that group is a novel, *An End to Flight,* by Vincent Banville, published by Faber in 1973, winner of that year's prestigious *Daily Express* Robert Pitman Award, and very quietly, without any previous notice, dedicated by the author to me. For the treasured gift of that honour, for the equally treasured close friendship we have enjoyed over the years, and for his unrelenting persistence in finally persuading me to write these memoirs, I have with the greatest happiness and no warning whatsoever, availed of the opportunity to turn the tables and return the compliment by joining him, along with my beloved wife and daughter, as dedicatees of this book.

One other 'New Irish Writing' debutante entitled to special mention is a young lady who sent me a story in 1969 which, though not of publication standard, displayed notable talent. Her name was Ita Daly, and as she lived in Dublin I phoned her, suggesting she might come in so that we could talk about her story. She agreed, and when she arrived I took her to The Mucky Duck for coffee and a chat. She, however, declined the coffee, saying she'd prefer a hot whiskey. I was quite stunned, though I later learned that she had chosen whiskey as the strongest possible drink to steady her nerves.

We talked about short story writing in general and her own story in particular. I encouraged her to write another one for me, which she did and which I thought good enough for the 'New Irish Writing' page. We met again – she was

extremely attractive as well as widely read – we fell in love
and in 1972 we married. As to her writing, she went on to
win the last *Irish Times* Short Story Competition as well as
two Hennessy Literary Awards, to publish a story collection
and five novels, the first two by Jonathan Cape, and the last
three by Bloomsbury to whom she transferred when Liz
Calder, who had been her editor at Cape, left to set up
Bloomsbury.

Our coming together, leading as it did to our marriage,
was the greatest stroke of luck of my life, but then getting
married hardly falls into the category of the strange and
unexpected, and though the decade of the 1970s could not
have brought me more happiness and success than it did, it
was ushered in by an episode that was certainly strange and
unexpected and that had no more than the most remote of
literary connections.

One evening very early in 1970 I received a phone call
from Mrs Maureen Lynch to say that Jack, who was then in
his second term as Taoiseach, wished to see me urgently in
his home and that if I could come immediately, a car would
be sent to collect me. The car arrived within minutes and
very quickly I was delivered at the Lynch residence. I was
welcomed by Mrs Lynch who told me that Jack was in bed
with the 'flu and she immediately showed me up to his room.

He was sitting up in bed, looking a bit tired but fully alert.
He welcomed me warmly, apologised for any inconvenience,
and said that he needed my help. He had to write his address
for the impending Fianna Fáil Ardfheis, but requiring to rest
as much as possible so as to be fully fit for the event, he was
unable to compose the speech himself. Would I write it for
him, basing it on an outline he would provide of the themes
on which he wished to elaborate? I agreed without hesitation

– it was a request I could hardly refuse – but I had severe misgivings, having never up to then been a political animal and since returning to Ireland was so involved in carving out a literary career that, as far as politics were concerned, I had no more than scanned the headlines.

Jack gave me a sheet of government notepaper, headed, to my surprise, 'Office of Minister for Finance', on which he had written his themes and underneath them a brief indication of the special aspects he wanted emphasised. The themes were 'Need for social consciousness', 'Strengthening of our economy' for which self-discipline was necessary, 'e.g. current wage increases are around 20% whereas national production increase is only about 4%', and the notes ended, apart from a P.S., with 'a little patriotism plug also'. The P.S. said, 'I'll try to think up a few more lines tomorrow' but in fact no further communication followed. In the brief conversation we had before I left he mentioned Northern Ireland, where the situation was already extremely serious but which was not included among the noted themes. He asked me to give that plenty of space, underlining that cooperation, consideration, friendship and understanding were to constitute the bedrock of our policy, with force offering no option whatsoever.

I wished him a speedy recovery, promised, as he had asked, that I would keep our arrangement completely confidential, told him I would get down to the speech immediately, said goodbye and was driven home. I worked on a draft all through the night, and when by the following night no fresh notes had arrived, I completed the address, polished it and typed it, some four and a half thousand words, and had it collected. It was the section about Northern Ireland that gave me the most trouble because, appreciating the delicacy of the situation, it was of cardinal importance that I express

Jack's attitude and policy with the strongest conviction and maximum sincerity. Apparently my words sounded the required note, for the morning after Jack delivered the speech, a phrase of which I had been particularly proud – 'amity, not enmity, is our ideal' – was headlined in at least one leading newspaper. Next day I received the following from the Department of the Taoiseach.

Dear David,
Thank you for your great help. As you will have read the affair went off well – yours were the best lines.
Yours sincerely,
Jack.

There is, at this point, a joke that is not inapposite. A certain Rabbi had such a fanatical love of golf that he took a flat next to a golf course so that he could play a few holes whenever possible. One Sabbath morning of clear skies and bright sun he woke up at dawn with a mighty, overpowering urge to take out his clubs and pay a brief visit to the course. He knew that to desecrate the Sabbath was the greatest possible sin, but there would be no one around to see him, and immediately afterwards he would hurry to the synagogue service and pray to the Lord for forgiveness.

He reached the course and teed up at the first hole. As he was loosening up with a few swings of his driver, Moses, looking down from heaven, suddenly spied him.

'Lord! Lord!' he cried. 'Look, the Rabbi, playing golf on the Sabbath! Do something, Lord.'

'My, my,' the Lord said. 'Yes, I'll have to punish him.'

At the tee the Rabbi took aim and swung. The ball flew high in the air, straight as an arrow, further than he had ever driven a golf ball before, descended in a graceful arc and plopped right into the hole.

The Rabbi was speechless for a moment. Never before in his life had he achieved a hole in one.

'Lord, Lord,' Moses protested. 'The Rabbi has desecrated the Holy Sabbath and You call *that* a punishment?'

'Yes,' the Lord smiled. 'But who can he tell?'

Well, Jack Lynch being no longer with us, I have taken the liberty of telling what I promised to keep confidential, but I feel that from where Jack now is he will look down with a smile and forgive me for revealing my part in the strange affair of the Fianna Fáil Ardfheis.

CHAPTER TWENTY-FIVE

Land Ahoy!

Where had it come from, that itch? Why now, after such a long time? Writer's itch. Not very well named. Real writers, good writers – what they suffer from is not writer's itch, but writer's block, when they put pen to paper but for some inexplicable reason nothing comes through. The other curse, the itch, is what non-writers suffer from, those who carry a writing bug inside them, but if they respond to it, what it breeds never lives. If it does breathe a while, its weakness is noted by friends who, being friends, keep mum. But the critics see it as it is, and the curtains are soon drawn. Yet the non-writer keeps opening them, doggedly cosseting his bug with little or no reward; or if he sensibly gives up, accepting that his possession of only a very mediocre talent is never going to get him anywhere, then the bug lies dormant until the time comes when it awakens and starts to produce what it is meant to produce – an itch.

But why had I scratched at it? All right, so Macmillan had published my first novel, *To Next Year in Jerusalem*, but they had rejected the second one. And that was over twenty-five years earlier. At which I had said enough is enough and got

on with my life. 'He who can does, he who cannot teaches' –
at best, that is. Otherwise he preaches, or reaches, or
screeches, or leeches. Anything to avoid trying to do what he
knows he cannot.

Yet here I was, on a beach in the West of Ireland, under a
warm, summer sun, with my wife next to me and our three-
year-old daughter playing in the sand, it's 1982, and the itch
is torturing me – after all that time.

I never liked lying in the sun. I could never get into a comfortable reading position, but there were still a good few
hours to pass until dinner time, so I thought the best thing to
do was try to work out why I was suddenly scratching at that
itch. Lateral thinking, that might tell me – except that I had
only the vaguest idea what lateral thinking was. But back-
ward thinking, that often worked. It was simple. Just trace
the trail of your thoughts back, thought by thought, until
you reach far enough back to where the trail had started.

I lay there, getting hotter and drowsier and half-dreaming
rather than thinking – and suddenly there it was. *The Irish
Times*, that morning, reading about Maeve Binchy's big,
block-busting, best-selling novel. Maeve Binchy, a busy, very
busy journalist, perhaps even busier than the literary editor
of the *Irish Press*, yet she had found the time to produce a
huge, and hugely successful, novel. No, she hadn't found the
time, she had *made* it. And here was I, a lazy sod, telling
myself that I couldn't possibly find the time to write a novel –
good, bad or indifferent. Notice, I thought to myself, you're
telling yourself that you couldn't find the time, not *asking*
yourself why you couldn't, or whether you really could if
you wanted to.

But why should I want to? I had the answer to that. It was
the reason I was scratching at the itch, the itch that that bug

had started after twenty-five years lying doggo. But that sort of bug does not just come back to life of its own accord; it does not have any automatic self-arousal alarm primed to go off after a set time. It is reactivated by a word, a phrase, a sentence, a thought – anything its non-writer host imagines to be an idea that he could, if he wanted, blow up into a plot. That's the point at which the scratching begins. Throw in a beach, sun, another week with no manuscripts to read, no book page to prepare, and news of the success of Maeve Binchy's penny candle burning like an inextinguishable bonfire in my mind, what could I do but scratch? Because what I was really scratching at was one sentence, a sentence I had read months, perhaps years earlier – I couldn't even remember where. But I didn't need to, because word for word it had embedded itself in my mind. I had never forgotten it: 'In the very early years of the 1900s some members of the Cork Hebrew Community planned to emigrate to Palestine, but their plans never materialised.' It was a plot for a novel sitting up and begging to be written. Of course it would need a lot of developing, a lot of invention. No point in following the empty trail of why the group's emigration plans collapsed. No interest in that; it was probably the usual reason I had often heard my father report after a community meeting: total disagreement on every item on the agenda. Besides, even if they had agreed and gone to Palestine, that's not where I wanted them. I wanted them in Cork, my hometown, a place I could write about, with the Cork Jews as my characters, Jews I knew, fictionalised of course, names changed.

I woke up suddenly to find myself sweating. I had been asleep and dreaming. Such nonsense! That was one dream I had no intention of following. A novel, bejay! I'd want to be mad. Hadn't I proved I couldn't write a novel worth a candle?

Forget that first novel. Any fairly literate, fairly young, aspiring writer could produce a publishable first novel if he was lucky enough to be a Jew, born in Ireland, with a brand-new sort of story to tell. But do it again? I had already tried and failed.

And then, under the hot summer sun with nothing else to do but scratch, the itch turned into a blister, the blister broke and the pus ran out. I fought like hell to mop it up, kept telling myself that thirty years had passed since that first novel. I was a completely different person then. I believed I was a writer. I believed I could write a novel. And I needed somehow to make enough money to pay off the *Irish Writing* debt. So I had the motivation, dammit.

The argument went on, two voices inside me that could not agree. What did I expect of Jewish voices?

    – *You're just too lazy.*
    – *No, I'm not. I work hard. I get into the office at eight every morning. Call that being lazy?*
    – *What about Maeve Binchy? You said she is probably at least as busy as you. And do you know how many pages there are in her novel?*
    – *Look, I could never write a novel as big or as successful as* Light A Penny Candle.
    – *Who's talking about big? Who said anything about successful?*
    – *Well, all right then, I couldn't write any sort of novel.*
    – *When did you last try?*

And yet behind the voices the itch was still there, still suppurating, until after a while I realised that the voices had suddenly stopped. And when they stopped, the itching stopped, and when that stopped, I stopped scratching. Why? Because out of the past I remembered Mr Friedling. Mr Friedling had escaped from Russia at the time of the Czarist-inspired pogroms. He had made it to Ireland, settled in Cork, and like his fellow-refugees peddled for years around the towns and villages of Munster, saving all he earned to set up in business. He became wealthy, the wealthiest man in the community. And then, one Friday afternoon during the IRA war against the Black and Tans, just as he was closing his business early to go home for the Sabbath, two men bundled him back inside, locked the door and put a gun to his head.

'Money,' the one with the gun said. 'C'mon, open the safe and hand it over or I'll shoot.'

Mr Friedling looked at the gun and shrugged.

'Go ahead and shoot,' he said.

They roughed him up, searched him, found some keys, but none of them was the key of the safe. No matter how much they threatened or hit him, he refused to reveal where it was.

'You're wasting your time,' he told them. 'So if you're going to shoot, shoot.'

They got nothing else out of him, nor did they get any money, and eventually they gave up and left.

It was a good story. Perhaps it was apocryphal, but everyone in the community believed it had happened. Mr Friedling was big and tough, and it sounded like him. I remembered him as an old man, still big, still tough, who came to synagogue only once every year, for the Day of Atonement, what was called in the Bible 'The Sabbath of Sabbaths'. The incident, true or false, had always appealed to me as something that would make a good short story, so I adapted it, called it 'Ransom', sent it to *The Bell*, and it was published. But 'Ransom' was written in 1954. Why should it come back to me now, almost thirty years later? I knew the answer to that too. I lay there half-buried in sand, pinned under the hot sun, and there was no way I could fool myself that I did not know. 'Ransom' had been waiting all that time because it was a story in search of a novel, the perfect first chapter for the novel I did not want to write. Along with that knowledge came something else from the past, the frisson that would race through my blood whenever some idea I had seemed nothing short of true inspiration.

Hold on, hold on, I told myself. How many times did you wake up next morning and find your inspired idea was about as brilliant as . . . as . . . yes, as a penny candle? But that argument couldn't get me free of the trap that lying on the beach reading about Maeve Binchy's novel had got me into. For Mr Friedling was still sitting in my mind, saying 'Go on, shoot,' and I knew that I couldn't think or talk myself out of it because even though the gun was no longer at his head, it was at mine. Already the gears had begun to mesh, Mr Friedling had joined the group of Cork Jews who were planning to emigrate to Palestine, and I had been conscripted into their company. There was no fighting it. The most I could get away with would be to lay down my own terms. I'd try to write the novel just as a challenge to myself, to see if after nearly three decades, I still had the *zitzfleisch*, the determination, and the necessary ability to end up with enough words on paper. Nothing high-falutin, nothing pretentious, just at best a reasonable read. No more, and, with luck, no less.

'Come on,' I said to Ita, 'collect Sarah and we'll go and get ready for dinner. I'm famished.'

I slept well that night, because when I went to bed I was thinking that I had just one week's holiday left before facing home not only to the accumulation of manuscripts to read and review copies to sort out, but also to getting down to planning the novel. I was never a follow-your-nose writer, never able to set out with only a character or a line of dialogue or just a good opening sentence, and go from there wherever that skeletal beginning might lead. With both the novels I had written – the published one and the unpublished one – the whole story had first been plotted, the characters named, described and their parts defined, and a synopsis of each chapter composed in full detail. It was the only way I could work, and being the only way, I would have to get that preliminary foundation laid down as quickly as possible. Without the foundation I wouldn't be able to start writing, and I knew my weakness. If I didn't get some words on paper straight off, my resolve would take advantage of every distraction and I might never get started at all. After all, I hadn't made a promise to anyone except myself, and it is not difficult to accommodate the persuasive logic that a promise to oneself is one's own to break.

However, once again I reckoned without Mr Friedling and his gift of the opening chapter. Lying out on the beach the next day under another perfect summer sky, I could think of nothing but the novel, and one and one started to make two. If Mr Friedling's story was to start the ball rolling, then what did the idea of the band of Jews trying to emigrate from Cork to Palestine have to do with it? Even if they did get to Palestine, what then? I had never been there myself, so I'd be biting off more than I could chew to try to write about the place. And if they didn't go to Palestine and the novel wasn't about Palestine, then what in the world *was* it about? '*Dummkopf*', I heard Mr Friedling saying, 'if it's not about Palestine because you don't know Palestine, then where *do* you know about, *dummkopf*?' Of course, my own country, where I had spent the first thirty years of my life and fifteen more since coming back. Bring the novel up to the 1920s, the Black and Tans, the IRA, the British Army. Set it in Cork, my hometown, when there was terror in the streets, curfews, ambushes, battles, blood, half the city burned down, when no one could be neutral, neither Jew nor non-Jew. Apart from Mr Friedling, other Jews had been involved one way or another and when I was young I had often heard their adventures recounted. In the National Library I could read up the files of the *Cork Examiner* for a day-by-day report of the situation and its highlights. It was all there for me. All I had to do was think up a story that would bring to life the place, the times and the people – the British, the Irish, and the Jews, a unique *ménage à trois* on a site which the Irish owned, the British held, and where the Jews, with no home of their own, had found sanctuary.

By the end of that week and the journey home I had it all worked out. Even the title came to me on the tide of ideas. In the *Haggadah*, the account of the Jewish captivity in Egypt recited every year at the Passover, was the sentence, 'And the Lord spake unto Moses, saying, "Know for a surety that thy seed shall be a stranger in a land which is not theirs."' Perfect! 'A Land Which Is Not Theirs'. It fitted each group. Months later, on a visit to Seán O'Faoláin I told him what I was writing.

'Have you a title?' he asked.

'Yes. "A Land Which Is Not Theirs".'

'No, no,' he insisted. 'Too clumsy. Not snappy enough. "A Land Not Theirs", that's your title.'

And it was.

Despite the sudden enthusiasm and heady confidence that had overtaken me, I knew better than to take it for granted that I would succeed in writing the novel. The streets and hostelries of literary Dublin were said to be populated by writers who for years had put it about that they were working on a novel, but no finished manuscript ever appeared. If indeed there were any such writers around, I wondered how they managed to bear the ragging and humiliation they must have suffered. If I ever found myself in a situation of that nature I would sit up night and day to write myself out of it. The thought immediately became father to the deed. I let it be known that I was writing a novel, hoping that if at any stage I began to flag, pride and the fear of being one of the hot air non-finishers would make me keep going.

To write a novel, whether it be one's first or twenty-first, is most of the time a painful, merciless, grim and forbidding experience – as indeed any creative endeavour is likely to be, but novel-writing takes longer than most. There are of course uplifting moments when one believes things are going well, but by and large the effort involved is indescribably exhausting.

I started to work on 'A Land Not Theirs' as soon as I could after returning from the West and the first two people I told were my wife and Philip MacDermott. Initially progress was slow and difficult, but when eventually I found my feet and began to develop a rhythm, two potentially important events took place. The first was that I met an agent from one of the leading literary agencies in London who was making a visit to Dublin. I told A – for reasons which will become clear, I'll refer to him as A – about the novel I had begun and gave him a one-sentence outline of the story. He expressed strong interest and asked me to keep him in touch with my progress. I had never had an agent but recognised that to be represented by a good agent was vital. The other development was that another Dublin visitor, Harold Harris, a director of the publishers Hutchinson, called in to ask me about any promising

Irish writers I could recommend. I gave him what help I could – visits of this nature from London agents and publishers were not infrequent. I did not say anything about my own project, but after his return to London the letter of thanks he wrote me for the information I had given him ended with: 'One thing I omitted to ask you was (a) whether you were writing a novel yourself, as I subsequently heard on the grapevine and (b) whether, if so, it is committed? Please let me know.' I replied, telling him about the novel I had started and promising that, if it ever came to anything, I would inform any agent who might be handling it of his interest.

Expressions of interest from two such quarters were, of course, more than welcome, but more important to me at that point was a steady flow of the right words in the right order on the page. Painful, merciless, grim and forbidding is how I have described the experience of writing a novel, and I soon discovered how accurate that description could be. I suppose I must already have gone through it all when I was writing my first novel, *To Next Year in Jerusalem*, but that was so long ago that it might have been the fate of some other writer, not me. And there was also the fact that I now had, for the first time, the experience of working with an agent – which turned out to be a bumpy learning process. My correspondence with A tells the tale.

On 11 May, 1983, he dropped me a line to ask what progress I was making and offered 'to look at anything at any stage'. I replied by sending him the first chapter, explaining that while I was confident about my material, I had doubts about my ability to deliver the goods. His reply was encouraging in that he thought what I had written was looking good and he urged me to keep going.

Spurred on by that I wrote all through the summer, and

by the following October was able to send another four chapters, some 23,000 words, in which the story 'was laid out or hinted at or signalled', along with a synopsis of what was still to come.

Again A's response was encouraging. I had, he said, 'some wonderful characters', the only thing missing being more colour, such as, for instance, details of what they wore, so as 'to allow us visualise them all'.

In December I sent more chapters with a promise to revise the earlier ones so as to 'get in more colour, as suggested'. I also had a suggestion of my own to the effect that as he now had 40,000 words, I hoped that might be sufficient to see what some publishers' reactions might be. In January, 1984, he sent these chapters to a leading publisher – not Hutchinson – but it took until May before they replied. It was brief: 'I'm terribly sorry to have taken so long with the David Marcus material; sorry, too, that after much reflection we do not feel enough confidence to make you an offer for it at this stage.' A's covering letter commented that what I had written still lacked colour and that he had not been 'keen on the idea of showing the book around at this stage'.

That reply gave me the feeling that A, himself, was no longer as enthusiastic about the book as he had been, so I wrote asking if that was so, and if it was, what had made him change his mind. He immediately phoned, telling me I should stop writing and he would annotate a few of the early chapters so as to show me what he meant by 'colour'.

Over two months passed with no further communication from A and no annotated chapters. As a result I felt I had no alternative but to write him that 'such a delay has revived more strongly than ever my suspicion that my novel is not really making much of an impression on you. Whether I am right or wrong in this belief is not the point – the point is that I hold it and, holding it, a trusting author/agent relationship is made impossible. I can't afford a holdup of more than two months and, more important, such a holdup makes it difficult for me to work up again to the pitch of confidence I had in the novel myself, or to feel at ease with a continuation of our business relationship.

'I am very sorry but it does seem to me that it would be better all round if you sent me back my MSS and we called it a day.'

A's answer was gentlemanly and understanding, in very much a 'soft answer turneth away wrath' tone. He wished me luck and returned my manuscript.

The more than two months during which I had stopped writing had been extremely unsettling. Having suddenly to cut off the adrenalin had brought on a feeling of creative vertigo, of being forcibly blown off the stimulative plateau I had occupied among my characters. To counteract it I had started to re-read what I had written, and the more I read, the more I distrusted A's opinion that the novel lacked colour. It had plenty of action, and even if action did not qualify as colour, what about the gallery of Jewish characters, what about the city of Cork, its streets and monuments and buildings? If all that wasn't colour, what was? I had been genuinely willing, indeed anxious, to learn, but as the days came and went and my world remained suspended with me locked inside it, I knew I had to break out and start it turning again.

To do so, however, was more difficult than I had expected. To have had an agent to whom I could send what I had written and get broadly encouraging feedback was more important in maintaining confidence than I had realised. Without the benefit of independent reaction and comment I felt deprived of compass points, with the result that further progress was slow and uncertain. I needed a new agent – and quickly. Fortunately I wasn't short of contacts on whose advice I could rely, and I was soon taken on by an agent who was not employed by any of the agency companies but had for some years been working independently. We soon had an excellent relationship, B – as I shall designate him – was full of enthusiasm for 'A Land Not Theirs', and once again I was able to work ahead steadily.

By now, probably in 1985, the end of the writing was in sight. Not too long afterwards, another publishing house, apart from Hutchinson, entered the field, Philip MacDermott being the man who awakened its interest. I had been keeping Philip informed of progress – indeed during 1983, when I found that editing 'New Irish Writing', being literary editor of the *Irish Press*, editor of Poolbeg Press, trying to write a novel, *and* make time for some sort of family life was a speedy trip to breakdown, I had resigned from Poolbeg. Philip realised that the break had been made inevitable by the pressure of so much work. To use the old cliché and say that we parted on the best of terms would be only half correct, for our friendship was never affected in the slightest, so we never really parted. He knew that 'A Land Not Theirs' was nearing completion, and as he was to be the Irish distributor for Bantam Press, the high profile American publishers who were preparing to set up a major associate British company in London, he brought me together with their manager, Mark Barty-King.

The three of us met over dinner, I gave Mark a full run-down on the novel, we seemed to be on the same wavelength and he asked me to ensure that a copy of the finished manuscript be sent to him. I passed the message on to my new agent, B, and then got down to the last chapters. There followed a few months of revision and polishing until, some thirty years after the rejection of my second novel, I had at last written another one. The pride of achievement, the euphoria of relief left me, paradoxically, bereft of words and deprived of the will to move. I remember that although it was late in the day when the final sentence was typed, as soon as I came back to life I made myself a cup of coffee. My intention was to stay up for however long it might take to read the manuscript right through, from first page to last. When I finished, I thought, 'Thank you, Maeve Binchy'. I had never forgotten it was her *Light A Penny Candle* that had spurred me to embark on something I thought was beyond me. I did not for one moment imagine that what I had produced would be even remotely successful; indeed I had no idea whether it would be published at all. But of course I lived in hope. As Samuel Johnson famously said, 'No one but a blockhead ever wrote except for money.' O.K. So I was a blockhead. Hadn't Mr Friedling called me a *dummkopf*? But just then I didn't care. What mattered was that I had reconstituted the part of myself I had believed was dead.

B's reaction to *A Land Not Theirs* was very positive and he sent copies to Bantam Press and Hutchinson, giving them plenty of time to read the novel and decide if they wished to make an offer for it. When both publishers said they were interested, he arranged to hold a phone auction on an agreed date. I was to be on hand at home to be kept informed.

As the appointed day drew near I felt not so much excited as curious. I no longer had to worry about whether the novel would be published. The question was by whom, Bantam or Hutchinson, and for how much. I had no special preference between the two publishers – Hutchinson, as Maeve Binchy's publisher, had a long and distinguished track record, but having Philip MacDermott as Bantam's distributor would clearly exert a strong influence on me if it came to a choice between the two. And as to what sort of advance the book might attract? I did try to restrain myself from thinking figures, and certainly Samuel Johnson's aphorism had been far from my mind at the beginning of this incredible adventure, but I found it impossible not to speculate. All I could feel certain of was that it would be rather more than the four hundred pounds advance I had received for *To Next Year in Jerusalem* in 1954. But how much more? Two thousand? Three thousand? Five thousand! I stopped at that point. To expect more would be a flight, not of fancy but of fantasy. Five thousand itself would be a pot of gold though I wasn't a leprechaun.

It was around noon on auction day when the phone started ringing. It was B. The first offer had come in. Seven thousand pounds! I couldn't believe it. I saw the figure in stars.

'My God! Are you taking it?'

'Don't be silly! That's only the start. It was Bantam. I'm expecting Hutchinson's call before lunch. I'll get back to you.'

And before lunch he did.

Hutchinson's – nine thousand pounds!

A break for lunch followed. I didn't eat any.

Soon afterwards Bantam went to ten thousand, to include paperback rights.

At this stage I was beyond any reaction. It was all too unreal for me.

Hutchinson moved up to twelve thousand, also covering a paperback edition.

Bantam increased their offer to thirteen thousand. Hutchinson upped theirs to fifteen, with some slightly improved percentages on ancillary rights. Bantam matched it.

B now intervened, suggesting that although the bidding probably had some more steam in it, we should stop it at fifteen thousand and I should choose which of the publishers to go with. His reason for such an unexpected suggestion was that if I pushed the money even higher and the novel turned out not to sell as well as hoped, any offer for my next novel would be adversely affected. Presuming that B knew what he was doing, and feeling, anyway, fifteen thousand pounds to be so stratospheric that a few thousand more would be neither here nor there, I agreed. I chose the Bantam Press offer and B notified both publishers accordingly.

It took quite some time for the 'walking on air' feeling to even begin to fade, for I had already started a new novel – based on the story of the Listowel Mutiny during the 1920s hostilities which I had read about when researching the military incidents of the times for *A Land Not Theirs* – and it was making excellent progress. However, my decision to become a Bantam Press author drew a very strong protest from Hutchinson. One evening, no more than a few days after they had learned of my choice, I received a phone call from Frank Delaney, who was at the time one of their literary advisers. Hutchinson had insisted that he take up their complaint with me, and although he had been ill with 'flu when they had contacted him, he got out of bed to phone me. Hutchinson were protesting that they had not been given an opportunity to make a further bid and increase their fifteen thousand pounds offer, and they wanted me to have the auction reopened. He said that they had been willing to go up to twenty-two thousand. I told him about B's advice and that I understood both publishers had been informed that stopping the bidding when he did had had my agreement. I added that the choice of Bantam had been mine alone and that though I was tremendously appreciative of Hutchinson's continuing interest, there was no question of my going back on my word. Frank accepted the situation with his usual understanding and went back to bed – and to give him his due, he gave *A Land Not Theirs* a very favourable review when it was published.

To give Bantam Press their due too, they not only heavily promoted the book, but held two publication parties for it, the first one in Cork where it was launched by the then Taoiseach, Jack Lynch, and the next evening in Dublin where Mark Barty-King did the honours. Reviews were mostly complimentary, though ironically the few that appeared in the British Jewish organs were strongly critical. Had the latter expected a more 'literary' effort while the Irish reviewers were intrigued by the Irish-Jewish element and usually praised the novel's readability, the quality I had aimed for from the beginning? Or, I wondered, were the British Jewish reviewers antagonised by my descriptions of British atrocities – all based on contemporary accounts – and the generally unfavourable picture of the British military presence in Ireland?

However, what most mattered to me was the response of the Irish reader, and here I certainly could not have wished for better. *A Land Not Theirs* was in the Irish bestseller lists for six months, No. 1 or 2 for the first four of these months, and it sold some five thousand copies hardback.

Undoubtedly the very satisfactory sales figure was greatly helped by my appearance on the Late Late Show, which I thoroughly enjoyed. Being interviewed by Gay Byrne was a completely stress-free experience, for his lightness of touch, affability and charm, his willingness to listen as well as talk, made me feel as if it was I who was the host and he the most charming of guests who had just dropped in for a chat. It made clear to me why he was such a lauded national figure, but it also made me recall an unfortunate occasion when I was editing the 'Ireland – the Arts page' in the *Irish Press* and had invited a particular person to contribute to the Irish heritage slot an assessment of the major changes that had come about in the beliefs and attitudes of the Irish people as a result of the Late Late Show. The person in question was someone of whom I had no knowledge whatever, but he had been recommended by senior members of the editorial staff whose advice I had sought. Although when writing to my prospective contributor I had given a specific outline of what I was looking for, what he sent me was an unrelieved eulogy of Gay Byrne, the TV celebrity. As a colour piece or profile of Gay it was splendid, but it was not what I wanted and 'Ireland – the Arts page' was certainly not its niche. I returned it to the writer with my apologies, referring to the clear specification I had provided, and asking if he would be willing to rewrite it along the necessary lines. He blankly refused. I did not publish his piece, but having commissioned it I arranged for him to be paid the fee I had originally offered. An editor's chair can suddenly develop a very uncomfortable bump. For me, fortunately, the Late Late Show's guest-chair had no such hidden dangers.

After *A Land Not Theirs*, good fortune continued to favour me. In the autumn of the following year, 1986, Bantam brought out my Listowel Mutiny novel, *A Land in Flames*, Corgi published the paperback of *A Land Not Theirs* and a year later the paperback of *A Land in Flames*, and in 1988 Bantam put the icing on my cake with a collection of my short stories, *Who Ever Heard of an Irish Jew?*, which Poolbeg later paperbacked. I wrote no more for over a decade until in the late 1990s I started a new novel. From very early on I realised it was a mistake but, having started it, I had to prove to myself that I could finish it, no matter that it would be worthless. And finish it I did. I never submitted it to a publisher and I have never read it since. If the experience has saved me for the rest of my life from the torture and ignominious awareness of writing yet another bad novel to be consigned to a damp cellar, it will have been worthwhile. As a novelist I can console myself that at least I had my day.

CHAPTER TWENTY-SIX

Hyphenated Americans

That the past often comes back to haunt one is, or used to be, more a hand-me-down short story cliché than the way things happen. To be thus haunted one has to have a past – the young, bearing no such burden, are unhauntable – and so more often than not one has to be renting the ante-room to advanced age for the past to pay a visit. In fact, however, as these visits are usually composed of high profile memories or nostalgic bon-bons, they are made welcome and sentimentally indulged. Rarely indeed do they material-ise as a real-life avatar, inspirer of the youth who became father to the man.

One afternoon in the spring of 1976 I was sitting at my desk in the Irish Press when front office phoned up to say there was a gentleman wanting to see me.

'Who is he?' I asked. 'Did he give his name?'

'He did,' came the whispered reply, 'but it was something foreign. I couldn't really catch it.'

Much puzzled, I went down immediately and approached the only stranger there, a man of above average height, very well built, with a full head of black to greying hair.

'David,' he said, extending a hand, 'great to meet you. Bill Saroyan.'

The daring young man on the flying trapeze himself, the first god in my pantheon of short story writers.

'I was over in Scotland, had a day free so I thought I'd take a chance and fly over to meet you.'

'Bill,' I almost shouted in surprise, only just checking myself from addressing him as Mr Saroyan, 'this is marvellous! Unbelievable! Look, how long have you got?'

'The whole day. Going back in the morning. I'm all yours, man.'

'Great. Give me a moment. I'll phone Ita, my wife, and tell her you're here and coming home to have dinner with us. Then I'll shut up shop and we'll go out on the town for the rest of the afternoon.'

Which we did. I remember little or nothing of the afternoon. Presumably we spent most of the time in a pub or café, because I do remember that we talked and talked. He did most of the talking – not that he wasn't a very willing listener, but I was more than happy just to sit at his feet. Of course I told him how, as a teenager, I came across his first story collection, *The Daring Young Man on the Flying Trapeze*, in the Cork Public Library and of its everlasting effect on me. That disclosure gave him great joy and he asked which of the stories in it I liked most. It didn't matter that it had been so long since I read the collection, many of the stories had formed part of my literary DNA so I was able to trot out some titles for him – its opening story, Seventy Thousand Assyrians, Seventeen, War, Sleep in Unheavenly Peace, and the title story itself. He nodded but said nothing about them until night came when Ita and I were sitting with him after dinner and then he said, 'I'm glad you liked Seventy

Thousand Assyrians. I liked it too. That's why I put it first in the book. Do you remember it?'

Of course I did. It was about himself, a down-and-out young Armenian who hadn't had a haircut in forty days and forty nights, so he went down to the Barber College in Third Street, San Francisco, for a fifteen cent trim. The trainee barber who attended him was a young Assyrian who 'sounded tired, not physically but spiritually'; the Assyrians had been a great people once, but now they were only 'a topic in history'. Just seventy thousand left in the whole world. And Saroyan had calculated that at that time his Armenians were not much better off – less than a million would have been as many as they could muster. I remembered it all.

'You understand it,' Bill said. 'You felt it, as the Assyrian felt it, as I felt it, and as you, a Jew, would have felt it.' When I first read the story it would not have been later than about 1940. I hadn't asked myself then why I felt it as I did, but now, in 1976, as we sat and talked, with six million Jews wiped out, I felt it even more.

Apart from the stories, what particularly fired me was the special preface he wrote for the Penguin edition some years later, explaining how the collection came into being.

Around Christmas-time, 1933, I learned that *Story* Magazine had accepted my story The Daring Young Man on the Flying Trapeze . . . this was my first acceptance by a magazine with national importance, and a national audience. I deliberately decided to take advantage of this opportunity. I decided, further, to do so with style.

I decided to write at least one short story a day for at least thirty days, and to send the stories to Whit Burnett and Martha Foley his wife, editors of *Story*.

. . . For about thirty-two days I wrote at least one short story a day and put it in the mail for the editors. Before beginning to do so, however, I wrote to the editors and told them what I was going to do . . . after they had read two or three of the eleven or twelve stories they had received from me by that time, they sent me a short note urging me to keep it up . . . When I was ready to rest, the editors had thirty-five or thirty-six stories from me . . .

This is the story, more or less. Every now and then I read over one or another of these stories. It does my heart good.

For me to read that preface now does not do *my* heart much good because I cannot imagine that Irish short story writers will ever again have a platform of national importance such as the *Irish Press* 'New Irish Writing' provided in publishing at least one new story every week, some sixty or so each year. Saroyan was familiar with 'New Irish Writing' because in 1975 he accepted my invitation to be the non-Irish adjudicator – Brian Moore being the Irish one – of the stories by previously unpublished writers contending for that year's Hennessy 'New Irish Writing' Literary Awards, just as in 1952, when I sent him a copy of *Irish Writing* and asked him if he would be guest-writer for a forthcoming issue, he immediately obliged with one of his typical, discursive, web-weaving stories entitled 'Four Hours for "Irish Writing"'.

Before he left Ita and me that night in 1976, he gave me two hundred dollars to buy any new Irish books of my choice and send them to him, which I gladly did. My parting tribute to him was to get my copy of *The Daring Young Man on the Flying Trapeze* and show him how much-thumbed

and cover-bedraggled it had become through so many readings. He took out his pen – red ink – grasped the book, opened
the fly leaf and wrote a moving message to commemorate his
visit. Almost two months later I had a long letter from him
telling me where he had been in the meantime, what he had
been writing and what he had been thinking. It ended 'My
best to both of you and keep sending the good stuff. So
Long! Bill.' He died in 1981. His memory, ever-welcome,
haunts me.

William Saroyan, Armenian-American, was the first
hyphenated American I had ever met and twelve years passed
before I came into contact with more of that double-fronted
American dynasty. One day in 1988 I was approached by the
Irish representative of The Irish American Cultural Institute
and asked if I would be interested in doing a lecture tour for
their Irish Perspectives programme. I had never been to
America, so this was an opportunity I could hardly pass up. I
took it for granted that I would be required to talk about
some aspect of contemporary Irish literature, which would
mean having to prepare a lecture in advance. I could take the
chance to talk about the genius of the Irish short story – to
do so in the land where the modern short story had been
born would be a privilege and a pleasure. I would bring Ita
and our nine-year-old daughter, Sarah, with me and together
we would have the time of our life. Yes, yessir, I indicated
that I definitely was interested.

Came the shock. What The Irish-American Cultural
Institute would like, what the members of their chapters
throughout America would be fascinated to learn about
from me was the story of Jewish history and experience in
Ireland. For a moment I was completely thrown. I had a little
knowledge of Irish-Jewish history prior to the turn of the

nineteenth century when the wave of refugees from the pogroms of eastern Europe, including my grandparents, brought to Ireland the nucleus of its twentieth-century Jewish population. However, a little research would fill out the tale. So I had no need to feel any worry about the Institute's chosen topic. Indeed, what caused me some initial concern was the proposed itinerary, fifteen cities in thirteen days. It seemed I would be spending almost as much time in planes as on the ground; indeed, as I had to make some half-dozen out and back connections through my hub airport, Detroit, I felt as if I had enough air-hours clocked up to claim my wings. Fortunately, my wife and daughter did not need to accompany me everywhere. On some occasions they were able to have two full days exploring a particular city before we met up together again. That way they saw much more of the US and its people than I did.

The talk I delivered was always well attended. Clearly I was something in the nature of a *rara avis* to these Irish-Americans, and also to the American Jews among them who usually made themselves known to me afterwards. The effect on them of my Cork accent was one of wonderment, reminding me of my joke about the two Chinese Jews, for not only did I not look Jewish, I didn't even sound Jewish. Some of the episodes I recounted evoked a special response from audiences, gasps at the story of my maternal grandfather's unbelievable good fortune in his escape from Lithuania when the train stopped at the border and the Russian guards, searching for Jewish youths trying to avoid conscription, mistook him for a non-Jew because of his blond hair. Many of my other historical titbits caused similar astonishment – that the first record of Jews in Ireland dated from 1078 when five came from England or Normandy to Turlough O'Brien, King of Munster, to plead that their brethren be allowed settle in Munster, but were quickly sent packing; that when Henry the Third of England was fighting the Welsh in 1244, he levied special taxes on his British subjects to pay for the war, decreeing that any Jew who did not pay up would be deported to Ireland; that in 1656 when Cromwell was spreading devastation and terror throughout the country, one of his advisers put to him a scheme to solve both the Irish and Jewish problems in a single stroke by making Ireland a National Home for the Jews. The mind grows dizzy at the thought of Ireland becoming Meyerland. Applause greeted the information that around 1740 a Cork Jew, Michael Praeger, emigrated to America where he became a founder-director of the Insurance Company of North America in Philadelphia, applause which in Philadelphia itself turned to cheers. However, I usually provoked a chorus of light-hearted boos when I followed that with the admission that when ultra-Orthodox Jews were leaving Ireland for the US, they were often known to recite 'And now, goodbye O Lord, we are going to America.'

By and large I found that hard, historical fact mixed with some light relief was the ideal prescription for a successful evening, so I was glad I was able to make my closing offering the story of the Irish priest, travelling in America, who came across in a small town a store with a sign over its door reading 'Cohen and O'Toole'. He went in, to be greeted by an old man with a beard and wearing a *yarmulkah*. 'I've just come in to tell you,' said the priest, 'how wonderful it is that your people and mine have become such good friends – even partners. That's a surprise.' The old man sighed. 'I've got a bigger surprise for you,' he replied. 'I'm O'Toole.'

For a stay-at-home like me that American tour was an education. Even though my time for sight-seeing was curtailed, the compensation was the experience of meeting scores of Irish-Americans whose dual-source lavish hospitality and personal warmth were quite breathtaking. My family and I were hosted everywhere we went by committee members of the Institute, some of whose houses were marble-pillared palaces, while others were small but beautifully-appointed apartments. In one city where I wasn't accompanied by Ita and Sarah I had the experience of being accommodated in a monastery where my room was as comfortable as a five-star hotel and my host a conversation-loving monk!

Our final venue, San Antonio, Texas, was certainly the most spectacular of the whole tour. It was evening when we arrived in the city, the temperature was around 90°, and the last lap of our journey to the home of the local priest where we were to stay was held up in the city centre by a parade. Bands, dancing, fancy dress, floats, all the abandon of what looked like a typical Mexican hooley, it was by far the most exotic, colourful and noisy parade we had ever seen. It took some time before we were able to reach the priest's house, only to find that our meeting had to be a brief hello and goodbye. Unexpectedly he had to leave immediately for some neighbouring town and had time only to tell us that the local historian, John Flannery, would be taking us under his wing in the morning, and to give us a hasty run-through his house before he left us to it and it to us.

After our long journey to San Antonio and the extreme heat, despite the lateness of the hour we were very glad to have a good night's sleep and be up fresh and breakfasted to greet our guide, John Flannery, who in fact was rather more than just the local historian. John Brendan Flannery was an instructor in economics and international relations at St Mary's University, San Antonio, who had emigrated from

Ireland at the age of 15 and settled in Texas in 1966. His knowledge of the State and of the history and roots of its Irish residents was immense – hence his reputation as 'local historian' – and before we departed next day he presented me with a copy of his absorbing, and lavishly-illustrated book, *The Irish Texans*.

He brought us on a tour of as many of the important sights of San Antonio as there was time for, pride of place being of course given to the Alamo, the fortress that had fallen to the Mexican forces in 1836 when many Irish-born settlers died. John Flannery's running commentary and brief account of the battle fought by Texans for its independence was a fascinating and stirring cameo of Irish-American history.

San Antonio was the second last city scheduled for my talk, the final being Boston, where I had spoken on the day of my arrival in the US, and where I would give a repeat prior to our departure home. A radio interview had been arranged by one of their local stations, and it gave rise to a particular question-and-answer exchange which for me ranks as a highlight of my US tour.

The interviewer, who was as sharply with-it as all American chat show presenters seem to be, went through the expected enquiries about my impressions of the cities I had visited and of America in general, moving on then to a brief run through Jewish-Irish history, followed by a light-hearted question – which I knew would wrap up the interview – asking if I had ever seen a leprechaun.

'No, never,' I admitted.

'But you have a lot of leprechauns in Ireland, haven't you?'

'Oh yes, but I haven't been lucky enough to spot one.'

'Any Jewish leprechauns?'

'No, not one.'

'No Jewish leprechauns! Why not?'

'We could never find a surgeon skilled enough to circumcise a leprechaun.'

The broadcast ended in an outburst of hilarity. It was the best spontaneous joke I had ever made!

CHAPTER TWENTY-SEVEN

The Joyce of Yiddish,
the Oy Vay of Irish

In 1968 Leo Rosten, an American Jew, wrote a book entitled *The Joys of Yiddish*. What is Yiddish? It is one of two languages I should be able to speak, but cannot. The other one is Irish, in which I was fluent when I left school but that fluency applied only to reading, writing and understanding. I never knew to what extent, or even whether, I could hold a conversation in Irish, because conversing in Irish was never a requirement. Apart from the simplest of sentences, it was not encouraged or practised by any of the different Irish teachers I had in secondary school throughout six or seven years. As a result of such a crass dereliction of duty to schoolchildren and to the native language, and the equally crass accompanying Government-imposed policy of compulsion, Irish was as unloved as Latin, and though not quite as dead, it was in these thirties and for decades afterwards struggling to stay alive. For me, however, although my love of Irish poetry led me to continue translating it for some years after I left school, not having any need or opportunity to speak the language, I never tried to, and so have always had to regard myself as an Irishman who did not speak his own language.

But what about Yiddish? The word means 'Jewish' but is not a synonym for 'Jewish'. It is the name of a language that is almost a thousand years old. Born in the early medieval period, it was a fusion of various tenth-century urban German dialects which became the vernacular of the Jews, and as the Jewish people were constantly forced to move from country to country, Yiddish was colonised by the language spoken in the places where the refugees settled.

Yiddish and Hebrew are entirely different. Hebrew was a sacred language, the medium for holy writings, religious services, theology and *Talmud*, and suitably modernised was declared to be one of two official languages when the State of Israel was founded in 1948, the other one being Arabic. Yiddish had been shunned since the revival of Hebrew, completed before 1920, because although it was 'the language of the heart' and the record of Jewish history, it was also the looking-back language of exile and suffering. Official antipathy to it in Israel lessened somewhat in later years and Yiddish newspapers, magazines and theatre were revived. But the transience of contemporary cultural fashions means that in no area can revival guarantee survival, and so the joke (?) recounted by Leo Rosten in *The Joys of Yiddish* – to which I am indebted for much joy and instruction – may again become apposite.

On a bus in Tel Aviv, a mother was talking animatedly, in Yiddish, to her little boy – who kept answering her in Hebrew. And each time the mother said, 'No, no! Talk Yiddish!'

An impatient Israeli, overhearing this, exclaimed, 'Lady, why do you insist the boy talk Yiddish instead of Hebrew?'

Replied the mother, 'I don't want him to forget he's a Jew.'

Why is it that although my parents spoke fluent Yiddish, I have only a smattering of Yiddish words and phrases? The reason, of course, is that although in my grandparents' homes in Lithuania only Yiddish was spoken, in Ireland they learned English by reading the newspapers and conversing with their children both in English and Yiddish. However, when two of their children met, married and became my parents, Yiddish – as I have explained elsewhere in these pages – was used by them in the home only as a secret language when they did not want their children to know what they were saying. So for me Leo Rosten's title, *The Joys of Yiddish*, becomes The Joyce of Yiddish, reminding me of the secret language of *Finnegans Wake* which academics and Joyce-worshippers spend years decoding and debating, but cannot speak.

And what do I mean by the *Oy Vay* of Irish? *Oy Vay* means 'Oh, pain', particularly emotional pain in spades, the equivalent of the Irish 'Och óchón!' It is often used in its fuller form, '*Oy vay iz mir*!' (Oh, woe is me!), a version I was very familiar with at home as it was frequently ejaculated by my mother to express her grief over any of my transgressions. So the '*Oy Vay* of Irish' is a voicing of lament for the Sisyphean strait of the Irish language today. What will be its fate? It is surely as unrealistic to imagine it would ever replace the English language in Ireland as it would be to expect Yiddish ever to replace Hebrew in Israel.

I ask myself what difference it would have made to me, as a writer, if my Irish had never fallen into desuetude. Would I have written in it? I know I wouldn't. Why not? For the same reason that I wouldn't have written in Yiddish even had I been able to speak it. Primarily what mattered to me was not the language I was using, but what I was using it for: my material. And primarily my material was my identity as a Jew and the subjective conflicts that engendered. Not – very definitely not – that I regretted the Jewishness of being a Jew. What I regretted was my inability to transform my material – my identity and its consequential, ever-present feeling of rootlessness – into great literature, and so that material became an incubus I periodically placated by producing novels and short stories which, despite the fact that they were published, sold satisfactorily and were liked by some, were for me irrelevant and forgettable. But nothing is ever forgotten. The deeper it is buried, the longer it lives. Yet there is a twin consolation: I am not a great worrier, living – as I have always tried to live – by the principle that if you have a problem about which you can do nothing, then don't worry, because to worry is to betray your principle *ab initio*; and I am certain that even if I had been able to write the great twentieth or twenty-first century Irish-Jewish novel about being a Jewish *déraciné*, it would not have solved anything. I would still be a Jewish *déraciné*.

Yet isn't Ireland my birthplace and my home? Yes, I was born in Ireland and, apart from thirteen years in London, have lived here all my life. But as Wellington said, 'Because a man is born in a stable, that doesn't make him a horse'; and while I'm legally an Irishman, and while being Irish may provide the tinder for my everyday passions, the Jew in me is branded on my soul as indelibly as the numbers on the arms of the Holocaust victims and survivors.

I have never visited Israel. I have never desired to go there, a reluctance based on two opposing fears: that I would like it and that I wouldn't. No doubt that makes me some sort of a mixed-up Yid, but I feel sure that to visit Israel must leave me even more mixed-up than before. If I went there and, for whatever reason, did not like it, I wouldn't be surprised or disappointed, because I have always considered the Jews to be like other people, only more so. Individually of course the majority of Jews/Israelis are as civilised as most other peoples. But people in the mass are a different animal, manipulable, as has been tragically demonstrated, and riven by apparently ineradicable traditional hatreds.

If, for argument's sake, I liked being in Israel – but no, even if I did, I cannot see myself as feeling it to be my home. I suspect that for me it is a matter of temperament. Loner-inclined, I would never, like Groucho Marx, want to be a member of any club that would have me, and the ghetto gene, my internal birthmark, would almost certainly rebel at the idea of settling in Israel. Being settled in Ireland from birth has put me in a completely different world, one in which I grew up and was educated and so was able to imbibe it at my own pace, one in which I could feel secure, in which I could become involved on my own bent. What it could not do was make of me a complete Irishman in the sense of that phrase which is now, thankfully, increasingly out of date. I am of Ireland, which is what matters. I know that, because I know that if both Israel and Ireland were taking part in the UEFA Champions League, I would want Israel to win, except if they were meeting Ireland. A draw at full time would, I suppose, be acceptable, but in that event I would look to Ireland to win the penalty shoot-out.

CHAPTER TWENTY-EIGHT

I Remember! I Remember!

My first meeting with Seán O'Faoláin was when I visited him in 1946 and invited him to edit my planned quarterly, *Irish writing*. I didn't meet him again until very shortly after I started the *Irish Press* 'New Irish Writing' page when he phoned and invited me to come and see him and his wife, Eileen. I have no recollection of that visit – I was probably too nervous for any memory of it to have survived – but I do recall the next one, made at my request. Its purpose was to ask his advice on whether I should accept Tim Pat Coogan's second-time offer of the *Irish Press* literary editor's chair.

Seán took me into his study, sat me down opposite his desk and half-hitched himself up on its edge to face me.

'Give me one good reason why you shouldn't take the job,' he said.

'The truth is I'm afraid of it. I've never done anything in that line before, and I'm so out of touch with things in Ireland.'

He snorted. 'I said one *good* reason. Fear is the very worst of all reasons.'

I remained silent. I knew he was right.

'All you need is someone, apart from Tim Pat, to tell you you'd be mad not to say yes. Well, that's what I'm telling you. It would be the making of you.'

This time *I* snorted. Seán laughed, lifted himself off his desk, rubbing his bottom.

'There's no more to be said. Come on, I'll make you a cup of tea. A drop of Paddy would be more to the point, but then you're not a drinking man.'

He led me back to the sitting room where Eileen was ensconced in her armchair from where she could look out at her beloved garden, and Seán was soon back with his afternoon tea tray.

He had been right, of course. Immediately he delivered his advice, I realised that all I was looking for was exactly the sort of support he represented – a trusted companion, as it were, in the new venture – and the forceful brevity of his chosen words had authoritatively dismissed any possible alternative. His confidence in me, which I took as implied behind his advice, reminded me, on my way home that evening, of the earlier occasion he had told me to go home and do it myself – when he declined, on that sunny afternoon in his garden, to be the editor of *Irish Writing*, but added many hints to help me on the way. Help – that, I saw then and see again now, was something O'Faoláin never withheld. He always gave it with a touch of style that disguised any trouble it might have put him to. There was the P.S., 'Make any use of this you like,' to the four-page letter he had sent me explaining why he couldn't write an article on 'Translating from the Irish' for my *Poetry Ireland* 'Irish Translations' issue. And while encouraging me to become the *Irish Press* literary editor caused him no inconvenience, what it led to certainly did.

To mark my appointment I asked him if he would allow me to interview him on his writing career. He agreed, but on my return to the office with the tape recorder I had used, I found that – probably due to my ineptitude with even the most simple device – not a word had been reproduced. Flustered with panic and stricken with embarrassment, I phoned and told him what had happened.

'Have you got a copy of your questions?' he said.

'Yes, I have.'

'Good. Send it to me and I'll let you have my replies.'

The replies were so detailed and extensive that they ran to half a page of the *Irish Press* on each of two consecutive days.

My frequent Sunday afternoon visits to Seán and Eileen became a highlight for me. Their wide-ranging exchanges were both educational and stimulating, but what really remains in my memory is the relationship between these two partners. For partners is how they came across. The cut and thrust whenever their opinions diverged, the assumed scorn of Eileen's rejections, the good-humoured resignation in Seán's supportive arguments, were the clear bonds of shared love between two equals. For me such sport was a promise of love's rewards, for being at the time happily committed to the writer, Ita Daly – and she to me – we were soon to regard ourselves as engaged. I was, consequently, very eager to introduce her to Seán and Eileen, a meeting which was the beginning of almost twenty years of golden moments and of a friendship between Seán and Ita which for him appeared to have a particularly special appeal.

Even at almost seventy – his age when these visits commenced – Seán O'Faoláin's masculine good looks were not only as impervious to the passage of time as they had appeared in photographs of his thirties, forties, and even fifties, but now that early allure had the composed credential of maturity. Always elegantly attired – Seán was never merely dressed – and always wearing his trilby at his accustomed rakish angle on the few occasions he came out for a brief walk with Ita and me, he still had an eye for the opposite sex. Now, however, its twinkle was not his only tribute to female beauty, or his only almost wistful indulgence of the romantic that, on his own recorded admission, he had always been. His pen still spoke for him.

We had visited him and Eileen a few times before our marriage, and in a letter he had occasion to write me in January of 1972 his final paragraph was, 'Why don't you bring out that Blessed Damosel of yours some Sunday: any, including next Sunday, if only you ring a couple of days beforehand so as not to frighten these 2 old Senior Citizens with too unexpected a shock of delight. We will give you afternoon tea (Fortnum & Mason's) or sherry cum lemon peel *à la* J.B. Yeats.'

Many were our visits after our marriage, always at his phoned request because I was still at least sufficiently in awe of him to wait for an invitation. I know that if his phone call had not come with reasonable frequency, both Ita and I would have missed it, for the welcome extended by the two Senior Citizens was unfailingly enthusiastic. He always seated Ita on a couch beside him so that he could the more easily engage her in conversation, and the mostly three-cornered discussions between the two of them and Eileen, with me putting in an occasional spoke, found Seán at his most sparkling, witty and complimentary. Ita was aware of the chemistry her presence set off, and because it was always light, flattering, natural and lovable, it wasn't ever in the slightest degree embarrassing for anyone present.

Almost all his letters were chock-full of gems of literary criticism, usually – though not always – about Irish writers.

When I sent him a copy of *Best Irish Short Stories 2* which I edited in 1977 for the now long defunct publishers Paul Elek – it was in fact my choice of the best new Irish stories from books and periodicals of the previous year – he replied with a two-page account of his reactions. I had one of Ita's stories in it, about which his comment was,

> Tell your golden wife that I have been thrice unfaithful to her. I read Kate Cruise O'Brien first, then Maeve Kelly, then Jennifer Johnston, and left her for Clare Boylan. (Yah, coward! You put all the 5 women on the cover.)' '. . . Kate C. O'B. could be a most welcome comic writer, as could also Clare Boylan.' '. . . That, if I were giving a prize, would leave Jennifer J., Maeve Kelly and Trevor, and Trevor would go out for the uncritical reason that he is beyond prizes. I wouldn't know whom to choose as between Jennifer J. and Maeve. J. did it so swiftly: her point is such a shock in (and shock to) the sentiments it is as admirable technically as the one circling line of a Matisse drawing – swoosh. But being who we all are *we* fill in the familiar outlines for her and she counts on that. Maeve has a subtler point (I confess I felt at times lost in her coils of symbolism) and *HAD* to work her needle delicately and long . . . For virtue I think I'd choose Maeve, and her sort of cool French pleasure, a theme worthy of a novel . . .' P.S. All the above most certainly not that my opinions are of the least import. They just prove that I got your gift book and in various ways enjoyed it so say Thanks the only way I can – like the Jongleur de Notre D.

> My (faithless) love to Ita.

In 1980 I sent him a copy of Ita's short story collection, *The Lady with the Red Shoes*, eliciting a reply which commenced, 'All my regards to Ita Daily, and nightly, with salt. No sweetness needed', followed by six pages of almost line by line comment, criticism and expert advice, prefaced, at one point, with 'In a phrase, dear-darling Ita (if you are, as I feel sure you will be, shown this letter) . . .' He ended the letter – I always particularly enjoyed Seán's endings – 'Chère collègue (the MCPs have calmly made the noun masculine but let's reject them), Please do, before I shuffle off this mortal coil, write me half a dozen stories like the ones here I so much like. Blessings to you, David, to Ita, Love.'

The most intriguing letter I ever received from him is undated and is evidently a critique of two stories of my own I sent him. He does not name the first of them though he does suggest a change of title to 'Brothers', but the clues are insufficient for me to identify the story; the second one he does name: 'The shorter "Bitter Laughter" is a perfect sketch.' There is no copy or record of such a story among my papers, nor have I the slightest recollection of it. What could it have been, I wonder, given that the title is a translation of a much used Yiddish phrase? How frustrating to have written a story Seán O'Faoláin thought 'perfect' but no longer to be able to enjoy it myself!

Undoubtedly, however, for Ita and me the most moving and precious of his letters is the one humorously headed 'Some date in December 1988'.

Dear Both,

At last '88'. The fax o' life. You are (or become) a short story. You two are become the longest and oldest (or is it youngest?) of our friends. Your only rivals for this fame in this remote Robinson Crusoe island are Dan Binchy and Paddy Lynch . . .'

The coda of this letter, mostly about his and Eileen's ailments and his own failing memory, is:

I have discovered a quite interesting author. I took him at random from my shelves. More than interesting. A discovery. Name: O'Faoláin. You see? I am a good former writer.

Our last visit took place some time after Eileen's death. Seán was in a Nursing Home, in bed, hardly conscious, hardly even recognisable as the lovely man we had known. I think he knew us. He certainly recognised Ita and held on to her hand as long as we were allowed stay.

Some months earlier, before his health had so badly deteriorated, we had arranged to take him out to lunch. At the last moment I was unable to go, so Ita went alone. When she came back, she passed on to me Seán's parting message. It was, 'Tell David I'm sorry he couldn't come. But not that sorry.'

Ever the gallant, for Seán O'Faoláin romantic Ireland had not been dead and gone, merely – like himself – ageing. With his passing, only memories remain.

Nowadays, when I think of Seán O'Faoláin I often think of Cork. The city where we were both born and grew up would not have shown a great deal of change in the twenty-four years between our respective births, except of course in Patrick Street, its main thoroughfare, one whole side of which, along with the City Hall, had been burned to the ground by the Black and Tans. Nevertheless, in writing *A Land Not Theirs*, my novel about the Cork Jewish community of those days before I was born, I had to ignore the city as I knew it and imagine it as Seán would have known it. In a letter he wrote me about the novel – actually it was a full-blown review of the book for my eyes only, his preferred Jongleur de Notre Dame way of saying Thanks – he sympathetically referred to this problem, so I was especially proud when Robert Nye, reviewing *A Land Not Theirs* for *The Guardian*, wrote '. . . for anyone who knows Cork, it captures the sights and sounds and smells of that city better than anything since Frank O'Connor in his prime.'

It is now getting on for half a century since I lived in Cork, but its 'sights and sounds and smells' grow in recollection even more evocatively as the city and I both enter the new millennium, Cork new-fashioned, I so relatively old-fashioned. A little over one hundred and fifty years ago William Makepeace Thackeray visited Ireland and wrote about Cork in his *Irish Sketch Book*. The Cork-born poet Augustus Young composed a verse-translation of extracts from that section which I published in 'New Irish Writing' in 1974, and much of it helps stir my pot of memories to the top.

For me an especially apposite stanza was that devoted to 'The Earnest Young Men'.

These are Ireland's Wandering Jews,
the earnest young Corkmen who choose
to leave it – to better themselves.
Youth well-spent on library shelves
courting the mind, they would be fit
companions for Hamlet. Take the ship:
return each year to Grand Parade
far-fetched wisdom to those that stayed.

He had a verse about Father Theobald Mathew, the Temperance Priest, in tribute to whose memory a statue was placed just before Patrick's Bridge, facing Cork's main street. The statue was, in my day, the terminus of the local bus service and it was there while waiting one afternoon for my bus, I witnessed an exchange that was *echt*-Irish, at least for the times that were in it. I told the story in my Introduction to *The Bodley Head Book of Irish Short Stories*, but as it is one of the most quintessential of my Cork memories, telling it again will wire me straight back to the past.

A station-wagon approached the bus queue kerb, its driver anxiously searching for a place to park. The area on either side of the bus-stop had, of course, to be kept clear, but there seemed to be just about a car's length free space between one of the white boundary lines and the row of cars parked beyond it. Into that space the station-wagon just fitted and out of the vehicle stepped the driver, an ageing, tweedy, law-abiding type. He immediately proceeded to inspect his position so as to make sure he was in no danger of being ticketed for illegal parking. What he saw brought a puzzled frown to his face. Certainly his four wheels had cleared the white line, but the rear of the station-wagon protruded over it and into the bus-stop's space. A technical infringement, at the very least? Undecided, he turned to the queue, and addressing no one in particular, asked, 'Do you think I'd get away with that?' For a while no one in particular hazarded an answer until an ancient, wizened, diminutive countryman took off his cap, slowly scratched his chin, and replied, 'Well, sir, 'tis like this: are yeh lucky?'

For me that answer encapsulated some basic elements of the Irish way of seeing as well as the pith of their way of saying. It had the touch of fatalism inculcated into them by centuries of religious rigour and inclement weather, a large dash of the superstition that was still rife in custom and convention, especially in rural areas, and a hint of the accommodations sometimes made necessary with *force majeur* on the temporal plane impressed on them by the weight of their country's history. And the very form of the reply – a question answering a question – was a summation of the whole Irish temperament, the implicit belief that in this world there were no clear answers; inklings and possibilities were the most one could expect.

Augustus Young's verse on Thackeray's 'The Flood' section reminded me of some of Patrick Street's older business premises whose fronts, because street-level entrances were often under water, had a second entrance up a flight of steps:

> Founded on marsh, Cork often floods
> and on makeshift rafts the young bloods
> gondolier the ladies from shop
> to shop, with umbrellas on top.
> A veritable Venice it is,
> Sunday's Well to The Mall. A mist
> rises at nightfall. From the sewers
> rats emerge and the flaneur poor
> perch on Patrick's Bridge, with doodeens
> smoke-happy, to study the ruins.

At least the 'flaneur poor' of Cork perched on Patrick's Bridge waiting only for the waters to subside is an infinitely kinder, more moving image than Frank O'Connor drew of Limerick in his Introduction to his translation of Brian Merriman's 'The Midnight Court', where 'leaning over the bridge in the twilight, looking up the river at the wild hills of

Clare from which old Merryman came down so long ago, you can hear a Gregorian choir chanting *Et expecto ressurectionem mortuorum*, and go back through the street where he walked, reflecting that in Limerick there isn't much else to expect.'

Thackeray's 'Leaving (by river)' is thus versified by Augustus Young:

Leave Cork behind in the death-throes
of swaggering hopes. Porticoes
of three new churches still unroofed:
statues unveiled, heroes rebuffed.
Through Lakelands where great Monkey trees
on Little Isle bow as you leave:
heavenly outlets from this place –
wish the same to its populace.

The poet's lines add an almost three-dimensional vibrancy to Thackeray's verbal sketches of Cork in 1843, but I do not imagine I would want a ticket for any time-machine to transport me back to these days. Yet I don't know – if one such conveyance were available, there are moments in Cork's storied history I would wish to have been present to witness. I close my eyes and the time-machine of imagination makes me one of the packed masses outside the Victoria Hotel being addressed by Charles Stewart Parnell; to Blackpool Bridge over which Sir Walter Scott drives in a carriage and pair, Maria Edgeworth beside him, before they transfer to a barouche to go and kiss the Blarney Stone; to another bridge, where stand the Rev. Arthur Nicholls and his bride, Charlotte Bronte, admiring Shandon and listening to its bells; to Beamish's Brewery for a pint of porter with Thomas Moore;

to old Christ Church whence emerges Edmund Spenser with his bride, Elizabeth Boyle of Youghal; to the Western Road where the cheering citizens unyoke the horses from Daniel O'Connell's carriage and draw The Liberator along themselves. And from the Western Road I float my memory-machine around the corner where from the front bedroom window of the home of my youth the only event of interest to see was the players in a cricket match opposite, but behind my closed lids I can watch Queen Victoria's carriage pass on its traversal of the Mardyke.

I open my eyes and it all disappears, except the framed drawing from the contemporary *Illustrated London News* of the Royal visit passing under the Mardyke Arch, which now hangs in the hallway of my home in Dublin.

The city of Cork and Seán O'Faoláin – one helped shape my youth, the other helped guide my path. I was lucky.

CHAPTER TWENTY-NINE

Going Out on a Spin

'The tragedy of old age is not that one is old, but that one is young.' Who said that? Oscar Wilde of course. But there is an alternative way of dealing with old age. Acceptance? Resignation? Fortitude? Keeping busy? All reasonable reactions, but what about a touch of Jewish humour?

Mrs Levy, ninety years old, went to see her doctor. After examining her, the doctor said, 'Mrs Levy, modern medicine can do many things, but it can't make you any younger.'

'Who wants to get younger?' Mrs Levy replied. 'I want to get older.'

A joke is all very well, but it can be really effective only once. Still, the idea is right: treat ageing with humour. Not with belly-laughter of course – unless you hope to be lucky enough to die laughing – but with the sort of humour that sends it up. Wilde's best sayings often arrive at his alternative truths by turning something upside-down or inside-out. It is done with original spin, which for me has a strong attraction. I have always felt that inside me is a Wilde man trying to get out, but not possessing a crumb of his genius, my sort of spin is to play with and on words. Like my old age one: 'When all is sad and dun, old age is a time of mellow fruitlessness.' Though old age doesn't have to be fruitless, bending something is often a good way of testing it, so I don't mind if some of my results bend the truth a little. At that stage it's just a game anyway, one way of playing out time. Which brings me back to my original buried treasure, that humour is the antidote, the syringe with which to prick the bubble of old age.

Of course it doesn't always work, the hardest person to convince of anything being oneself. And as one enters the vestibule of old age only once in life, that's the time to bear in mind Flann O'Brien's *aperçu* that only people of no experience have theories. Then again, as times change *tempus* fudges, and in today's world of dotty.com millionaires, Harold Nicolson's comment that success should come late in life to compensate for the loss of youth prompts one to wonder what in these millionaires' old age will compensate them for *their* loss of youth. Perhaps the question won't arise, for the trend is for youth itself to become an out-of-date, non-existent concept.

Growing old induces contemplation. The more that nourishment for pursuits of the mind are driven out of the market by the mindless processes of dumbing-down, and the more one sees the extent of corruption in public life and of dereliction of duty in political life, then the more angry one gets. I get very angry very much, but having a lot to get angry about is one of the big consolations of old age. It makes me spin. Hence my cynical spin: duty is only skin-deep.

My pilfering of 'beauty' from the foregoing is in a way an act of protection. Nowadays beauty is an endangered species, subjected to exploitation by wholesale and retail commercialisation. It exists now in the lie of the beholder. Even the beauty of nature, the beauty of the world of one's youth, is in one way or another, in one place and another, being ravaged. Historic buildings, whether officially protected or not, the skyline, cityscapes, all subject to vandalisation by developers under the brandishment of improvement. Who ever heard of nature needing to be improved! Their thing of beauty is a ploy forever, a sophisticated form of crime. None of your common, thuggish smash-and-grab, it's now grab-and-smash.

And art? Art, how are yeh! Sick. It's the do-it-yourself age. You have no voice but you can one-finger pluck a guitar, so with just a little luck you'll be a hit. If you're female, all you have to do is play your rump card – audiences cheer when sex rears its ugly rear. If you're down and out and haven't a place to sleep, you'll find an unmade bed in London's Tate Gallery of Modern Art that you can dive into and wake up an artist. It's the same with poetry: write a piece of worthless prose that has been chopped up without rhyme or reason, and hey presto you're a poet. Art used to reflect life, the difference being that in life the important thing was what one did, whereas in art it was how one did it. It used to be the only truth. Now it's not even the only lie. There are now no rules, no standards, and hardly a critic sane enough and brave enough to say that most of the emperors have no clothes. The aim of the poet should be to make the real unreal and the unreal real, but nowadays most poetry is something seen through prose-tinted spectacles. For the sake of a quiet life I'll put up with sacred cows, but I draw the line at sacred cow-dung.

Once upon a time when I got lost in words, I managed to slow the spin and question where I got my penchant for these verbal gyrations. I wrote down some of my favourite efforts, and seeing them on paper in black and white, seemed somehow to sound on the air the aural music that had kept the words silent in my mind. The penchant had produced pen-chants. But the question remained – whence all this minor-key logorrhoea? I decided it probably started with my grand-uncle Sopsa. He was an inveterate fantasist who believed all his creations, and he had a bevy of nephews, my very ungrand uncles, who would probably have invented him if he had not already existed. Instead, their competitive house-game was to outdo each other in making up ribald names for members of the original Cork Hebrew Community.

Cork? How come such a crazy gang of Jewish refugees fleeing the pogroms of their native, Czarist-ruled Lithuania should plonk themselves down in Ireland? And not even in Dublin, its capital, but in Cork, a place they would never have heard of. Tucked away among the bays of its southern coastline, it was often referred to by bumptious metropolitans as 'the arsehole of Ireland'. But Cork turned its posterior to this excretory insult. Hadn't it the biggest deep-water anchorage in all the then British Isles? Wasn't it the port of call for the magnificent, smoke-farting continental and American liners? Which, the legend goes, is how those fuddled, bedraggled, wandering Jews came there, for, having no English and hearing, as their ship docked, the calls of 'Cork, Cork', they took it to be their intended destination, New York, and so disembarked. My uncles had their own version, that 'Cork, Cork' was thought to be 'Pork, pork', thus causing the Kosher-Orthodox travellers to make for the shore *en masse*.

Whether or which, in the penultimate stage before preparing to meet one's Taker – or baker, if descent to an oven rather than ascent to a heaven is one's fate – the word-world of poetry provides the most satisfying of consolations. Not that I feel yet ready to risk a hostage to misfortune, but such a persuasive and soothing recourse sometimes takes one unawares. Favourites of my youth, those years of presumed immortality, swim up as if from nowhere. A verse such as Walter Savage Landor's 'Finis' returns:

> I strove with none, for none was worth my strife.
> Nature I loved and, next to Nature, Art:
> I warm'd both hands before the fire of life;
> It sinks, and I am ready to depart.

All very nice and cosy, but if anyone asks for me, I'm not yet quite ready to depart. Somewhat more to my current temper would be the opening verse of Emily Dickinson's 'Because I could Not Stop for Death':

> Because I could not stop for Death,
> He kindly stopped for me;
> The carriage held but just ourselves
> And Immortality.

I never find myself ready to accept Hamlet's prescription that '. . . the readiness is all', being more pugnaciously attuned to Dylan Thomas's 'Do Not Go Gentle Into That Good Night', described by Seamus Heaney as 'one of the best villanelles in the language':

> Do not go gentle into that good night,
> Old age should burn and rave at close of day;
> Rage, rage against the dying of the light.

But old age and death are parent and offspring, the difference between them being more than just that of tense: present imperfect old age is regret-ringed, body-betrayed, fear-stricken; death, the worst of those fears, is the devil that makes the future perfect by turning into an angel who stills every fear.

Today medical science predicts a not far off life span of well over a hundred years, but threescore and ten is still the approximate time when many begin to look back, if not in anger, then at least with a tired tut-tut over the mistakes of their past. I am not one of the tut-tutters – not that I didn't make mistakes – but I long ago resigned myself to accepting that the tide is always out for water under the bridge. Consequently, it is the occupation of my immediate past and the plan of inaction for my immediate future that most disturb me. The disturbance occasioned by my immediate past arises from a feeling that by committing to print the memoirs in the foregoing pages, I have been writing my own obituary which, obituarily, may amount to no more than a somewhat mixed brag.

Ironically, however, that particular worry was atomised by the turmoil that exploded in my mind the moment these memoirs were completed, instantly wrecking the no-plan for my immediate future. The explosion had a name, a four-letter word with which I had once been plagued: it was 'itch', that of writers.

In his recent book, *The Summer of a Dormouse*, John Mortimer, originator of the irresistible 'Rumpole of the Bailey' TV scripts, laid bare some of the perils visited on him by the creeping process of his own old age. He had not yet been tested by the warning of the ninety-three-year old playwright Christopher Fry who told him that 'after the age of 80 you seem to be having breakfast every five minutes', his more commonplace complaints being the increasing difficulty of guiding his feet into their stockings, the dangerous and strength-sapping struggle entailed in getting out of the bath, the pains of arthritis and the annoyance of failing eyesight. Writer's itch was not mentioned.

I have a list of my own aggravations. My mind has not begun to go – yet – but my memory has. Words fail me, meaning I often all but fail them when finding that only after long hesitation, brain-box perplexedly raised heavenwards, can I succeed in bringing to mind many that were once my daily friends. Further, if in any way feasible, I have to avoid book launches, readings and other literary functions, because I know those present will include many close acquaintances whose names have fled me. I once tried to persuade similarly afflicted friends that we should form a club for members who, on such occasions, would wear a badge announcing 'I drop names', but none would take me seriously. No joke, however, are the intermittent physical niggles, like knee joints that suddenly refuse to bend painlessly, teeth that only agonisingly will bite crusts from the hand that feeds them, and worst of all, fingers that can no longer be guaranteed to alight unerringly on the piano keys my most-loved composers chose.

But now, making all the foregoing fade into the background, the writer's itch that last assailed me after a thirty year respite has, only half that span later, returned. Why? Perhaps it is its punishment for my transgression in writing this autobiography and thus shocking both of us out of our retirement. I am reminded of the Jewish Day of Atonement 'Kol Nidrei' prayer in which one begs for pardon for a whole catalogue of sins, both the witting and the unwitting, and even others one could not possibly have committed. I should have remembered the poet Louis MacNeice's warning:

The sunlight on the garden
Hardens and grows cold,

We cannot cage the minute
Within its nets of gold;
When all is told
We cannot beg for pardon.

But even if we could, how would it help me who does not believe in a hereafter or in a controlling God? If I am wrong, about that, what then? I call on my illustrious co-religionist, the poet Heinrich Heine, who on his deathbed in 1856, speaking of Divine forgiveness said, 'Naturally, He will forgive me. *C'est son métier.*'

INDEX

A Land in Flames (Marcus),
234
A Land Not Theirs (Marcus),
220–235, 257–258
agents, 225, 226–229
auction, 230–232
reviews, 233
Abbey Theatre, 40
Abse, Dannie, 202
Adler, Larry, 205–206
alcohol consumption, 134, 186
whiskey, 53–56
Allen, Robert, 132, 134, 135
American Library, The, 67
American Mercury, 46
Amis, Kingsley, 176
anti-Semitism, 7–10, 12,
76–79, 157–159, 203
Armstrong, 20
art, 265
atheism, 192–196
Auden, W.H., 13

Bach, J.S., 23
Bantam Press, 229–232, 234
Banville, John, 204, 205
Banville, Vincent, 212
Barea, Arturo, 101
Barna, Viktor, 91
Baron, Abie, 122–123,
128–129
Baron, Manny, 122

Baron, Sid, 122
Baron's, Oxford Street,
122–129, 137
Barty-King, Mark, 229, 233
Battersby, Eileen, 201–202
BBC, 149
Beatles, The, 20
Beckett, Samuel, 100
in *Irish Writing*, 101–102,
149, 150, 172–173, 183,
202, 205
Waiting for Godot, 137–139
Beethoven, Ludwig von, 21,
23, 87, 202, 203
Behan, Brendan, 82, 173
Bell, The, 2, 37–38, 42, 167,
221
and Marcus, 103–104
Belloc, Hilaire, 32
Bellow, Saul, 201
Berlin, Irving, 20
Best Irish Short Stories, 255
betting, 4–5
Binchy, Maeve, 218, 219, 220,
222, 230
Black and Tans, 221, 224, 257
Bloomsbury, 213
Board of Trade, British, 64–65,
69, 79, 84, 97, 170
*Bodley Head Book of Irish
Short Stories, The*, 259
Bogarde, Dirk, 201

Bogdanov, Michael, 164
Bolger, Dermot, 210
Boll, Heinrich, 176
book reviewing, 199–204
Borodin, Peter, 210
Boucicault, Dion, 130
Bowen, Elizabeth, 167, 176
Boyd, John, 200
Boylan, Clare, 255
Boyle, Elizabeth, 262
Boyle, Patrick, 202, 205
Bradman, Don, 87
Brahms, J., 203
Braine, John, 205
Brandon Books, 207
Braybrooke, Neville, 208
Broderick, John, 205
Bronte, Charlotte, 261
Buckley, Cornelius ('Pug'), 3
Bull, Peter, 138
Burgess, Anthony, 205
Burnett, Whit, 238–239
Butler, Hubert, 208–209
Byrne, Gay, 233–234

Calder, Liz, 213
Campbell, Michael, 82–83
Campbell, Patrick, 81–82,
    95–96
Carlisle Jewish Club, Dublin,
    88–91
Carroll, Paul Vincent, 100
Catholic Church, 81
Chartered Insurance Institute,
    135, 140
Chaucer, Geoffrey, 50, 51
Chopin, F., 21, 23

Christian Brothers, 88, 174
Christy (picture-framer), 144
Churchill, Winston, 133
Clare, County, 165–166
Clarke, Arthur C., 201
Clarke, Austin, 100
Cluskey, May, 164
Coghill, Lady, 53, 56–57
Coghill, Sir Neville, 50–60
Colum, Mary, 84
Colum, Padraic, 84, 99
Coogan, Tim Pat, 180–183,
    202–203, 210, 251–252
    and 'New Irish Writing',
        170–171, 173–174
Cooke, Alistair, 201
Corgi Books, 234
Cork, 118, 133–134, 161
    bookshops, 197–198
    Jewish community, 6, 119,
        137, 190, 266
    in *A Land Not Theirs*, 219,
        221–224
    Marcus on, 257–262
Cork, County, 95
Cork Dramatic Society, 147
Cork Examiner, 42, 224
Cork Jewish Youth Club,
    88–91
Cork Public Library, 36–37,
    165, 237
Cork Symphony Orchestra,
    145
Corkery, Daniel, 95, 147–148,
    167
cricket, 14, 87–88
Cromwell, Oliver, 242

Cronin, Anthony, 99
Crosby, Bing, 20
Cumann na mBan, 78
cummings, e.e., 84
Curragh, Co. Kildare, 75–76
Cusack, Cyril, 202, 210–211
cycling, 92–94

Dahl, Roald, 176
Dail Eireann, 204
Daily Express, 212
Daily Herald, 182
Daly, Ita, 218, 222, 225, 237, 253, 254, 257
  marriage, 212–213
  short stories, 255–256
  USA trip, 240, 241, 243
Daring Young Man on the Flying Trapeze, The (Saroyan), 237–239
Day Lewis, Cecil, 13
Day of Atonement, 221, 269
de Valera, Eamon, 123, 165, 166
de Vere White, Terence, 205, 206–207
Debussy, C.A., 23
Deevy, Nell, 40–41
Deevy, Teresa, 40–41, 42
del Monte, Toti, 20
Delaney, Frank, 176, 232–233
Dickinson, Emily, 267
Dickson, Lovat, 109–113, 115, 116
Dillon, Edward, & Co., 176
Dolmen Press, 29, 99, 152–153, 200

'Dooley, Mr' (F.P. Dunne), 100–101
Drishane House, visit to, 50–61
Dublin
  canal, 153–154
  King's Inns, 13, 16–17, 23, 33
  Marcus returns to, 151–159
Dublin Magazine, The, 37–38, 167
Duil, 45
Dunne, Finley Peter, 100–101
Dunsany, Lord, 62, 100

Eason's, 82
Eden, Sir Anthony, 201
Edgeworth, Maria, 261
Eliot, T.S., 13
Elyan, Larry, 26–27, 28
emigration, 142–143
Envoy, 167
Evangelist, Brother, 8–9, 11
Evening Press, 160–164, 169, 175, 200

Faber, 210, 212
Farrell, James T., 100
Ferguson, Sir Samuel, 31
Feuchtwanger, Lion, 101
Fianna Fail, 213–216
Fisher, Eddie, 141
Flannery, John Brendan, 243–244
Foley, Martha, 238–239
Fowles, John, 205
Francis, Dick, 201
Fricker, Brenda, 210

Fridberg, Maurice, 28
Friedling, Mr, 221–222, 223,
    230
Friel, Brian, 95
Fry, Christopher, 268

Galbraith, J.P., 201
Gate Theatre, 164–165
Gemini Productions, 163–164
Geraldo, 20
Germany, 124–125, 157–159,
    247
Gershwin, George, 20
Gogarty, Oliver St John, 83,
    100
Goldberg, Gerald, 13
Golding, Bill, 164
Goodman, Benny, 20
Gordon, Mr, 131
Great Southern Railway, 75
Greene, David, 210
Greene, Graham, 151, 201
Greer, Germaine, 201
Grieg, E.H., 23
Guardian, The, 258
Guildhall Insurance Company,
    130–137, 140, 142, 183
Guy's photographers, 11–12

Haggadah, 10, 224
Hall, Henry, 20
Hamish Hamilton, 153, 174
Hammerstein brothers, 20
Hanley, James, 100
Harrison, Harold, 225–226
Hart-Davis, Rupert, 115
Healy, Shay, 164

Heaney, Seamus, 267
Hebrew, 247
Heifetz, Jascha, 119
Heine, Heinrich, 270
Hennessy Literary Awards,
    176, 213, 239
Henry III, King, 242
Higgins, F.R., 99
Hilda (Baron's), 123, 124–125,
    127, 128
Hill, Susan, 205
'Hill, Peter' (Michael
    Campbell), 82
Hitler, Adolf, 33, 123
Hobson, Harold, 138
Hogan, Desmond, 174–175,
    209
Holocaust, 10, 33–35, 124–125,
    158–159, 238, 249
horse-racing, 4–5, 134, 175
Houlihan, Con, 200, 210
Hussein, King, of Jordan, 201
Hutchinson, 225–226, 227,
    229
  novel auction, 230–233
Hutton, Len, 87
Hylton, Jack, 19–20

Ibsen, Henrik, 99
Illustrated London News, 262
Ingrid, 154–159
Intermediate Certificate, 11–12
Irish American Cultural
    Institute, The, 240–245
Irish Bookman, The, 167
Irish Censorship Board, 29
Irish Independent, 3

Irish language, 71, 246–247, 248
poetry translations, 29–32
Irish Press, The, 218, 229, 236.
see also 'New Irish Writing'
'Ireland –The Arts', 210–211,
234
Marcus literary editor,
180–183, 184, 199–213,
251–252
'Novel a Day', 203–204
resident critic, 204–205
Irish Republican Army (IRA),
76, 78, 221, 224
Irish Times, The, 30, 168, 169,
172, 208–209, 218
Marcus review, 114
'On Becoming Sixty', 147
'Quidnunc', 81
reviews, 206–207
Short Story Competition, 213
translation published, 27–28
Irish Writing, 167, 170, 171,
172, 182, 194, 239, 251,
252
archive lost, 148–149
financial problems, 64–67,
79, 83, 106, 220
first issue, 46, 49, 50–51,
62–64, 80–81
launch, 81
Somerville interview, 60–61
International Issue, 101
No. 2, 83–85
Pinter tribute, 149–150
plans for, 42–46
progress of, 97–105
Israel, 247, 249–250

Jameson, Storm, 101
Jenkins, Alan, 205–206
Jewish community
in Cork, 6, 119, 137, 190,
219, 221–224, 266
in Ireland, 240–242
Jewish Sabbath Day
Observance Employment
Bureau, 119–122
Jewish Social Club, Cork, 6
Jockey Joe (bookseller),
197–198
Joe (Baron's), 123, 125, 127,
128
John (picture-framer), 144
Johnson, Samuel, 230, 231
Johnston, Denis, 81, 202
Johnston, Jennifer, 152–153,
255
Jonathan Cape, 213
Jordan, Neil, 205
Joyce, James, 36, 51, 102–103,
118, 167, 248
Joyce, Stanislaus, 102–103

Karloff, Boris, 53
Kavanagh, Patrick, 62, 94, 99
Keane, Eamonn, 164
Keane, John B., 94–95
Kelleher, John V., 99
Kelly, Frank, 164
Kelly, Maeve, 255
Kemp, Cyril, 91–92
Kennedy, Robert, 164
Kersh, Gerald, 3
Kiely, Benedict, 29, 99, 171,
199

Kilkenny Magazine, The, 167
King's Inns, 13, 16–17, 23, 33
Kinsella, Thomas, 99, 202
Kreisler, Fritz, 20
Kristallnacht, 1, 10, 34

Lady Chatterley's Lover
   (Lawrence), 4
Lady With the Red Shoes, The
   (Daly), 256
Landor, Walter Savage, 267
Larkin, Philip, 201
Late Late Show, 233–234
Laughton, Charles, 202
Lavin, Mary, 83, 100, 211
Leonard, Hugh, 210
Leventhal, A.J., 100, 202
Levinge, Bertie, 92–94
Limerick, 260–261
  'pogrom', 78, 147
Listowel Mutiny, 232, 234
literary periodicals, 167–168
Lithuania, 5, 77, 190, 241,
   248, 266
London, 4, 5
  Baron's, 122–129
  emigration to, 106
  Guildhall Insurance Co.,
    130–137, 140, 142
  Marcus in, 65–67, 68–73,
    118–150, 151
  parents in, 142–143, 148
  play produced, 162–165
London Assurance, The,
   130–131, 142
Longford, Lord, 99
Lord Dismiss Us (Campbell), 83

Loss, Joe, 19
Lynch, Jack, 13–17, 180, 233
  speech-writing, 213–215
Lynch, Maureen, 213

Mac Giolla Ghunna, Cathal
   Buí, 26
McCann, Sean, 160–164,
   169–170, 171, 175
McCarthy, B.G., 80
MacDermott, Philip, 211–212,
   225, 229, 231
MacDonagh, Steve, 207–208
McGahern, John, 174
MacGreevy, Thomas, 40
MacKenzie, Ian, 111, 113–114
McKinney, Blanaid, 210
McLaverty, Michael, 171, 205
MacLiammoir, Micheal, 199
MacMahon, Bryan, 95, 100,
   171
MacManus, M.J., 99, 199
Macmillan, 84, 116, 217
  To Next Year in Jerusalem,
    109–115
MacNeice, Louis, 13, 62,
   269–270
MacReamoinn, Sean, 152
Madden, Deirdre, 210
Mangan, James Clarence, 31
Marcus, Abraham, 17, 38–39,
   44, 46, 64
Marcus, Chookie, 151
Marcus, David. *see also Irish*
   Writing; New Irish Writing
  acting, 6–10
  appendicitis, 46–49

attitude to religion, 187–188, 190–196
bomb threat, 178–180
called to the Bar, 25
fear of failure, 182–183
on growing old, 263–270
and Jewish identity, 246–250
journalism, 160–164
literary editor, 180–183, 199–213, 251–252
marriage, 213
musical interests, 18–24, 86–87
radio talks, 184–190
return to Dublin, 151–159
search for faith, 192–193
sports, 87–94
university studies, 13–17
US tour, 240–245
writes Lynch speech, 213–216
writing ambitions, 2–3, 12–13, 217–220, 269–270
first novel, 106–115
A Land Not Theirs, 220–235
translations, 25–32
Marcus, Elkan, 22
Marcus, grandfather, 5, 77–78
Marcus, Louis, 89–90, 142, 151–152, 200
Marcus, Mr (father), 4–6, 18–19, 49, 248
character of, 145–146
leaves Cork, 142–143
picture-framing business, 143–145

Marcus, Mrs (mother), 18–19, 67, 146–148, 248
character of, 146–148
leaves Cork, 142–143
Marcus, Nella, 145
Marcus, Sarah, 218, 222, 240, 241, 243
Marcus, Sopsa, 266
Mathew, Father Theobald, 259
Matthews, Denis, 202
Maurois, Andre, 101
Mendelssohn, Felix, 23
'Merchant of Venice, The' (Shakespeare), 6–10
Merriman, Brian, 25–26, 28–30, 162, 164, 166, 260
Merriman Summer School, 165–166
'Midnight Court, The' (Merriman), 25–26, 28–29, 99, 165–166, 260
Marcus play, 162–165
Marcus translation, 29–30
Miller, Glenn, 20
Miller, Liam, 29, 99, 152–153, 160, 200
Milton, John, 72
Moore, Brian, 167, 176, 239
Moore, Thomas, 261
Morrissey, Mr, 47–49
Mortimer, John, 176, 268–269
Mozart, W.A., 21, 23
Murphy, Seamus, 202
music, 18–24
piano, 86–87

na gCopaleen, Myles (Flann
	O'Brien), 71
Nash, Heddle, 19
National Library, 224
Nazism, 1, 33–34, 202–203
'New Irish Writing', 180, 182,
	199, 207
	progress of, 169–177
	young writers, 209–210,
		212–213, 229, 239, 251
	book publications,
		211–212
	Cork verses, 258–261
	young writers, 209–210
New World Writing, 67, 108
New York Times, 114
New Yorker, The, 45, 82
Newman, Dickie, 135–137,
	139
Nicholls, Rev. Arthur, 261
Nicolson, Harold, 264
Noonan, Gillman, 205
Northern Ireland (NI), 1, 95,
	214–215
Nye, Robert, 258

O'Brian, Patrick, 100
O'Brien, Conor Cruise, 99, 205
O'Brien, Edna, 173–174, 176
O'Brien, Flann (Myles na
	gCopaleen), 264
O'Brien, Kate Cruise, 255
O'Brien, Turlough, 241–242
Observer, The, 138, 205
O'Cadhain, Mairtin, 210
O'Casey, Sean, 83, 99, 109,
	202

O'Conaire, Padraic, 95
O'Connell, Daniel, 262
O'Connor, Frank, 27–29, 36,
	100, 109, 167, 171, 258
	autobiography, 202
	and Irish Writing, 44–45, 62
	on Limerick, 260–261
	reissues, 211
O'Dea, Jimmy, 82–83
O'Donnell, Peadar, 37,
	103–104
'O'Donnell, Donal'. see
	O'Brien, Conor Cruise
O'Driscoll, Denis, 195
O'Faolain, Eileen, 251, 252,
	253, 254, 257
O'Faolain, Julia, 176
O'Faolain, Sean, 2, 36, 37, 95,
	100, 103, 104, 167, 171,
	224, 258
	book review, 80–81
	on Irish translations, 30–31
	and Irish Writing, 42–43, 62
	judge, 176
	and Marcus, 251–258, 262
	resident critic, 204–205
O'Flaherty, Liam, 36, 45, 62,
	95, 100, 167, 205
	and Irish Writing, 70
	old age, 263–264
O'Mahony, T.P., 95
O'Mara, Joseph, 18–19
O'Rahilly, Dr Alfred, 14–15,
	84
O'Suilleabhain, Eoin, 164
O'Suilleabhain, Sean, 210
O'Sullivan, Seamus, 37

Palestine, 1, 219, 223
Parnell, Charles Stewart, 261
Pascoli, Giovanni, 102
Paul Elek, 255
PEN Cogress, 1953, 101
Penguin Books, 63–64, 238
Penguin New Writing, 38
piano-playing, 22–24, 86–87
Picasso, Pablo, 22–23, 202
Pinter, Harold, 149–150
Plunkett, James, 100
poetry, 209–210, 265–267
   translations, 25–32
Poetry Ireland, 30–31, 98–99, 252
Poolbeg Press, 211–212, 229, 234
Porter, Cole, 20
Praeger, Michael, 242
Presentation College, Cork, 1, 3, 87–88
   Marcus leaves, 11–12
   'Merchant of Venice', 6–10
Pritchett, V.S., 32, 176

Radio Éireann, 147, 151–152, 160
railway journeys, 74–78
'Ransom' (Marcus), 221–222
Reid School, 23
'Religion of Love, The' (Marcus), 108
Robert Pitman Award, 212
Robeson, Paul, 20
Ros, Amanda McKittrick, 202
Ross, Martin, 60, 95
Rosten, Leo, 246, 247–248

Royal Festival Hall, London, 119, 137
RTÉ
   Marcus talks, 184–190
   religious interviews, 193, 194–195
Ruane, Medb, 30
Rubinstein, Artur, 119
rugby, 14, 95
Runyon, Damon, 82
Ruskin, John, 198
Russell, Diarmuid, 99
Russell, Francis, 100–101
Russell, George (AE), 99
Russia, 77–78, 221
Ryan, Phyllis, 163–164

Sagan, Francoise, 204
Sage, Mr, 23
St Fin Barre's Cathedral, Cork, 133
St Martin's Press, 111, 113–114
St Paul's Cathedral, 133–134
Salkeld, Cecil Ffrench, 100
San Antonio, Texas, 243–245
Saroyan, William, 37, 100, 176, 236–240
Sartre, Jean-Paul, 100
Sassoon, Siegfried, 182
Saul (Baron's), 123, 125–127, 128
Savoy Cinema, 20
Scannell, Vernon, 202
Schumann, R.A., 21
Schwartz, Maurice, 5–6
Scott, Sir Walter, 261

Second World War, 2, 33–35, 51, 64–65, 147, 202–203

Shakespeare, William, 6–10, 138

Shanahan, Gerard, 22–23, 40

Shaw, George Bernard, 63, 66, 84–85

Sheehy Skeffington, Owen, 114

Shillman, Bernard and Molly, 16

short stories, 2, 36–39, 167–169, 234, 256

Ita Daly, 255–256

magazine for, 39, 42–46

'New Irish Writing', 169–177

Poolbeg Press, 211–212

'Ransom', 221–222

Saroyan, 237–240

sports, 94–96

Silone, Ignazio, 101

Silverstein, Mrs, 119

Simenon, Georges, 101

Sinatra, Frank, 20, 141–142

Singer, Isaac Bashevis, 201

Smith, Terence, 41–42, 43, 46, 62, 80–81, 99

soccer, 88–91

Solomon, pianist, 20

Somers, Dermot, 95

Somerville, Dr Edith, 50, 52, 57, 59–61, 62, 95

Special Branch, 179–180

Spenser, Edmund, 262

Sperrin-Johnson, Dr, 15

sports stories, 94–96

Squire, Sir John, 109–113

Stephens, James, 45–46, 62,

84, 102, 108, 109

meeting with, 68–73

Story Magazine, 238–239

Stuart, Francis, 100, 202–203

Sunday Times, The, 138

Sweet Cry of Hounds, The (Somerville), 60

Swift, Jonathan, 99, 202

table tennis, 14, 90, 91–93

Tate Gallery of Modern Art, 265

Tatum, Art, 20

Taylor, Elizabeth, 140–141

Thackeray, William Makepeace, 258–261

Thomas, D.M., 176

Thomas, Dylan, 13, 62–63, 72, 84, 85, 267

'Thought For The Day', 187–190

Threshold, 200

Thurber, James, 82

To Next Year in Jerusalem (Marcus), 106–115, 217, 226

Toal, Maureen, 164

Toomey, Mr, 131

Tostal, An, 100, 102

Trevor, William, 176, 202, 205, 255

Trinity College Dublin (TCD), 84, 100, 206

Trinity Players, 164

Trumpet Books, 64, 67

Tynan, Kenneth, 138

Ulysses (Joyce), 107
United States of America
   (USA), 240–245
University College Cork
   (UCC), 12–16, 33, 80
Ussher, Arland, 165

vegetarianism, 132–133
Victoria, Queen, 262
Vincent, Brother, 11–12
Virgil, 79
virtues, talks on, 185–187

Wain, John, 176, 202
Waiting for Godot (Beckett),
   137–139
Walsh, William, 100
War of Independence,
   221–222, 224

whiskey drinking, 53–56
White, Jack, 28
White, Sean J., 99
*Who Ever Heard of an Irish
   Jew?* (Marcus), 234
Wilde, Oscar, 263
Williams, Tennessee, 201
Williamson, Bruce, 114

Yeats, Jack B., 22–23, 40
Yeats, W.B., 31, 83–84, 109,
   202
Yiddish, 5–6, 67, 246–249
Young, Augustus, 258–261,
   260
Young, Edward, 187